Man of War

Man *of* War

· ·

My Adventures in the World of Historical Reenactment

CHARLIE SCHROEDER

HUDSON
STREET
PRESS

HUDSON STREET PRESS
Published by the Penguin Group
Penguin Group (USA) Inc., 375 Hudson Street, New York, New York 10014, U.S.A. • Penguin Group (Canada), 90 Eglinton Avenue East, Suite 700, Toronto, Ontario, Canada M4P 2Y3 (a division of Pearson Penguin Canada Inc.) • Penguin Books Ltd., 80 Strand, London WC2R 0RL, England • Penguin Ireland, 25 St. Stephen's Green, Dublin 2, Ireland (a division of Penguin Books Ltd.) • Penguin Group (Australia), 250 Camberwell Road, Camberwell, Victoria 3124, Australia (a division of Pearson Australia Group Pty. Ltd.) • Penguin Books India Pvt. Ltd., 11 Community Centre, Panchsheel Park, New Delhi – 110 017, India • Penguin Group (NZ), 67 Apollo Drive, Rosedale, Auckland 0632, New Zealand (a division of Pearson New Zealand Ltd.) • Penguin Books (South Africa) (Pty.) Ltd., 24 Sturdee Avenue, Rosebank, Johannesburg 2196, South Africa

Penguin Books Ltd., Registered Offices: 80 Strand, London WC2R 0RL, England

First published by Hudson Street Press, a member of Penguin Group (USA) Inc.

First Printing, June 2012
10 9 8 7 6 5 4 3 2 1

Excerpt from "I Feel Like I'm Fixin' to Die Rag," words and music by Joe McDonald. Copyright © 1965, renewed 1993 by Alkatraz Corner Music Co. Used by permission.

REGISTERED TRADEMARK—MARCA REGISTRADA
HUDSON
STREET
PRESS

LIBRARY OF CONGRESS CATALOGING-IN-PUBLICATION DATA
Schroeder, Charlie, 1972-
    Man of war : my adventures in the world of historical reenactment / Charlie Schroeder.
        p. cm.
    ISBN 978-1-59463-091-0 (hardcover : alk. paper)   1. Military history—Anecdotes.
2. Historical reenactments—Anecdotes.   3. Schroeder, Charlie, 1972—Anecdotes.   I. Title.
    D25.5.S357 2012
    355.4'8—dc23

                                                                                2011048485

Printed in the United States of America
Set in Adobe Garamond Pro

*Penguin is committed to publishing works of quality and integrity.
In that spirit, we are proud to offer this book to our readers;
however, the story, the experiences, and the words
are the author's alone.*

To Wendy. Sorry about the hair.

ACKNOWLEDGMENTS

This book wouldn't exist without the reenactors who shared their time, knowledge, uniforms, tents, weapons, boats, provisions and bug spray with me. In roughly the order we met, I doff my kepi to them now: Lou Lopez, Matt Charapata, Randy Beard, Brian Abela, Vinnie Francischetti and Dan Armstrong; Robert Niepert, Buddy Jimmerson, Rich Howe and the rest of the 7th Michigan and 5th Florida units; Arik Greenberg, David Michaels, Mike Scott, Brandon Barnes, John Olinger, Lorie Ann Hambly, Jim Pieper, Dan Peterson, Julius Feigelson and the Fort Lafe staff; Rik and Tarrah Fox, Josh Wojda and Bruce Willis; Jane and Robert Whiteside, Marilyn Hess, Angie Potter, the Studzinksi family and Craig McGirr; Donlyn Meyers and the Smoke and Fire staff, Tony Baker, George Neal, the members of Schuyler's Company (especially John Osinski, Kevin Richard-Morrow, Harvey and Mary Alexander, Tom Quinn and Jonathan Pirillo) and the Old Fort Niagara staff, in particular Jere Brubaker, Eric Bloomquist and Bob Emerson; David, Reb and Bill Manthey; Rick Russell and Greg Ketchem; Patrick Hubble and family; Jack Garrett, Ed Berland, Brian

Agron, Tory Parker, Kay Tracy, Henrik Olsgaard, Rick Mantegani, Annie Petersen and all my fellow Vikings of Bjornstad.

Chuck Lyons at the San Gabriel Mission drummed up local media interest in my walk and many friends either accompanied me, "volunteered" to be a Sherpa soldier or cheered my hike on from afar via Twitter and Facebook. They are: Loren Tarquinio, Hiro Saito, Ray Perez, Arthur Yuen, Cliff Eberly, the Rein Family (Ayr, Perry, Maisie and Angus), Simeen Maghame, Eric Beckett, Tom O'Leary, J. Ana Flores, Ian Helfer, Laura Flanagan, Michael Goldfried, Jay Reiss, Rebecca Feldman, Sylvie Reiss, Justin Lukach, Carrie Yutzy, Allison Klein, the Hovanesian family (Jarmen, Edi, Sean and Alan), Ryan Noll, Mollie Burns, Eliza Burns, Scott Haverstick, P. J. McSparran, Ped Demling, Curt Lam, Keith Patterson, Amanda Miller, Chris Donovan, Sabrina Martin, Joseph Klein, Nandita Shenoy and John Aboud.

Mike Gerber, the great Josh Karp, Drew Fellman, Krissy Clark, Pamm Higgins, Adam Fifield and Michael May either read early drafts or advised me on the writing/reporting process. David Johnston volunteered his photography skills and Skye Moorhead lent us her studio. Also, a big thanks to the Naked Angels Theater Company and Potluck Playhouse members who let me read excerpts at their respective reading series.

Josh Johns, Nate Althouse, Justen Byler, Cathy Brown, Todd Miller, Noel Poirier, Marianne Heckles, Mara Creswell McGrann and Cassie Creswell all helped clarify some of my very hazy memories of high school history class. Rodney Channing Welch III cleaned off his sofa so I could crash on it during my Bay Area visits. The kind Bona Lee Kim made my mission walk informational flyer and Patti Thompson offered technical expertise. Thanks to Liz Engel and Dan Regan, who patiently lent an ear during my many moments of title angst. *Dank geht an Ruth Sarah Erkens für ihrere großartige Übersetzungsarbeit.*

At Hudson Street Press and Penguin, a hardworking and enthusiastic team has supported me every step of the way. You couldn't ask for a better battalion than Caroline Sutton, John Fagan, Ashley Pattison, Courtney Nobile, Liz Keenan and Katie Hurley. The talented Meghan Stevenson deserves the biggest "huzzah" of all, however. She took a risk on a first-time author (me) and provided finely detailed editing at every step of the writing process. I raise a goblet of mead to you and then I chug it.

Jonathan Lyons believed in this project before anyone else and delivered excellent counsel throughout the entire process. He helped shape the proposal and manuscript, and, as an agent, went way, way beyond the call of duty. Bomb, you the.

My parents, Robert and Gail Schroeder, and my brother, Rob, read drafts, suggested funny lines (my dad's "Friar Chuck"), title ideas (my mom's "Pooping in the Woods"), support (my brother's "I think you've become a little too obsessed") and tremendous patience during the year and a half of my often hermetic writing life. Sorry for being so AWOL.

And finally, my wife Wendy put up with my mischief making more than any spouse should, enduring my physical and mental absences (not to mention my unsightly hairstyles). She is truly my better half and as cliché as it sounds, I literally couldn't have written this book without her. *Ngoh ngoi nei.*

Man of War

CHAPTER ONE

Sleepless in Stalingrad

B*ang.*
The Russian sniper had been perched up in a tree, about ten feet off the ground and shrouded by branches. I hadn't seen him from where I was, 150 feet away, half crouched over in bone-dry reeds. The only indication that he was there, straddling a thick bough, was the burst of fire I saw shoot out of his rifle. It flashed quickly, like a small angry dragon. Because the spark was so vivid, so direct, more yellow than orange, I knew that his weapon had been aimed at me. A few hours earlier I'd been told by the reenactment organizers that if I saw such a pointed conflagration, it meant I'd been "killed." Now it was time for me to take what one of my fellow combatants called a "dirt nap." Which I was more than happy to do, because my back was killing me.

After an hour-long break in which I unwisely lounged under a tree within spraying distance of an incontinent stallion, I was back on my feet marching with my fellow soldiers up a long dusty road. But I'd rather have been dead. Dead meant sitting down by the side of the road and chugging water. Dead meant resting my feet and massaging my calf muscles. Dead meant taking a time-out from being a grunt.

It wasn't the three-mile hike that crippled me and made my back seize up. It was lugging the twenty pounds of military gear: a rifle, C rations, canteen, shovel, parts of a tent, sixty blanks, gas mask canister, mess kit and my rolled-up greatcoat. Had I been to the gym in the last three years it might not have affected me all that badly, but I hadn't. If I had to be honest, I probably hadn't walked more than a couple miles in the last three years. I was an out-of-shape, soft twenty-first-century American who'd just traveled back in time, and the thin leather Y-straps that held all my gear in place were digging into my shoulders like a three-year-old who'd never trimmed his nails. I wanted to go back to the future. Now.

Vroom.

A large hybrid military vehicle with wheels in front and caterpillar tracks in back, called a half-track, roared by, kicking up a cloud of dirt that coated my dried lips and stung my eyes. It was late afternoon in early October, the sun directly in front of me and autumn low. I looked down to avert my eyes from it. That's when I saw the small swastika sewed onto my jacket's right breast pocket. *What am I doing?* I wondered. *How did I end up here, in the barren plains of Colorado, reenacting the 24th Panzer's drive on Stalingrad?* But deep down I knew the answer. I'd come because I wanted to learn about history.

The plan was for our division of Nazis to spend the night in an abandoned one-room schoolhouse, perched atop a rise in the otherwise flat high-desert terrain. The ninety of us would all take turns sleeping— napping, really—then once we were rejuvenated we'd relieve other squad members who were hunkered down in foxholes and keeping an eye out for the Russians. Once the clock struck 3:00 a.m., the entire 24th Panzer would launch a surprise attack on Stalin's Red Army. All seventy of them.

But with every labored step it was becoming more apparent that reaching the schoolhouse might be the most grueling part of our mission. Stretching far ahead, the one-lane dirt road rose out of the valley at a steep and steady incline. After our last skirmish with the Russians in a thick cluster of cottonwoods, I was covered in burrs. My legs buckled with every step. My squad leader, Matt, who marched behind me, could tell I was worn out and suggested I hitch a ride the next time a motorcycle passed by. As bad as I felt, it could have been worse. One soldier was throwing up from dehydration and a few other weary men threatened to quit if they didn't start seeing more combat.

Vroom.

A motorcycle approached, looking very *Hogan's Heroes.* I held up my arm like I was hailing a taxi. The driver stopped. Climbing into the sidecar, I wedged my rifle between my legs and clamped my mouth shut so no dirt would get in. As we rumbled up the road I began to wonder what the point of the Drive on Stalingrad reenactment was. I wasn't fighting for a cause, I wasn't getting paid, my face and neck were sunburned and my hands were caked with dirt and briar lacerations. I hadn't slept, brushed my teeth or washed in thirty-six hours. With every rotation of the motorcycle's tires my sleep-deprived mind inched a little closer to delirium. I'd come looking for a history lesson, to learn about the Battle of Stalingrad, but so far all I'd learned about was suffering.

By the time we finally reached the old schoolhouse—shuttered, I'm sure, because most people aren't crazy enough to live in this desolate part of Colorado—I'd lost any enthusiasm I had for the reenactment. Spotting a rusty merry-go-round, I hobbled over to it, plopped down and buried my face in my hands.

"Hey, propaganda minister, how's it going?" I looked up to see Cliff, the squad's youngest Nazi reenactor, gleefully skipping up the road with his two other Hitler Youth pals. Fresh faced and ruddy with a bandana neatly tied around his neck, Cliff gave off the impression that he was out for a leisurely predinner stroll, not an intense march into no-man's-land.

"Uh, well," I said, trying my hardest to sound upbeat. "I'm out of shape."

"That was intense for us too!" he said, clearly not picking up on my subtext of misery. "That was rad!"

Directly opposite me, low in the eastern sky, the moon crept over the horizon. Behind me the sun hung on the same angle. It was as if the two balls were on a long, invisible seesaw. At that hour—what I can only guess was 6:00 p.m.—the sun was the heavier of the two, but only by a little, so that it fell toward the earth at an imperceptibly slow pace. As it sank, the moon rose just as slowly. It was almost unbearable to watch this inevitable, unstoppable exchange between the two, their falling and rising, the light and impending dark, the waning warmth and encroaching bitter cold. At base camp the night before, huddled inside a sleeping bag and trying desperately to fight off the twenty-degree temperature—and the dissonance of ninety snoring, farting men—I didn't sleep a wink. Tonight it'd be just as cold except there'd be one major difference: we wouldn't have sleeping bags.

My mind started racing to what lay ahead: no sleep tonight + a surprise attack on the Russians at 3:00 a.m. + soldiering again all day tomorrow + event lasting until midnight tomorrow + likely no sleep tomorrow night + catching a plane back to L.A. at 6:30 a.m. = no sleep for seventy-two hours and guaranteed madness. Former Nazi POW Jean-Paul Sartre may have said, "Hell is other people," but he obviously never spent any time with Nazi reenactors. Otherwise I'm certain that he would have revised his famous line to read, "Hell is Nazi reenacting."

I shuffled over to the one-room schoolhouse and stepped inside. *Crunch, crunch.* My hobnailed boots had ground up something hard. The room, not much larger than a one-bedroom apartment, had been stripped of everything except an old stove located behind where a teacher once stood. *Crunch, crunch.* I took a couple more steps and again the ground cracked under my feet. "Careful, Charlie," Matt said. "This place is caked in rat shit." In the fading light I could barely see the dried excrement, white and globular, like congealed paint splotches. I pressed my boot down again and a dollop shattered like glass. "They say this stuff is toxic so don't lie down on the floor until I'm finished sweeping," Matt said. The room had retained the afternoon heat well. It was at least fifteen degrees warmer than outside—a major relief given that the mercury was supposed to drop into the twenties again. I couldn't have cared less whether rat dung was toxic or not; all I wanted to do was get some rest. If it meant spooning with feces then so be it.

Outside, guys dug foxholes and pitched tents while a cook in a white smock fired up the field kitchen. I could see steam rise from a large kettle where the world's blandest potato and leek soup simmered. Once we had cleared out all the rat crap I helped a few guys spread out our tent canvas on the creaky wooden floor.

After easing myself down on it, I slipped my arms into my overcoat like it was a Snuggie and placed my wool gloves under my head. Then I folded my arms mummy style and shut my eyes. But I couldn't doze off. People kept walking in and out, people kept talking.

I missed my wife, Wendy, terribly—I felt sick to my stomach the way I did after we'd met in Hong Kong and fallen in love. A major investment bank had hired us and a few other actors to teach its employees how not to sexually harass each other. In the scene we performed, Wendy was my underling and the object of my affection. I like to tell people that when we met I was sexually harassing Wendy onstage and that once the scene ended I tried to sexually harass her offstage too. We'd been inseparable for three weeks, then I got on a plane and flew eight thousand miles back to New York, not sure if I'd ever see her again. Somewhere over Taiwan, I remember feeling nauseous, like someone was kicking me in the gut. At the time I hurt so much I considered unbuckling my seat belt and parachuting back down into her arms. Now as I lay on the schoolroom floor, I felt exactly the same way. I'd have given anything to transport myself back to the future, to snuggle with her under our freshly washed duvet, to slip my head between our two feathery pillows, to squeeze her tight and bury my nose in her shoulder. If I could just be home with her now, I swore I'd never complain about all her idiosyncrasies: how she never throws out junk mail, how every horizontal surface in our apartment doubles as her "desk" and how she takes corners at twice the posted speed limit. I even silently promised to stop teasing her about watching all those *Charmed* reruns.

I didn't know it at the time, but nearly halfway around the world, in Mian Poshteh, Afghanistan, the 240 Marines of 2/8 Echo Company were taking shelter in an abandoned school as well. Bereft of water, electricity, beds or bedrooms in a "vacant, dirty building," as *New York Times* reporter Dexter Filkins would write, "They sleep on the floor, a dozen to a room, or they sleep in the dirt outside, shirtless in the heat. They fight every day. When the Marines don't attack the Taliban, the Taliban attack the Marines."

How do real soldiers do it? I wondered. How do they spend months, *years* away from their wives and children? How can they survive the real danger, the everlasting pain, the heartache that must linger within them and never go away? I hadn't given much thought to the men and women of our military—of *any* military—but I did then, and now I always will.

"We've got to vacate." A voice in the darkness wrenched me back to the present. I wondered for a moment if I'd fallen asleep, if I was being summoned for guard duty. Then some shadowy figure shined a flashlight in my face. "Let's go guys," he said, "*now.*"

"What's going on?" I asked, rising slowly.

"There's a guy outside, claims he's got the lease on the schoolhouse . . . and he's *pissed.*"

A handful of groggy soldiers gathered their belongings—tent tarps, shovels, canteens, rifles—and headed outside into the frigid, starlit night. A pickup truck was idling in the middle of the road not far from the schoolhouse, its high beams illuminating the dirt strip that stretched from here to eternity. Swarms of Nazis bundled in long overcoats scurried about, moving supplies, filling in the craters they'd dug for shelter. Steam from the field kitchen wafted into the air in thick plumes.

I sniffed around for information but it was hard to gather. Apparently the Drive on Stalingrad (DOS) organizers had gotten approval from a local landowner to hold the event here, but not all the neighbors knew about it. So when an uninformed cattle rancher drove by and saw ninety Nazis setting up camp for the night—not to mention the tank, half-track, motorcycles, horses and that steaming *Gulaschkanone*—he *freaked*. Now the event's organizers were trying to calm him down so things wouldn't get really out of hand.

I dumped all my supplies next to a ditch that some guys were filling in and asked them what was up, if they'd heard any updates, but they hadn't. One of them, a tall, doe-eyed guy, shrugged his shoulders. "This happens with this hobby," he said, tossing another shovelful of dirt back into the hole. But his thick-lipped friend, bundled in a head scarf, was livid. "People usually look at us and think, 'That's cool,' but this guy . . ." He gestured at the parked pickup. "Why does he have to ruin everything?"

Over time the truth came out about why the rancher was so irked. Turns out he didn't have a lease on the schoolhouse, but he was a Vietnam vet with three bullet holes in his chest to prove it, and he did not think Nazi reenactment was "cool" *at all*. "Why don't you go educate people about [Nazism] instead?" he asked from the safety of his truck.

The air was tense and I put the odds that he was carrying a gun at roughly 100 percent and the chance that his ammunition was blank—like ours—at approximately zero. For all the sophisticated historical weaponry that everyone brought to this grown-up version of cowboys and Indians, this was the first real danger we'd faced all day. At one point while I was eavesdropping on the tense convo, one of the Nazis went nose to nose with him, really got up in his grill. That didn't help matters. Soon two other pickup trucks—friends of the rancher—arrived and parked about fifty feet away at a nearby crossroads. With headlights shining and motors idling it was a passive-aggressive posture that bellowed, "Don't mess with Colorado." One fair-haired Hitler Youth who couldn't have been more than twenty muttered about the vet, "Leave it to some dumb redneck to ruin it for everybody."

While the standoff continued, the rumor mill churned. The event was going to be canceled; we'd have to move for the night; etc., etc. It didn't take long for morale among the troops to disintegrate. At one point I overheard a group of guys from Texas bemoaning the "long walks and little battle." A couple members of their squad had already dropped out, and the rest of them were now considering throwing in the towel. "Too much walking, not enough shooting," one said. When I heard one of them utter the word "motel," I pounced on him.

"Please take me with you!"

"What squad are you in?" he asked.

"Um," I said. I couldn't remember its name. In a panic I blurted out, "California!"

"That's not a squad name," a shadowy figure with closely shorn hair replied.

"Please," I begged. "I can't feel my toes anymore." Another hour or two outside and I feared I'd be the (very) last German casualty on the Eastern Front.

One of their guys who'd quit had hitched a ride back to base camp. Now he was returning in his truck to pick up the rest of the deserters. "Oh, all right," one of them said, taking pity on me. "Meet us at the crossroads in fifteen minutes."

"Okay, great, yes, than you so muh! Than you so muh!" My cheeks were so cold I could barely form the words.

"Oh boy, here come the cops," a guy in a Sergeant Schultz helmet said. I turned to see a squad car pull up, siren and lights off. The rancher had dialed 911.

The car stopped in front of the schoolhouse, grille to grille with the pickup, headlights beaming bright. A bald man in a beige sheriff's jacket got out. A gold star was pinned to his chest. He started chewing the fat with one of the Nazis, but I couldn't hear what they were saying. They chatted for a while as if what had happened was a minor infraction—like riding a bike on the sidewalk or something—and it looked like things were getting resolved. It looked like the reenactment would continue. Then in the distance we all heard a low rumble. It sounded like one of those apocalyptic rattletraps from *Mad Max*. Loud, really loud and quickly getting really louder. The men immediately recognized what it was. Their looks of horror telegraphed their disbelief. It was the Russians. They were launching a surprise attack. Nobody had told them there was a time-out on the field.

Like lightning, two Russian BA-64s, 4 x 4 light armored vehicles, charged over a small hill, pedal to the metal. *Rat-a-tat-tat! Rat-a-tat-tat!* Before anyone had a chance to flag them down, they were opening fire on the slack-jawed krauts. Bursts of flames spit out of narrow slits, like a motorized four-wheeled dragon. *Rat-a-tat-tat! Rat-a-tat-tat!* The concussion was deafening, the trail of dust so great that it nearly obscured the vehicle behind it, which was firing as well. *Rat-a-tat-tat! Rat-a-tat-tat!* The driver of the first vehicle never saw the flailing Germans; he just spent all his rounds and tore off into the darkness of the high desert.

A crowd of panicked Germans ran toward the second vehicle, waving their arms, whistling and yelling, *"Stop! Stop! Stop firing! Cut it! Knock it off!"* But vehicle number two kept speeding ahead, spitting three-foot flames, until finally it ground to a halt when it almost ran over a desperate reenactor. The dark sky had lit up with flashing blue and red lights. It was the cop. He'd turned his patrol lights on and his eyes were bugging out of his head.

"That scared the shit out of me," he said, his hand inside the squad car, reaching for who knows what. "And I don't carry blanks."

Once the dust had settled and everyone's hearts resumed their normal rhythm, the cop turned back to the Nazi he'd been talking to.

"Did they have M4s in World War I?" he asked, referencing the type of gun on the BA-64s.

The Nazi looked at him in disbelief and then somewhat incredulously replied, "World War *II.*"

I didn't stick around long enough to see how things ended. The truck with Texas tags arrived at the designated corner and I hopped in its bed with half a dozen reenactment vets who couldn't take how hardcore the Drive on Stalingrad really was. I braced myself as we sped away, hunching over to avoid the arctic wind that was blowing over the roof. I prayed that none of the remaining Nazis would shoot us shirkers in the back, like we'd been warned. But no "bullets" ever came.

The mood in the truck was grim. A heavyset guy who was sitting with his back up against the cab muttered, "I was looking forward to this for five months . . . made sure everything was authentic . . . for *this*?" Nobody bothered to respond.

· · · · · · · ·

All this came about because of something that had happened three months earlier on a hot July Sunday. On that day, Wendy and I went to Old Fort MacArthur Days (OFMD), a fund-raiser and reenactment timeline event at a former army installation, twenty-five miles south of Los Angeles. For a ten-dollar entry fee, visitors could traverse the fort's sun-baked hillside and chat with the members of seventy-five different reenactment groups. Lots were there. Romans, Vikings, Civil War soldiers and many more from the past two thousand years of Western civilization were camping out on the grounds in period tents. Dressed in historical clothing, they demonstrated how people used to live and fight; they eschewed showers and refrigerators, slept on the ground and cooked over campfires. All together they formed what OFMD's organizer Lou Lopez called the "largest multicultural living history event west of the Mississippi." As Lopez told me, "Any group reenacting any time period can encamp on the grounds of the old fort. So long as they're authentic."

I spoke with him just outside the Delaware Light Infantry encampment. Behind us a blacksmith dressed in a long, soot-stained apron was pouring boiling hot lead into a cast and demonstrating how Revolutionary War–era musket balls were made. "If someone wants to portray a caveman and he can speak authentically, I'll dig him a cave right there," Lopez said, pointing to a hillside where some medieval knights were admiring a Napoleonic reenactor's steed. Lopez, a Hispanic Wallace Shawn minus the lisp, wasn't just the event's organizer, he was a participant, dressed as a Rough Rider from the Spanish-American War: suspenders, denim shirt, Teddy Roosevelt hat and all. The only indication that he hadn't just traveled through time to talk with me was the pair of glasses he wore that darkened whenever he stood in the sun.

That day Wendy and I talked to dozens of reenactors: barber-surgeons and antebellum ladies, territorial marshals, even pirates. I found it fascinating to learn about history in a three-dimensional, interactive way. To ask questions of people who loved a time period so much they felt compelled to dress like one of its inhabitants.

While I didn't know much about history, I'd recently started to take an interest in it. In fact, one day not long before OFMD, Wendy asked me what subject I'd major in if I could go back to college. To my surprise, I blurted out, "History," even though I didn't own any history books and never watched the History Channel.

To be honest, for nearly all of my thirty-seven years I considered the subject to be boring. I'd always been more interested in "now" and "later" than "back then." I liked to follow trends and be on the cutting edge, to share the latest YouTube videos and buy the newest music. I liked change and forward progress. In college I studied avant-garde theater and during the eight years I lived in New York City I acted in all sorts of wacky experimental theater pieces. Once I painted my face blue; another time I performed in a show that mostly took place in the dark. I even stood onstage and courted a broomstick while Frankie Valli's "Can't Take My Eyes Off You" played in the background.

And yet the older I got, the more fascinating history seemed. I guess because now I have a history myself. After all, with age comes the ability to recognize that, as Mark Twain once said, "history doesn't repeat itself, but it does rhyme." Since graduating from college I've lived through two financial crashes, a couple of wars and three presidents. When Wendy and I went to OFMD, America was going through a sort of midlife crisis. The airwaves, cable TV and Internet were grinding out stories of discontent: cries of a "socialist" president, corporate corruption, "Don't Tread on Me" flags and people donning tricorns and reenacting the Boston Tea Party. Watching all this play out from the sidelines I felt like it wasn't just in my interest to study history, but my *duty* as a citizen of the world. To learn about who we are and how we came to be, so I can better understand the place I live.

That said, I'd be lying if I said my interest in history was solely about civic duty or curiosity. It's also something I've needed to surround myself with since moving to L.A. in 2003, something to make me feel grounded, like I'm standing on rock, not sand. I grew up in a 1738 log cabin, whose logs were marked with Roman numerals to determine the order of its construction. My Amish neighbors lived a pre–Industrial Revolution lifestyle. I went to college in Maine at a school that was founded in 1855 and later moved to New York, one of the country's oldest cities. But, like I said, when I was thirty-one I moved away from all this history to the West Coast so I could pursue an acting career in film and television. Living in the newest of new American cities—a place where 1950 feels ancient—I felt disconnected from my traditional upbringing. I needed to feel rooted in something more substantial than L.A.'s plasticity and geographic sprawl.

Yet despite growing up in an old house, next to anachronistic neighbors, history was the last subject I cared about as a kid. For my high school history teacher, who awarded extra credit to anyone who attended our school's basketball games, it seemed like it was the last subject he cared about too. He devoted the entire first day of class to teaching us how to park our cars. "Park to escape" was his mantra. He kept saying it until we all promised to back our cars into our parking spots so we could make a hasty exit. "If you get stuck in the parking lot after school it won't be my fault, class, it will be *ass fault*."

And, if my friends are any indication, I'm not unique. We're the generation raised on MTV and video games, who went to school when the classics were being replaced with computer training. Rather than studying the works of Greek philosophers and learning Latin, we were figuring out how to save documents on floppy disks.

Of course, it's totally unfair of me to blame my teacher, school system or generation for my flimsy grasp of all things historical. As a kid all I wanted to do was get an A in history class so I could enroll in a good college then land a well-paying job on Wall Street and make a lot of money so I could buy a BMW.

So when I heard about OFMD it seemed like the perfect environment to learn about a subject that I was coming around to. When I got there, however, I realized that another part of the reenacting world appealed to me too: its vibrant, eccentric subculture.

Ever since I'd landed my first professional acting gig at a Renaissance faire when I was twenty-one, I was curious to learn about people who voluntarily spend their weekends dressed in historical clothing. At the faire—no matter how hot or muggy it got—someone always came dressed in armor and chain mail. If I wasn't getting paid $150 to wear pantaloons and a doublet I wouldn't have been caught dead on a summer day in that much old clothing. My friends and I snarkily referred to these people as "Ren rats," and laughed whenever we saw guys dressed in homemade chain mail constructed from beer can tabs. But for every knight bedecked in Budweiser, there were dozens who looked dashing. On any given street in the shire one could see "Elizabethan girls" donning long milkmaid dresses and sword-carrying men sporting finely tailored jackets and hose. Many looked as if they'd just stepped out of a painting. It seemed as though they took re-creating history very seriously. Who were they? I wondered. And why did they dress up? What attracted them to this particular era? What, if anything, did they learn by "inhabiting" a character from the past? These questions stayed with me for sixteen years, and after walking around Fort MacArthur I still didn't have my answer.

• • • • • • • •

After Wendy and I got back from OFMD, I started to research reenactment groups. To my surprise I learned that there's no umbrella group, no official organization that unifies all reenactors. Sniffing around, I came across a few large, sophisticated events that sounded totally fascinating. There was a Viking melee in Maryland, the re-creation of an 1812 sea battle in New York State and even a group of Ukrainian guys who like to reenact Vietnam.

Still, as surprising as it was to discover what was out there, it never occurred to me that people would actually *want* to bring the most vilified group in modern history back to life. One lazy Saturday afternoon, however, while lying in bed, laptop propped up on my legs, I thought I'd give it a shot. I started to google "nazi reenactment," but only made it as far as "nazi ree" before the search engine yielded three results: "nazi reenact-ors," "nazi reenactment" and "nazi reenactment uniforms." People *did* want to bring them back to life and they thought nothing of sharing their hobby with the world. I was so shocked, I nearly dropped my computer.

That afternoon I visited nearly a dozen Nazi reenactment sites. Each dedicated to re-creating a specific unit of the Wehrmacht, the armed forces of Nazi Germany: 9th Waffen SS Panzer Division, 11th SS Panzergrenadier Division Nordland and Kampfgruppe Knittel, to name a few. Their sites were designed with gothic lettering and featured photographs of uniformed members flanking tanks, posing with rifles or caught mid-"combat" carrying one of their "wounded" *Bruders* off the "battlefield." Sometimes I couldn't tell if the old, grainy black-and-white photos were real or staged.

On each site's home page a disclaimer barked—*"Achtung!"* or "Please Read!" or "Very Important!"—declaring that the groups were "nonpolitical" and that they "do not condone or support any neo-Nazi or race supremacy agenda." On the 9th Waffen SS Panzer Division site it proclaims that they're "Fighting to keep history alive!" and that they want to "help educate the public about what America's enemies looked like and why victory over them was such a monumental achievement." Underneath the group's mission statement is a link to its store where one can buy mugs, steins, license plate frames, mousepads, wall clocks, coasters, throw pillows, T-shirts and even thongs with the German cross and other various SS insignia on them.

After sifting through a number of sites I eventually found my way to Driveonstalingrad.com and found this description of its upcoming event:

[The] Drive on Stalingrad is a campaign-style WWII living his-tory event. The event is portraying the first week of September 1942 in southern Russia, west of Stalingrad. The event will cover

12 miles of terrain over three days. There will be thousands of acres of maneuver room for the armored vehicles at the event. Combat involving open steppe, fortified villages, bunker lines and bridges will make the event a multifaceted living history experience. Everything from processing PW's to night combat in collective farms make this an event not to be missed!

The attention to detail was astonishing. Rigid uniform and field gear requirements stipulated that no one wear "wide collar greatcoats," that one's boots "must have appropriate hobnails" and that "all equipment and uniforms must be either original or high quality reproduction." If any wannabe participants had any doubts as to what to wear, he was to remember that he was re-creating the "summer of 42." On one page someone had transcribed the exhaustive rules for how to play a period card game called skat, and on another were listed sixteen different rules of engagement, including:

- There will be no mock executions.
- There will be no shooting of POW's.
- The Nazi salute is not to be used at any time.
- Remember! Most German soldiers did not speak Russian just as most Russian soldiers did not speak German. Don't gab! Your [sic] not supposed to understand the other guy!
- Do not clutter up the area where the fighting is taking place . . . there is nothing worse then [sic] 20 guy's [sic] standing around in the middle of a fire fight shooting the breeze because they are "dead". Remove yourself if you are wounded and able, Stand up and surrender if directed or lay there dead until the fight passes you.
- Remember! reenact for the guy on the other side of the front line! Give him a good show. He will return the favor I promise!

To further convey the event's intended grittiness, I followed a link titled "What to Expect," which led to an archival photo of two soldiers—likely Russian—lying atop a pile of rubble and aiming their rifles at an unseen enemy. (At least I think they were archival photos.) They were so grainy I wasn't entirely sure when they were taken. After all, it seemed these guys were so determined to be authentic, they may have even staged history to promote the event.

A couple weeks later I e-mailed Randy Beard, the DOS's German reenactor coordinator and commander. I mentioned that I was a writer and asked him if I could participate. He was skeptical at first, saying that many people "have an axe to grind and have a problem with, in their perception, grown-ups playing army and wearing swastikas." I replied, telling him I had "no axe to grind, only curiosity and an open mind." When he responded shortly thereafter, he told me that the "event is wide open to those who have a sincere interest and a calling for this particular flavor of living history." He told me I'd be assigned to the "west . . . Erste zug (1st platoon)," and put me in touch with two men, Matt Charapata, the leader of the "Western Gruppe"—reenactors participating from Western states—and Brian Abela, his assistant.

After I paid a thirty-five-dollar entry fee that helped to pay for a groupwide insurance policy, I was contacted by Matt and Brian. Like the event's website, they stressed authenticity: no modern glasses frames were allowed; all food had to be wrapped in tinfoil or waxed paper so it looked "period." As Matt told me, "Nothing kills the atmosphere like a can of Pringles and a bottle of Evian." I was happy to oblige, but I was worried that keeping it real meant that I couldn't use my notebook and voice recorder. So I asked Brian for suggestions. "Can you use paper and a clipboard instead of a notebook?" he asked. "And a wooden pencil instead of a pen?" "Yes," I said. I also agreed to say that I was a *Kriegsberichter*, a German war correspondent, if someone were to ask me why I was writing. As for my uniform, Matt had extra fatigues—the cost to outfit a German reenactor can run up to $2,500—and would lend them to me.

During my first phone conversation with Matt, a chatty construction worker from Ventura, California, he seemed intent—almost preoccupied—with convincing me that he was not a real Nazi. "I mean, my grandfather was Jewish and my grandmother was Polish . . . *hello-o*," he said. Like Beard, he was also apprehensive about having a writer tag along. Apparently the German magazine *Der Spiegel* once did a "hatchet job" on the group and they didn't want any more bad PR. "If you want to join the Aryan Nation, go to Coeur d'Alene," Matt said, referencing the northern Idaho city where the group has marched. "We have zero tolerance for actual Nazism. Even if you have a tattoo, you're outta here." He assured me that his controversial hobby stemmed from his interest in military history. His two stepfathers both served in the military and because "zillions of people" do GI impressions, he decided to go German. In war games someone always has to play the enemy. If I still had any doubts about what to expect, Matt felt compelled to clarify, "We'll be soldiering, not *sieg heiling*."

· · · · · · · ·

A week before the event, Brian e-mailed me a three-page PDF of young Nazis photographed from different angles. "[We're] pretty strict about hair," he told me. The men in the pictures were unmistakably Third Reich: fresh faced, Aryan and angular, with Hitler-style hair, short on the sides and in the back, but long enough on the top to part.

The night before I flew to Colorado I took the printout to a strip mall salon down the street from my apartment. Sandwiched between a Laundromat and a greasy spoon Italian restaurant, the four-seat establishment advertises seven-dollar haircuts, a selling point that had always kept me away. But when I got Brian's e-mail, I knew it'd be the perfect place for my new do. After all, I always thought Hitler looked like the victim of a cheap haircut. With any luck one of their staff could make me look just as awful.

"*Really?* You vant to look like dees men?" my stylist, Loreta, asked when I showed her the photos. Her black hair was streaked with blond stripes and she spoke with a thick Armenian accent. An episode of the Animal Planet show *Bear Attack!* blared on a flat-screen mounted to the wall.

"Yeah, uh, yes," I stammered. I hadn't quite figured out my backstory and wasn't sure how to respond. "It's for a movie. I'm an actor and I just need it for this weekend. It's a war movie. I play a soldier." I was talking way too much and way too fast and she could probably tell by the sweat on my brow that I was totally full of it.

"Yes, yes, yes," she said, trying to shut me up. "When you done, you come back. I *blend.*"

She flicked on her clippers and three and a half minutes later I looked like a Nazi. I was nearly bald in the back and on the sides, but on top my hair was still long, and parted diagonally just like the Führer's. *So ist das Leben.*

The next afternoon, about half an hour after touching down in Colorado Springs, I was sitting in the living room of Dan Armstrong's suburban split-level. The windburned forty-seven-year-old federal employee was designated as my point person and had picked me up at the airport. Across a coffee table topped with candles wrapped in cellophane sat another reenactor, Vinnie Francischetti. A Scott Bakula look-alike, the fifty-eight-year-old promotional products businessman had driven ten and a half hours from Montana, through a blizzard, to participate in the DOS, and had just woken up from a nap he'd taken in Dan's den, an area he calls his "military room."

Ever since I learned that people reenact as Nazis, I wanted to know more about why they do it. So with time to kill before driving to the event site, I asked Dan. The former air force weapons loader told me that most reenactors are military collectors and military buffs infatuated with tactical warfare. Not surprisingly, most are politically conservative, most own guns and, he estimated, about 40 percent are either active or former military, which may explain why they're attracted to re-creating WWII's most sophisticated armed forces. "In general, people who do a German impression don't do other impressions," Dan said. Not because they identify with Germany per se but "because German impressions are so expensive." At the end of WWII most German military uniforms and equipment were destroyed, and this put a premium on their resale value today. But Dan, who'd be dressed as a German at DOS, diversifies, and reenacts on the Allied side as well, where he pretends to be a GI in his grandfather's unit. He's even done a Japanese impression.

Still, while both Dan and Vinnie told me they loved the hobby, they also admitted that it was "stupid" because it's so time-consuming and expensive. Vinnie, who moonlights as an ice hockey referee, uses the side money to buy original gear like a Luftwaffe Leica camera. "I'm not sure it works, but I'll give it a shot," he said, pulling it from its battered original leather case and showing it to me.

Soon another reenactor named Tommy arrived at Dan's front door. A heavyset former deputy sheriff with a wispy mustache that curled around the corners of his mouth, he limped inside, leaning on a cane to steady himself. Tommy wore a black T-shirt printed with a face that blended Barack Obama's with Heath Ledger's Joker. Underneath it was the word "Socialism."

"I brought you that belt, Vinnie," he said, placing a thick black leather strap on the coffee table and easing himself into a chair. As I'd soon find out, Tommy recently had to forcibly remove an inmate from his cell and wrestle him to the ground. While he was subduing the inmate, two other officers—weighing a combined 450 pounds—arrived to assist, piled on top of him and crushed his two lower vertebrae. Now he struggled to remain upright—and awake from what I assume were painkillers. His eyes drooped and he spoke in slurred whispers.

Tommy had been reenacting since he was sixteen—for the past twenty-four years—but was sitting out the DOS because of his recent injuries. When he found out that I was a newbie he rolled his eyes and referred to the hobby as "living misery." When I asked him why, he asked me if I'd ever been in the military.

"No," I said.

"Boy Scouts?"

"No."

"Have you ever been camping?"

I had to think about that one. "Twice, but once was in my backyard and in the middle of the night I got scared and headed inside."

He shook his head and laughed.

"I was six!"

Trying to appear somewhat manly, I told him about the second— and last—time I camped, in Peru, on an ecotour. "The mosquitoes were as big as my thumb!" I said. "They ate us alive!" But evidently the misery of moth-sized mosquitoes extracting quart bags of blood couldn't compete with "living misery." Tommy just leaned his chin on the cane's handle and sighed.

· · · · · · · ·

Even though it was early October, we'd be reenacting the events of the first week of September 1942, when the Wehrmacht was advancing above and across the steppe toward Stalingrad. We'd be playing the 24th Panzer, an armored tank division. There'd be lots of vehicles: a tank that a Texas reenactor had mostly built from scratch, a half-track, motorcycles with and without sidecars, jeeps, a radio truck, two large supply trucks and even a couple horses. "Reenactment is usually pretty broad," Dan said. "But not this. This is a little snapshot in time."

Once the German forces arrived in Stalingrad, the war's most intense fighting commenced. "For every German soldier killed," Dan said, "four to five Russians died." But even that wasn't enough for Hitler to defeat Stalin. "Seven or eight Russians needed to die for that to happen. Stalin refused to lose so he just kept throwing people into combat—women, children, men up to the age of fifty-five. It was bloody. *Bloody*." Ultimately, after a brutal winter campaign, the Germans surrendered in early February and retreated back to Berlin. The defeat marked a turning point for the Third Reich. It was, as Dan told me, "the beginning of the end."

Toward the end of our conversation, while Vinnie and Dan chatted with one another, Tommy divulged that, despite all the websites' disclaimers, "some guys like to wear the swastika a little too close to their heart, because they lean a little . . . *to the right*." Others gravitate to it because, as Tommy told me, "it fills the emptiness in their life. Their real life sucks. They're mall ninjas that work as security guards during the week, but on the weekend they get to play 'General Field Marshall.'"

Since Tommy was speaking so candidly I asked him if he knew of any Jewish Nazi reenactors. To my surprise, he did. "One in New Jersey and one in Texas," he mumbled. Apparently the guy from Texas once wore his Nazi uniform to a restaurant, folded a napkin into the shape of a yarmulke, placed it on his head and started singing "Hava Nagila." As Tommy put it, "That's when we said, 'Okay, no more going out to restaurants dressed as Nazis.'" I sat there for a moment and tried to think of a follow-up question, but nothing came to me. I was, for the first time in my life, speechless.

· · · · · · · ·

After the sun dropped behind Pikes Peak it was time for us to head to the site. Vinnie and I hopped into his well-traveled Dodge Caravan. All the seats had been removed to make room for an old mattress that he caught catnaps on during his long drive from Montana. We followed Dan's Acura east into the darkness and the Colorado plains.

Most of what I knew about Nazis came from Hollywood and old film reels, images of Hitler *sieg heiling*, red swastika armbands, intense fist banging, crazed speeches, white supremacy and genocide. But I wanted to know *why*. What happened to turn so many Germans into monsters? So I broached the subject with Vinnie. "What exactly is a Nazi anyway?"

"Someone who's a member of the National Socialist German Workers' Party." He spoke quickly—perhaps a leftover from his New Jersey upbringing—and with a curious cadence of flat Montana blended in with the gruffness. I was just about to say that I wasn't looking for an explanation of the abbreviation, when he added, "You know, like Obama. Someone who wants the government to run everything."

It struck me that I was in the middle of one of those blue state/red state culture clashes I'd seen play out on TV. In one corner was me, the NPR-listening, *New York Times*–reading, foreign film–watching, progressive urbanite, friend to gays, Jews, people of color and artists; and in the other corner was Vinnie, talk radio–listening, rural conservative, gun-toting, don't trust the government as far as you can throw 'em guy. *All those years spent traveling abroad to experience foreign cultures*, I thought, *when all I had to do was fly to Colorado.*

After I got my footing, I asked Vinnie if, by the government running everything he meant the Troubled Asset Relief Program, or TARP.

"Yeah. We would have been much better off if we let those companies fail. It would have been hard, but they would have emerged stronger. I guarantee it."

I gingerly offered up that it was the Bush administration that created TARP, all the while keeping in mind the loaded gun he told me he keeps in the glove compartment.

"Yeah, but Obama passed legislation through and wouldn't let anybody read it," he said with a conspiratorial growl. If I was more on the ball at the time I would have suggested that the military, fire and police benefit from taxpayer dollars too, but a heated political debate at the start of a two-day weapontastic mancation probably wasn't a very good idea.

After driving for over an hour on a dark two-lane road, Dan ground to a halt at a rural intersection. For a moment he paused as if he was double-checking that this nondescript country road was the right one. Then the Acura's wheels turned to the right and his high beams revealed a dark dirt road. We followed close behind and as we turned, I saw a small, arrow-shaped sign stuck in the ground that read, "DOS."

The plains stretched from here to the Mississippi River, nearly a thousand miles away, and from what I could see in the bright moonlight, it didn't look like much got in their way. On the horizon, small, distant lights—probably from farmhouses—twinkled. It was the perfect place to stargaze, the kind of sky where you can see the Milky Way, the kind of sky that always makes me feel infinitesimally small and the differences between Vinnie and me seem utterly ridiculous.

After about five miles of dust and dirt, we saw the flicker of a bonfire on the horizon. Soon we pulled into a makeshift campground where about thirty cars were parked along a barbed wire fence. "Base camp," Vinnie growled. A handful of tents—some "general purpose" big, some individually small—had been erected along the road. We got out and walked across uneven ranchland toward the fire. It was very cold and I was severely underdressed in my jeans and Windbreaker. Perhaps that's why, even though we didn't have to be dressed in our uniforms until 9:00 the next morning, a dozen men were already wearing their ankle-length greatcoats, *Feldmutze* (field hats) and head scarves, and warming themselves by the conflagration.

A few guys huddled around a steaming field kitchen, where a cook dressed in a white smock poured coffee into their tin cups. I shoved my hands in my pockets to stay warm, but my knees shook uncontrollably. After a bit I struck up a conversation with a Nazi who looked like Matt Damon, circa *Saving Private Ryan*. Before long I mentioned that I grew up next to an Amish farm. "Okay, see if you can tell the difference between these," he said and then proceeded to deliver two sentences, one in "old" German and one in modern German. They sounded completely different to me—that was the point—and in the dark, with only the campfire illuminating his face, Nazi hairdo, swastika and greatcoat—and the guttural vowels spilling forth from his mouth—I felt uneasy, like I'd been transported to, well, just west of Stalingrad in September 1942. It was the first "period rush" I'd experienced—what reenactors define as a "you were there" moment—and the event hadn't even begun.

· · · · · · · ·

The sounds produced from the noses, mouths and asses of ninety snoring, farting men make for a layered, atonal polyphonic symphony—a ninety-part motet, perhaps?—but as an audience member, wrapped tightly inside a sleeping bag, I found their marathon performance unbearable. I listened to it all night from inside the tent I shared with a dozen other reenactors—from its minimalist beginnings to its full crescendo and climax at around 4:30 a.m. when the bass, tenor and baritone voices all combined to create a deafening chorus.

"Reveille." Somebody stuck his head in our tent at daybreak and gave me a completely unnecessary wake-up call. I gathered myself and emerged from the tent bleary-eyed and nearly stepped on a mound of cow dung. I stopped the first guy I saw—dressed head to toe in army green—and asked where I could find a Porta-Potty. He looked at me like I was nuts and said, "Dig a hole."

Men were huddled in groups just like the night before, drinking coffee and trying to stay warm. The sun was low and blinding and in every direction I looked the land was flat and treeless. I heard a bird chirp but couldn't see it. I wondered if it was the plover I'd read about that attracted birdwatchers to the area. Near the road was a small hand-painted sign, hidden in the dark when we pulled in, that read, *Achtung! Feindeinsicht u. Beschuss* [sic]. Enemies in Sight and Shooting.

I signed in at a registration desk near the turn-in and was handed a small manila envelope by a teenage girl dressed in civvies. "Don't open it until you're killed," she said.

"Okay," I replied.

I met Matt Charapata by a long trailer hitched behind a black Hummer. He was about my age, bald, and had a big nose and was running on fumes. Like me, he hadn't slept well, and he was flitting about making sure everybody in the Western Gruppe had supplies. He handed me my full German kit: low boots, wool pants with suspenders, a wool tunic, a steel helmet and an A-frame—essentially a backpack without its shell—fitted with hooks and leather Y-straps to secure all my supplies. He also gave me a K98 rifle. It was solid wood and steel and a lot heavier than it looked, like a fat lead pipe.

After changing into my rather uncomfortably large uniform—I felt like a Nazi Beetle Bailey—I got into a conversation with three teenage Nazi reenactors. Brent, Harrison and Cliff were all students, aged seventeen to nineteen, who helped make up the 12th SS as part of the California Historical Group, a four-hundred-plus-member organization dedicated to, as its website proclaims, "remembering and paying tribute to the combat soldier of WWII." "Dude, I rock the SS for public events," a ruddy-cheeked Cliff told me when I first met him. They were loading their A-frames with cans of food that had been wrapped in period-style labels. Reenacting Nazis, they told me, isn't just something they do at hard-core private tacticals like this one; they also show up in uniform at air shows and timeline events.

Cliff had skipped school for the DOS and was the first seventeen-year-old I've met who admitted that he gets "really emotional about history." When not dressing up as a Nazi, he hosts old movie nights at the historic Grenada Theater in Ontario, California. During our conversation, he got so ramped up about the past that he frequently bobbed up and down in excitement. "I'm just passionate about rad shit that happened," he told me. "I mean, World War II was *epic*. The repercussions are still so fresh. Japan can't have a standing military, Israel was created, the United Nations was founded . . ."

Cliff's friend Harrison, a lanky red-haired freshman at Arizona State, tucked a gingham scarf underneath the collar of his tunic and told me he started reenacting after playing the video game Medal of Honor, Allied Assault. One day, while battling against an anonymous online opponent, the stranger on the other end of his headset asked him if he reenacted. He hadn't, but soon he would. Now he maintains two MySpace pages, one for his "modern life" and one for his hobby.

All three young men felt that reenacting was the best way to learn about the past. "History in a book is black and white," Cliff said. "When you come out here, though . . . it takes you back. This is what really happened and you're scared as hell. It's suspenseful. You get lost in it. It's like a weird vacation where you get to fill in all the blanks. Reenactors are the only ones who give a damn about history."

Harrison agreed. "I like to look through the eyes of one soldier," he said. "To sit in a foxhole and keep talking to another soldier so I don't freeze my ass off. It's great to get away from my PlayStation."

"Just because you were a soldier in the Wehrmacht didn't mean that you believed everything Hitler stood for," Brent said. "People were people. Not all of them were politically motivated. The Russians were brutal too, but you never hear about that." It's true I had never heard of that, but I would later, when I read Antony Beevor's book, *Stalingrad: The Fateful Siege*. In it, he includes numerous anecdotes that paint Stalin for the monster he was. One involved injured Soviet POWs, who, upon being released by the Germans, "were sent straight to the Gulag . . . following Stalin's order that anyone who had fallen into enemy hands was a traitor. Stalin even disowned his own son, Yakov."

All three guys described themselves as conservative. Each told me that the more they learned about the past, the less they trusted the government because all governments in World War II were guilty of war crimes and propaganda, not just the Germans. When I referenced the staged Jessica Lynch rescue and Pat Tillman friendly-fire cover-up, Brent nodded his head vigorously and referred to these incidents in Iraq and Afghanistan as "same shit, different toilet."

On the one hand, I admired these kids. They were half my age and knew far more about history than I did. Before I started working on this book I'm embarrassed to admit that I'd never even heard of Stalingrad. But another part of me wondered if they were aware that, by spending their weekends "rocking the SS," they were—intentionally or not—romanticizing a group that wanted to exterminate entire groups of people.

When I broached this with them Cliff told me his friends think Nazi reenacting is "badass," but that adults, specifically those who "grew up in the sixties" still have a problem with it. "My grandmother hates Germans," he said. But his experience has been different. Once when he was waiting tables, Cliff overheard an elderly man speaking German. Turned out he was a former Nazi. "He was a really nice guy. When you meet people, they don't resemble the stereotype," he said. "It helps to separate the soldier from the war."

It's hard to believe, but at their age I once considered hanging a swastika flag in my college dorm room—not because I was a socialist or an anti-Semite, but because I too thought it looked "badass" and didn't know any better. I grew up in a town that was nearly 100 percent white, mostly Protestant, and of the 1,500 or so students in my high school, *I think* only one was Jewish. During my freshman year of college, while pursuing a girl, I noticed that a black classmate of ours was being sexually aggressive toward her at a party.

"They're all like that," I said.

"Oh, my God," she said. "You're such a racist!"

"What are you talking about?" I was stunned and offended. I couldn't understand what I said that was so horrible. "If you think that's racist, you should come to my hometown and hear what some people say."

I thought of my own youthful ignorance while talking with other guys at base camp. I wondered if any of them had considered that some people might be offended by their hobby. I wondered if they kept their hobby a secret from some friends. I also noticed that what I considered to be the most significant event of World War II, the Holocaust, was a mere blip on the screen to many of the reenactors. Whenever I brought it up to people, they acknowledged that it was "not such a good thing," but to them it was only a small part of a larger, deadlier war. A war in which nearly 70 million people died, including the 6 million who perished in the Holocaust.

"Wake up, [genocide] happens," Brent said, citing the ethnic "cleansing" that happened in WWII, as well as more recently in Rwanda and the former Yugoslavia. "Sherman said, 'War is hell.' The worse it is, the faster it's over. Horror produces results. Fear produces results." With such tough talk I thought I might have three future commanders of our armed forces on hand, but none wanted to serve. As Harrison put it, "My parents said, 'We've spent too much money on you for you to get killed.'"

. . . .

It was shortly before noon now and warmer. Everyone had rolled up their greatcoats and strapped them to their A-frames. We were summoned around the tank for a prebattle debriefing and "pep talk." Unlike public events where enemies mingle with one another before fighting—like two football teams shaking hands at midfield—we wouldn't see any of Stalin's Red Army until we were officially at war. This was our chance to get psyched about kicking some Commie *Arsch*.

Our commanding officer, Randy Beard, a slightly chubby Robert Mitchum, stood atop the tank, cigarette in hand, one foot propped up on its turret. He wore a *Schirmutze*, an officer's visor cap, and *Staub Schutzbrille*, dark celluloid dust goggles. It looked like he'd gone swimming in full military regalia, like Michael Phelps in a creepy Halloween costume.

He cleared his throat and shouted, "Can you hear me?" His voice was raspy.

"Jawohl!" the troops replied. Either everybody had done this before, or I'd missed a dress rehearsal.

"Today . . . ," he said, pausing for dramatic effect, "is history! Surrender to the event! You are Germans in southern Russia. You're going to get tired, sleep deprived and miserable. When it sucks—and I promise you it will—remember, that's why you came."

Beard warned us that danger awaited us—in many forms. The Russians had a "shitload of mortars and grenades," and there'd be rattlesnakes too. Lots of 'em. He'd seen five in the last day and a half, an unusually large number for early October. "If you hear a rattle," he warned, "don't be Steve Irwin." Then, to drive home the fear, he said, "The only way to make this event more dangerous is to use real bullets."

Before we were dismissed, Beard's bald, bespectacled sidekick, the second in command, called the *Zweite Zug* Lieutenant, or simply *Zweite*, climbed atop the tank and addressed us. "Seeing as how Deutschland is a Christian country," he said to widespread laughter, "we'll have a prayer." We took off our helmets and bowed our heads.

The prayer was in German, but I still managed to pick out a few words, like *Frau, Gott* and *Russische Kommunistische.*

. . . .

By the first week of September 1942, Germany and its allies had rolled across the dusty, barren steppes of southern Russia toward Stalingrad, a city of 500,000 people on the banks of the Volga River. Capturing the major industrial center would make it a lot easier for the Germans to penetrate the Caucasian oil fields and it would also be a symbolic victory: Hitler bitch-slapping the city named for his pinko Commie nemesis—the equivalent of the Russkies sacking a place called Hitler Town.

The Luftwaffe had already bombed much of Stalingrad, killing nearly forty thousand people. The Volga was on fire, Germany's 6th Army had taken 26,500 prisoners and now its tanks were on the outskirts of Stalingrad and "we," the 24th Panzer, were advancing fast. Okay, so maybe not that fast.

We marched south toward the blinding sun, down a long, sand-colored road. Our squad was split in half, nine of us on the left shoulder, ten of us on the right, evenly spaced out and in perfectly straight lines. I was near the back of the right flank. Matt, who was our squad leader, trailed me to help us maintain our spacing. Every now and then, Randy and the *Zweite* would trot past us on their horses, followed by two guys in a *Zündapp*, a German motorcycle with a sidecar.

"We're live, guys," Matt reminded us as we trudged forward. "They could be out there." Unless they were gnomes hiding behind shrubs, however, they weren't. The only thing I could see was thorny brush, big sky and a snow-capped Pikes Peak some one-hundred-plus miles due west.

The DOS wasn't the only war to take place in these parts. From

1863 to 1865, when Colorado was still a territory and the Civil War was raging, the U.S. Army forced local Plains Indians from their lands onto reservations. One particularly gruesome incident, known as the Sand Creek Massacre, took place not far from here in 1864, when Col. John M. Chivington commanded seven hundred drunken troops to raid an encampment of Cheyenne and Arapaho Indians. They slaughtered 133 people, mostly women and children, and later paraded their body parts through the Denver streets. One can only imagine what the Plains Indians' ghosts thought as they watched a legion of white guys marching off to fake-kill each other.

Soon we crested a gentle rise that revealed a valley bisected by the road. On either side cottonwoods provided a welcome burst of greenery. "Must be water down there," one of the guys said. Our unit broke off to the right into the low shrub, while the rest of the soldiers continued on down the dusty road. The ranchland's sandy, fragile terrain had eroded into tiny shelves and crumbled under my feet. Cacti shaped like small prickly cucumbers sprouted from the ground. Snake holes, three inches wide, disappeared underground. Brittlebush and thorns latched onto my woolen pants whenever I brushed by them. All my gear put so much pressure on my back that a sharp pain shot up through my neck.

"Mahk shoo day cahhh see ooo," Matt said.

"What?" I asked. I'd plugged my ears with wax so I wouldn't go deaf once we started shooting. Now all I could hear was a muffled, oceanlike echo.

"I said make sure they can't see you." There were twenty of us walking along a hillside with no cover whatsoever. Anybody within a mile could see us.

Suddenly we heard gunfire in the distance.

"Evehboduh crowtch dohn!" Matt barked.

"What?"

"Everybody crouch down!"

I dropped as quickly as I could into a thicket of burrs. I got up and they were everywhere: my hands, the backs of my legs, my butt, my calves, everything seemed to be punctured by the clingy starbursts. I tried to get rid of them, but no matter what I did I only managed to transfer them to other parts of my body. I finally gave up when I heard a rattle. I spun around, but I couldn't see anything. Images flashed through my head of rattlesnakes leaping out of the shrubbery and sinking their fangs into my neck.

To ward off any impending strike, I crouched down and started kicking my legs out like a Cossack. As I did this I noticed an army of ants scurrying over the ground. Pressure built up in my bowels. I'd had a lot of nightmares leading up to the event, about how things might go wrong, but I never considered what to do if *this* happened—*if I had to go potty.* It would take me at least a minute to get my pants off. To calm my nerves I stood up and walked around. So what if the Russians saw me? *This isn't real!* I thought. *The bullets are blanks! If I get shot, I'm not actually going to die!*

I saw young Cliff facedown in a scrub bush blooming yellow wildflowers and hurried over to him. After a moment I posed the only question I could think of: "Have you ever seen the movie *The Hurt Locker*?" He shook his head.

Our other units had lured the Russians into a copse of cottonwoods. Now Matt ordered us to circle in from the rear and surround them.

What had been distant gunfire was now close and growing in intensity, machine gun *rat-a-tat-tats* overlapping with tank *booms.*

When we finally got to the battle, our tank was lobbing grenades packed with baby powder into a cluster of trees. When each landed, a plume of white smoke mushroomed into the air. We walked through tall, brittle grass, staying low to avoid detection. A couple hundred feet away in the tall trees, shadowy figures darted to and fro, opening fire on one another. It was hard to tell who was who, so I kept my rifle on safety. I didn't want to kill one of my own men. The rest of my squad fired at anything that moved, all while advancing cautiously through the grass.

"Shay wish yo shad!" Matt yelled at me.

"What?" I asked, cupping my hand against my ear.

"Stay with your squad!" he yelled.

The soldiers advancing en masse through the bone-dry reeds made for such a good picture that I pulled out my camera and snapped a photo. While I was doing that, they advanced without me.

I tried to catch up with them, ignoring orders and standing up to quicken my pace, but only managed a couple steps when I saw it: a flash of fire discharging out of the barrel of a rifle, ten feet up in a tree, 150 feet away. It had been aimed at me. I'd been shot before I ever got a round off.

As per orders, I pulled out the tiny manila envelope from my pocket and opened it up. I unfolded a piece of paper that was tucked inside, as slim as a Chinese fortune. It read:

KIA! THOUGHT YOU WERE DREAMING, BUT CHOKED ON YOUR BLOOD, NOW GO TO SLEEP.

That's gross, I thought.

I raised my rifle over my head and walked out of the grass toward the "medic," a civilian girl who was sitting on the tail of a pickup truck at a nearby crossroads. Her feet dangled a few inches above the ground and she wore an orange hunting vest, jeans and sneakers. She took the envelope from me, slipped another piece of paper into it—the description of my next death—stapled it and gave it back to me. "Thanks," I said. "War is hell." She half nodded.

I filled up my canteen with water from a large plastic jug and sat on the ground, unhooking all my gear. Soon dozens of other dead soldiers congregated at the crossroads and played armchair quarterback, recounting how many Russians they killed and how they ultimately met their demise. At one point a German soldier led about twenty Russian POWs to the intersection—including the only two women reenactors I'd see at the event. They'd all placed their hands on their heads and were pouting. The guard pointed his rifle at them and yelled in German for a bit, but it didn't have the intended effect. Mostly the Russians looked at him with get-over-yourself eye rolls. Authenticity has its limits. It's perfectly fine to re-create some parts of history, they seemed to be saying, but push it too far and you cross the line into Creepyville.

I'd traveled to Colorado to learn about what happened at the Battle of Stalingrad, a six-and-a-half-month siege that Antony Beevor calls "perhaps the most important battle in history." But since I reached the event site I hadn't heard anybody talk about it. Nobody talked about the 1 million soldiers and civilians who died, or how it was one of history's most gruesome battles, where frostbitten soldiers would unwrap their bandaged hands and feet only to watch their fingers and toes "stay behind." No one talked about how significant the German loss was, and how it was the beginning of the end for the Wehrmacht. From their surrender in the brutal cold of February 1943, they'd make a long, slow retreat back to Berlin, where, ultimately, on April 30, 1945, Hitler would blow his brains out.

Instead, on a lunch break held on the banks of the nearby stream, the reenactors mostly traded tales about military suppliers they ordered gear from. "Cheap-ass bastards only have stuff with one stitch," said one. I learned they call people like him a "stitch Nazi," someone who's so particular about the construction of his uniform that he'll literally count how many stitches are used. Apparently reproduction uniforms constructed with two stitches on the seams are better made and more "authentic."

It seemed like spending the weekend in a time machine was what really made them happy: to eat tuna out of cans that had been wrapped in white paper, to stab a tube of salami with a knife and bite into it, to tell stories they'd read about Napoleon. And yet as I sat under a tree resting my eyes, turning my face toward the warming sun, I couldn't help noticing a few glaring anachronisms: the Nazi eating a bagel, the repeated quoting of *Platoon*. But nothing, not a word about Stalingrad.

· · · · · · · ·

Later that night, after I hitched a ride with the Texans, the pickup truck pulled into base camp. I hopped out, scooted over to Vinnie's van and grabbed a spare key that he'd placed atop one of his tires. "Just in case you get back before I do," he'd growled. After climbing inside, I blasted the heat and lay atop his old mattress. After only nine hours of war, I was a civilian again. And I couldn't have been happier.

The next morning, I sat in the van's driver seat and considered a herd of cattle who'd strolled over to a barbed wire fence. I was happy to be back in the real world, listening to a baseball game on the radio and munching on a PowerBar. At one point, I took out a book I was reading, Tony Horwitz's *A Voyage Long and Strange*. I read a sentence or two then slipped it back in my bag, because nothing was longer or stranger than what I'd just been through.

I stayed dressed in my uniform until early that afternoon. Before I took it off, I dug around inside my pockets and found the manila envelope stapled shut, with my fate sealed inside. I opened it up and pulled out the slip. It read,

KIA! FIRST A THUMP,
THEN YOU FELT THAT YOU WERE DROWNING,
THEN GONE.

That's gross, I thought.

I could feel something else in the envelope so I pulled it out too. It was my registration card. I flipped it over and read what was on the back, the "DOS Ten Commandments." One was so important it garnered two spots, numbers 1 and 10. It said, "Stay with your squad."

CHAPTER TWO

The Way We Weren't

Although acting like a German soldier didn't yield many historical lessons, I did learn a few things in Colorado. Namely, that life would be awful without fire, potable water, soap and plumbing. If you don't think they're an integral part of our modern lives, I suggest trying to go twenty-four hours without just one of them and see how you feel at the end of the day. You'll be dirty, thirsty, cold and stinky, which was exactly what I was.

So after living in such a deprived world, it should come as no surprise that when I returned to modern life I acted like a gluttonous freak, stuffing my face with junk food, taking hour-long showers and sleeping in late just so I could experience the luxury of our Serta Perfect Sleeper. And yet despite suffering through simulated war for only two days—and let's be fair, for one of them I sat in a van and listened to a baseball game—my interest was piqued. The DOS was so extreme, so different from the Fort MacArthur timeline event, that I wanted to know more about the world of reenacting. Why people did it and why they chose to commemorate or reenact a particular moment in time. Why civilians willingly chose to experience "war." Why people liked to spend their weekends without any of modern life's creature comforts.

But the experience also gave me an idea. What if I could reenact my way through history? To learn not only about the hobby but maybe, just maybe, about the past too? I remember at OFMD watching the reenactors parade by the crowd in chronological order. First a group of Roman soldiers filed by, then Vikings, then big hairy men in kilts and on and on until it ended with guys dressed quite surprisingly as Vietnam GIs. I pictured myself embedding with the units and I hoped doing so would give me a better understanding of the past and maybe even the present.

"What do you think?" I told Wendy my idea. She looked at me like I was bonkers.

"You know I support whatever you do," she replied.

"Yes," I said.

"Except that one time NPR wanted you to report a story from inside a coffin. That was macabre."

"And I completely understood your concerns back then, but this would be such a great experience."

"Well . . ." I could see her wheels turning. "Promise me that if you do this you won't die."

"Real die or fake die?" I asked. "Because fake dying is part of the experience."

"I'm not even going to respond to that."

"So is that a yes?"

"Yes."

I gave her a hug and bolted into my office to research some more time periods. I wasn't sure what to do next, but I was determined that whatever happened, I was not going to go AWOL.

. . . .

Half my extended family lives in Florida. Both sets of my grandparents vacationed there. Outside of the four states I've lived in, I've probably spent more time there than anywhere else. But the small town of Brooksville near the center of the state, the "real" Florida, if you will, was as foreign to me as Azerbaijan. The first thing that struck me when I pulled into town was its stately redbrick courthouse. It was three stories high and four tall columns framed its front. As I parked my rental car across the street and gazed toward it, I half expected to see Matlock emerge from its front door. Leading up to its steps was a small courtyard flanked by two stately live oak trees that I also felt weirdly drawn to. I think it must have been their *Midnight in the Garden of Good and Evil* vibe that sucked me in, because I stood under their overlapping canopies and photographed them for the better part of five minutes. Still, no matter how much I knelt down, bent over and twisted my phone toward the sky I couldn't adequately capture their clingy vines of Spanish moss. The tentacles were so dense, in fact, that only a few dapples of early morning sunlight could reach the sidewalk.

After standing under the mythical trees for a while I felt like every bit the southern gentleman so I sauntered to a nearby street corner, where a statue of a solemn and youthful Confederate soldier held court over all the passersby, which, given that the sidewalks were deserted, amounted to me.

I studied the memorial for a bit, took a picture and jotted down some notes: "Dedicated by the United Daughters of the Confederacy in 1916. Chiseled from limestone? Quote under Confederate flag says 'Love Makes Memory Eternal.' Soldier holding rifle."

I had a few hours to kill before the Brooksville Raid, Florida's largest Civil War reenactment, so when I spotted a neon tube bent to look like a steaming coffee cup I headed toward it. Signs announced that it was GM's Bistro and it was open. I walked inside, took a seat in a booth and started to peruse the menu. Within minutes the restaurant's owner, James Tsacrios, pulled up a chair. He reminded me a bit of Stephen Sondheim in his crisp oxford shirt and neatly trimmed beard. Judging by the way he looked at me, I must have reminded him of Charles Manson—or perhaps Allen Ginsberg, but only on a good day. I'd grown a bushy beard for the reenactment and was wearing a pair of orange glasses. It wasn't a good look, and I got the sense he thought I was either a serial killer or a beatnik and wanted to keep a close eye on me, in case I pulled out a cleaver or broke into an impromptu poetry slam and scared off the other four patrons.

Once I explained my historical quest, however, Tsacrios opened up, albeit in a tone that convinced me the place was bugged. "The limbs of those trees are, um, very *strong*," he said, looking in the direction of the two live oaks. I turned around toward the courthouse.

"Yes, they're very beautiful," I said.

"No. When I was young, I asked my grandfather when the last time those limbs were, uh, *used*," he continued. "He just rolled his eyes and said, *Recently.*"

Looking in the direction of the trees I started to catch his drift. Images of old black-and-white photos and scenes from *Mississippi Burning* flooded my imagination. Sturdy trees that looked a lot like those live oaks always figured prominently in those grisly frames. The trees weren't beautiful, they were ugly, improvised gallows that ended men's lives. For a moment I was transported back to Brooksville's checkered past. I saw a mob of angry whites standing under the body of a black man. I'd never been to a town where lynchings took place—at least not that I knew of—and I suddenly felt sick, knowing that not five minutes earlier I'd stood under those trees and admired them for their beauty.

Online comments from people who've visited Brooksville frequently mention how it feels like a place where they've "stepped back in time." And those people are right, it does. But the last thing many of the town's eight thousand residents want to do is turn back the clock. If there's any indication of Brooksville's historical political leanings, consider that what had been settled as Melendez in 1845 was renamed Brooksville eleven years later, shortly after the pro-slavery South Carolina congressman Preston Brooks pummeled the abolitionist Massachusetts senator Charles Sumner with a cane on the U.S. Senate floor. After the Civil War, things didn't get much better for freed slaves. Jim Crow laws were instituted and during a dark, thirty-one-year period that lasted until the 1920s, Hernando County lynched ten times more blacks than any other Florida county. Even after the lynchings stopped, racial tension continued to flare up. As recently as 1982, *Sports Illustrated* profiled Brooksville native and Philadelphia Eagles defensive tackle Jerome Brown's disruption of a KKK rally in front of the now symbolic courthouse.

When I visited Brooksville, it seemed as though things had started to improve. I saw interracial couples at the local Walmart and two young black guys I talked to outside a gas station said the only people who give them a hard time are the local police.

"They give us shit about our tinted windows and aftermarket exhaust pipes," "L" said through his ruby-capped teeth.

"Why?" I asked.

"They're illegal."

"So aren't they just doing their job?" I asked.

"But white guys have it and they don't get pulled over like we do."

"It's all that statue," his friend Desmond said, through gold-capped teeth.

"Which statue?" I asked.

"The one down at the courthouse."

"The Confederate soldier?" I asked.

"That's what it is."

"I'm confused. What does the Confederate soldier have to do with the cops?"

"That is the cops," he said.

Times were tough in Hernando County when I visited in January 2010. Nearly 15 percent of its residents were out of work, the third highest rate in the state. I saw flyers taped to gas station windows advertising "gold parties," where people could trade their gold jewelry for cash. Many of the storefronts were shuttered and the ones that remained in business—a pharmacy, an antique store and a couple restaurants—showed little signs of life. As in so many other small towns across America, business had fled Brooksville for suburban strip malls and after the economic collapse of 2008 its town center was left gasping for breath.

That weekend's reenactment seemed to be the biggest thing going. Posters were stapled to telephone poles and that morning's *St. Petersburg Times* had devoted three pages to it, calling it "Hernando County's Largest Public Gathering." Historical battle maps, photos of Confederate and Union reenactors and a profile of my contact for the event, Robert "Colonel Bob" Niepert, filled its pages. I even saw a large and lavishly detailed mural painted on the side of a women's clothing store that depicted Union and Confederate troops engaged in an intense battle. Next to it a placard read:

THE BROOKSVILLE RAID
REENACTMENT HELD EVERY THIRD
WEEKEND IN JANUARY

Given the actual historical event's modest size I was surprised at how popular the reenactment had become. "The raid was a blip on the radar," Colonel Bob told me a few weeks before the event. "It wasn't much of a battle; it was more of a skirmish. It only lasted a couple days." But despite the fact that only 240 Union troops and a handful of civilian irregulars "saw action," today the Brooksville Raid attracts up to four thousand participants—and it happens every year over Martin Luther King Day weekend.

· · · · · · · ·

As unbelievable as it may sound, the first people to reenact the Civil War were Civil War veterans themselves. During Gettysburg's fiftieth anniversary—at the so-called Great Reunion of 1913—over fifty thousand Confederate and Union veterans reenacted Pickett's Charge. Well, sort of. Mostly, the elderly vets hobbled across the battlefield, their most dangerous weapon being the canes that helped keep them vertical. They met at a designated meeting point and shook hands, officially putting the differences of the country's bloodiest war behind them.

It wasn't for another forty-eight years, during a Civil War centennial celebration at Manassas Battlefield, that civilians got in on the fun. Now every year in the United States hundreds of Civil War reenactments take place. Much as Ken Burns's Civil War documentary likes to remind you that "the Civil War was fought in ten thousand places," at times it feels as though the same goes for the war's reenactments. There's an event nearly every weekend and one in almost every state. Some take place near famous battlefields like Gettysburg and Manassas, while others occur in towns (and states) where the Civil War wasn't even fought, like Lamoni, Iowa, and Boscobel, Wisconsin. A few have melodramatic movie-appropriate names that scream "Tom Selleck Hallmark Hall of Fame Movie," like the Skirmish at Gamble's Hotel; others, such as Summer of Hell: The Battles of Gaines' Mill and Malvern Hill, could easily be the next Wes Craven vehicle. While most raise money for local historical societies and keep the paying public cordoned off behind safety ropes, others remain private tactical affairs, not unlike the Stalingrad event I participated in. I found out after about a minute of research that the Civil War is, by far, the most popular era to reenact, not only in the United States, but throughout the rest of the world. And because of its relative affordability, this war is often the first period that folks new to the hobby reenact. Estimates place the number of American Civil War reenactors at fifty thousand, with an additional ten thousand or so abroad.

I probably could have participated in any number of Civil War reenactments, but I chose Brooksville because it promised to be such a different experience—*practically antithetical*—to the Stalingrad one. For one thing, it was in Florida so I wouldn't freeze my butt off. For another, it was a public event, so I wouldn't march off into the great unknown and risk never returning. Plus Colonel Bob's company—the group I'd embed with—weren't über-concerned with authenticity. "If your uniform can pass for 'real' from ten feet away, well, that's just fine," Colonel Bob told me a few weeks before I flew to Florida. So-called mainstream reenactors, Colonel Bob's company camps with other like-minded hobbyists in trailers and RVs. "We don't go for that sleeping on cold ground stuff," he said in his gravelly southern drawl. Thrilled that I wouldn't be spending the night shivering in a foxhole, I ventured to a local sporting goods store and loaded up on modern camping equipment: a tent, bedroll, mummy sleeping bag, tarp, compressible pillow and lifetime supply of baby wipes and earplugs. I felt confident, heading to Florida, that I'd last long enough to see the end of the Brooksville Raid.

Weather, intensity and lax uniform standards aside, the biggest reason I wanted to reenact the Civil War in Florida was because Tony Horwitz didn't. In 1998, Horwitz wrote *Confederates in the Attic*, a wildly popular book about contemporary southerners' obsession with the Confederacy. Horwitz travels mainly through former Confederate states and tackles hot-button issues like the Confederate flag and Disney's proposed Civil War theme park near Manassas. He spends time with the Civil War historian Shelby Foote and with Alberta Martin, purported to be the oldest living Confederate widow.

But he spends the most memorable chapters—at least for me—with a hard-core Civil War reenactor named Robert Lee Hodge. Among other wacky things, Hodge tries to perfect the look of a bloated corpse and spoons in a trench with fellow reenactors to stay warm. During one chapter the two men go on a weeklong, sleep-deprived "Civil Wargasm," a sort of Greatest Hits road trip in which they visit the war's must-see sites. I was so enthralled by Hodge's fanaticism that I couldn't put these sections down. And apparently I wasn't the only one. In fact, whenever I mentioned the words "Civil War," "reenactment" and "book" to any human being, what I often heard back was, "Oh, you mean like *Confederates in the Attic*." In some ways I found this very flattering—after all, Horwitz is a Pulitzer Prize winner—but in other ways, I found it to be really friggin' annoying because I felt like he stole my idea ten years before I ever had it.

Still, even though Florida was the third state to secede, Horwitz didn't visit it, probably because today Florida doesn't exactly conjure up the images most often associated with the South or because, aside from the Battle of Olustee, nothing all that memorable happened there during wartime.

Florida was the Confederacy's least populous state, with only 140,000 people, half of which were slaves. While there may not have been very many Floridians, there were lots of cows, especially around Brooksville, an agricultural area located less than twenty miles from the Gulf of Mexico. Its strategic position, abundance of cattle and readily available salt (boiled down from nearby waters) transformed the area into a sort of breadbasket for the Confederate army. Cows were slaughtered, their meat was preserved in salt and then it was shipped north to hungry troops.

Toward the end of the war—which of course nobody knew was the end of the war—the North initiated a strategy to cut off food and supplies from the Southern troops. Railroad lines were destroyed, farms set ablaze and cattle slaughtered. On June 30, 1864, federal troops stationed in Fort Myers sailed north about fifty miles to the town of Bayport. They came ashore, marched inland over the next few days, burned local farmers' crops, barns and houses and created a path of destruction en route to Brooksville. You won't read about the Brooksville-Bayport Raid in any of the great Civil War books or hear the late Shelby Foote spin a yard about it in Ken Burns's documentary, but you will hear plenty of talk about it in the one place where they do remember, Brooksville.

. . . .

I've never eaten at the fast-food chain Chick-fil-A, but I like its mascot. For one thing the illiterate Holstein cow is clever. In advertisements he holds a hand-scrawled sign that reads, "Eat Mor Chikin." For another he's huge. At least, the inflatable version of him that I saw marking the entrance to the raid's reenactment site.

I pulled in to the 1,200-acre Sand Hill Scout Reservation from a busy four-lane highway and stopped at a registration desk. I paid my two-dollar participant fee and signed a couple forms promising I wouldn't kill anybody. One of the attendants, a blond woman in her fifties, handed me an orange lanyard and participant badge and told me to wear it around my neck for the duration of the event. Slipping it on, I thought of how the stitch Nazis would have scoffed at such a historically incorrect "necklace."

I hopped back in the car and continued to drive down a long paved road that divided two vast grassy fields. Off to my immediate left, a couple dozen merchants were setting up food stalls and large canvas tents. Farther down, a large blue-and-white-striped tent loomed like a recently landed spaceship. I felt like I was at a county fair, not something striving for nineteenth-century authenticity. At any moment I expected to spot a kettle corn stand, and then, as if on cue, there it was, a kettle corn stand.

Colonel Bob had told me to follow signs marked "Hardy's Brigade" and, after nearly a mile of now bumpy, curvy roads, I pulled into a makeshift campsite framed by tall sand pines and roped off with thin pink ribbon. RVs and campers lined its perimeter. Backing my rental into a small clearing, I nearly tore off the side-view mirror of a red pickup truck with a Sarah Palin bumper sticker taped to its cab window. (But not on purpose, I swear.) I found Colonel Bob just past the camp's epicenter, a smoldering campfire and an easel holding a whiteboard scrawled with the weekend's scheduled activities. In a makeshift horse pen he was grooming a dark red stallion with a black mane and tail.

Colonel Bob had long, wavy gray hair that cascaded out of his slouch hat, and a salt-and-pepper mustache—sort of a modern-day Buffalo Bill. "You're going to need a uniform," he said, looking at my street clothes. He pointed his cigarillo across the campground toward a short, squat man with a goatee, named Rich Howe, who had extra uniforms in his camper. I walked over and Howe held out a pair of gray wool pants that were so wide Fat Elvis would drown in them. "These won't fit without suspenders and all the buttons are missing," he said with a wide grin. "Looks like you're gonna need to go shopping."

Colonel Bob's company doesn't pledge allegiance to either the Union or the Confederate flag. Rather, they "galvanize," dressing in blue or gray to even out the battlefield when the colors are lopsided—which is pretty much all the time. On any given day the Colonel commands either the 5th Company Florida (Confederate) or the 7th Michigan (Union). At Brooksville I'd don uniforms from both companies. Flipping sides like this earns his company two nicknames, the "Cross-Dressers" and the "Biggest Losers" because they lose both of the two battles.

Before I knew it, I was walking to a merchant area called Sutler Row for some late afternoon shopping with Buddy Jimmerson. The stout forty-four-year-old was still dressed in his Confederate gray from an earlier school demonstration. "If you go on your own, you'll never know which buttons to get," he said.

About a hundred feet into our walk, we emerged from a small cluster of pines into the Confederate camp proper. All signs of twenty-first-century life vanished. Rows of small canvas wedge tents filled a clearing carpeted with pine straw, and smoldering pits exhaled the unmistakable aroma that is campfire. At one camp, a group of wild-haired Confederates played a game called cornhole, a sort of cross between horseshoes and Skee-Ball. When one of the guys tossed a beanbag toward a hole cut into a piece of plywood and missed badly, his opponent quipped, "Fuck, Bart, even a Yankee coulda done better 'n dat." All his friends cracked up and Buddy could tell it'd caught my attention. "Most of these guys 'round here would never wear blue," he said. "They'd rather die." *Good!*

Sutler Row amounted to a grid of large canvas wall tents that housed the wares of nomadic merchants—"sutlers"—like those who used to follow and sell to Civil War soldiers. Modern-day sutlers follow reenactments across the country, like hawkers at a state fair. Everything for sale under the tents' roofs was Civil War period or themed: hoop skirts and frock coats, haversacks and gaiters, chevrons and belt buckles; gunpowder and replica weapons; CDs with names like *Tenting on the Old Campground* and books with titles like *Hearthside Cooking* and *Thoughts on Men's Shirts in America, 1750–1900*. We stopped at a number of stores—places named the Regimental Quartermaster and Loafers Glory—looking for the exact right buttons, and eventually we found some plain silver ones at a store called Sidekick Sutler. They shared a display case with about twenty other styles. Buddy was right. I would have never known that they were the ones to buy.

Ever since my family's first vacation to the South, when my dad kept saying, "You see the way they look at our Pennsylvania license plate? They're still fighting the war down here!" I always wanted to know if that really was true. So on our way back to camp, I asked Buddy, who works at the Tampa Bay airport.

"I don't think the war's still being fought, per se," he said, spitting a wad of chewing tobacco onto the sandy soil. "But there's a difference. There's a northern way and a southern way. Northerners think it's rude to say 'Yes, sir' and 'No, sir.' But not me. I teach my kids to say that. That's the southern way." But another difference got under his skin. "Northerners come down here and tell us how to run things. Well, that may not be the way we do it. You're in the South now. This is how we do it." It wasn't unlike the perspective the South had before secession. At that time, the rapidly industrializing northern states were modernizing and abolitionists were pressuring the federal government to abolish slavery across the union. The straw that broke the camel's back was when Abraham Lincoln was elected. The South was convinced he'd use his federal authority to abolish slavery, and soon after his election southern states started to secede. As Joseph J. Ellis writes in *Founding Brothers: The Revolutionary Generation*, slavery was "the central and defining problem" between the founding of the country and its ultimate abolition.

I couldn't help but think as I saw men dressed in Confederate flag T-shirts that said, "Heritage Not Hate" that the pain of losing the Civil War and the South being destroyed still stings. Unlike the World Series or Super Bowl, where nobody remembers who finished second, when it comes to the Civil War everybody knows who lost and when you live in a place where battles were fought you see reminders of it everywhere.

By the time we arrived back at the campground it was dark and Buddy disappeared into his camper to rest for the following day's battle. Seeing a few other members standing under the fluorescent-lit overhang of a pop-up camper, I introduced myself to them. Bill, Gary and

Jack were dressed in civvies and at least forty years older than the average Civil War soldier—and had chosen to spend their golden years on the battlefield rather than the golf course. Each man sipped his liquid of choice out of a "mucket," a stainless steel mug/bucket hybrid popular with Civil War reenactors.

I tried to engage the men in a discussion about Civil War history and the series of events that led to secession; how, as each new state entered the union, it was either "free" or "slave" and how that affected the balance of power in the federal government; how in 1861, at only eighty years old, the United States was less "united" than "states" and how the growing and fervent abolitionist movement was pressuring the government to end the immoral practice of slavery. But every time the real war came up the conversation circled back to a trip the men took to Gettysburg a year and a half earlier.

That year, at the battle's 145th anniversary, they fought alongside an estimated fourteen thousand other reenactors, five hundred horses and one hundred cannons. (Which sounds impressive until you consider that *forty-one thousand* reenactors—the capacity of Wrigley Field—clashed at the 135th anniversary, earning it the title of world's largest ever reenactment.) People came from all over the world to the 145th, and a lot of them wore gray, hoping to capture the rebel spirit that attracts so many people to the southern cause. "When you saw all the Confederate troops marching out of the woods, it was like someone had poured mercury down the hillside," said Jack, a dead ringer for Denver Pyle. "When it was all over, all you could see were dead bodies . . . *everywhere*. I'd say fifty percent of the Yankees had tears in their eyes."

But it wasn't just the 145th's scale that made the men giddy, it was the chance to be in a film. A crew hid in the tall grass and behind trees and recorded the battle for a movie, *Gettysburg: Darkest Days, Finest Hours*. Produced by LionHeart FilmWorks, a Virginia-based studio specializing in reenactment movies, the four-hour DVD may lack pace, good acting and drama, but it makes up for that in a detailed retelling of the battle and crisp high-def photography. "They interviewed us before we went off to battle, as if we were real soldiers," Jack said excitedly.

In fact, the experience left such an impression on the men that I had a hard time figuring out what was more profound for them, walking in the footsteps of history or having been a part of something akin to a Woodstock for reenactors. So I asked. "Man," Gary, a gaunt, soft-spoken former firefighter, said, "I guess I'd have to say . . . *both*."

. . . .

The next morning I and about twelve mostly middle-aged soldiers showed up at formation near the company's horse pen. Drowning in oversized gray wool pants and squeezing into a kid-sized slouch hat, I was delighted to see that my long trousers concealed my malapropos footwear, a pair of well-worn black Campers. Wearing contemporary Spanish shoes would, if spotted, earn me the label of "farb," a derogatory word that denotes anyone who dons anachronistic apparel. (Its etymology purportedly derives from the 1961 Civil War centennial when someone commented on another reenactor's historically challenged uniform and declared, "*Far be* it from me to criticize [what you're wearing].")

I stood at what I imagined attention looked like—rigid back, straight feet, arms by my sides. While Colonel Bob inspected our uniforms, a bearded Falstaffian company member named John Butler handed me a replica 1862 Enfield musket that weighed slightly less than a stop sign.

"You've shot a gun before, right?" he asked.

"Yes, sir," I said. "In fact, I just did a World War II reenactment where we shot K98s." He grinned at me as if I'd just told him I was president of the NRA. I didn't have the courage to tell him that I failed to get off a shot.

"Right, well, then you're plenty experienced."

But of course I wasn't. Even though I grew up in the sticks I'd only ever fired an air pump BB gun and a .22, two mechanically simple weapons that I fired at empty Coke cans. Firing something as arcane as a musket, however, was totally alien to me, and standing there holding on to it, trying to comprehend its intricate loading system, I regretted not studying up on how one worked. So I faked an air of martial assuredness and copied what all the others did. I slipped a couple leather pouches onto my belt—one filled with prerolled gunpowder, the other with small copper percussion caps that would help ignite my historic weapon.

After a brief safety inspection in which John scrutinized our muskets for any minié balls—real ammunition—we marched onto the battlefield for colors, a formal gathering in which representatives from both sides present their company flags. A couple chest-high fortifications, called breastworks, divided the otherwise expansive, coarse-grassed field. A small opening revealed a patch of blue sky in an otherwise gray one. I couldn't help but draw parallels between it and the soldiers' colors. Confederate gray outnumbered Federal blue nearly five to one. (Confederates called Union troops "Federal" as they represented the national government.) Despite the fact that half of the Union troops who fought in the actual raid came from the U.S. Colored Troops, all 1,281 reenactors were white. When I asked Colonel Bob why, he told me he knew some black reenactors but said in general "black guys just aren't into reenacting." He added, "But they should be. The U.S. Colored Troops were fighting for their freedom."

After colors our unit stayed on the field to drill our military maneuvers.

For a while we marched in a line two by two, shoulder to shoulder, then Jack ordered the pair of men in front of me to fall back so that we were four across. After that we all lined up in a row, so that everyone, all twelve of us, stood side by side, shoulder to shoulder. Then Jack yelled, "By files left!" and we'd pivot, like a pinwheel, counterclockwise, until we faced forty-five degrees to the left.

All this choreography took a long time to get right. Someone— usually me—fell out of sync and broke up our line so that we bumped into one another like the Bad News Bears. I didn't know what was going on, why it was all so elaborate or why it was so regimented. For a moment I thought we were practicing for a ceremony or maybe even a talent show, but eventually it dawned on me that this was how Civil War soldiers actually fought—in a close, compact group, as a mobile, human wall.

After half an hour of this we needed a break. Jack stood before us, hands on hips, looking like, well, the manager of the Bad News Bears. "Any questions?" he asked. I raised my hand hesitantly.

"So . . . this way of fighting . . . did Robert E. Lee come up with it?" I barely got the word "with" out of my mouth when the other soldiers cried, *"No!"*

"These are Napoleonic tactics!" Jack said.

I'd learned—and forgotten—that factoid from Ken Burns's Civil War documentary. Confederate commander Lee and Union commander Ulysses S. Grant both studied Napoleonic fighting tactics during their years at West Point. But the French general's highly influential strategies were devised for late eighteenth- and early nineteenth-century weaponry, when bullets flew as wobbly as a Phil Niekro knuckleball. By the Civil War, however, as a result of advancements in barrel coiling, minié balls flew straighter—a lot straighter—making Napoleonic tactics obsolete and transforming a bunch of guys standing shoulder to shoulder from a human wall into *standing* ducks. That's one of the reasons why almost 600 soldiers died *per day* during the war, 596 more than the number of U.S. soldiers who died every day during the worst fighting in Iraq.

John strode to the front row and pulled out a small paper tube filled with black powder from a leather pouch on his belt. "Never pour gunpowder down the barrel if the hammer is engaged," he said, meaning the part of the gun that slams down after you pull the trigger. "If there are embers inside it, it will ignite. If your barrel is pointing at your face, it could blow it off." He bit off the top of the tube, spit the paper on the ground and poured the grainy powder down his rifle barrel. "Now you do the same."

As I pulled out a charge, I caught a whiff of sulfur, a rancid smell I hadn't inhaled since the fourth grade, when I, my brother, Rob, and a neighborhood friend, Ray, pilfered a can of gunpowder off Ray's Civil War reenactor dad. We smuggled the can to a nearby Mennonite school and sprinkled the powder onto a patch of pavement, well out of sight from passing cars. While Rob and Ray prepared for our mighty conflagration, I drifted off into the schoolyard, so the only indication I had that something had gone terribly wrong was the loud *whoomph* sound I heard, followed closely by my brother's panicked screams. Unaware that the powder would ignite into a fireball, he'd dropped a match onto the pile, just inches from his face.

He spent four days in the burn unit bandaged up like the Elephant Man. It was the scariest day of my childhood, and I vowed never to touch gunpowder again.

"After you pour gunpowder down the barrel," John said, snapping me out of my flashback, "place a cap on the nipple." He pulled a tiny brass percussion cap out of another pouch. I reached toward my belt and did the same.

The most efficient Civil War soldier took twenty seconds to load and shoot one bullet, but it took me about a minute to load and shoot a little bit of powder. There were so many steps. I tried to come up with a mnemonic device to help me remember the order of things, but I couldn't, so I drilled the sequence over and over in my head. The last thing I wanted was a repeat of the "Mennonite School Incident."

Reach into pouch
Pull out tube of gunpowder
Bite off top
Spit out paper
Make sure hammer is not engaged
Empty powder down muzzle
Cock hammer
Pull out cap
Pinch cap on nipple
After commander yells "Ready!" cock back hammer one
    more click
Pull trigger on the "F" in "Fire!" and only on the "F"

How Civil War soldiers labored through all these steps while bullets and artillery fire whizzed by their heads is beyond me. Consider that more than 25 percent of Union soldiers and 33 percent of Confederate soldiers died in a war that lasted less than four years. In today's numbers that's equivalent to 5.9 million men. Many signed up to fight in the adventure of a lifetime but quickly realized they'd volunteered for a living hell.

. . . .

Before I went to Brooksville, a number of reenactors who do other time periods expressed concern for my safety. A French and Indian War reenactor told me that Civil War reenactors were "crazy." A Greek hoplite reenactor—think the movie *300*—begged me to "stand behind someone" so I didn't get shot by an actual bullet. I thought they were exaggerating—or just being extra cautious—so I started researching on the Internet, which was not a good idea.

Apparently there have been tons of "oops" moments at Civil War reenactments. In 1998, at Gettysburg's 135th anniversary, a French reenactor borrowed a pistol from another reenactor and accidentally shot someone in the neck. At a Raymond, Mississippi, event in 2001, a reenactor got shot through his testicles. In August 2008, again at Gettysburg, a seventeen-year-old reenactor was injured when he was shot in the foot by a powder blast. Later that year in Virginia a reenactor shot another participant in the shoulder. Bad blood between a Confederate and Yankee reenactor spilled over at the Battle of Stanardsville in 2009, culminating with the Confederate shooting his opponent in the face with a blank.

To my chagrin, blowing off my face and getting shot in the nuts weren't the only ways to end up on the DL. After a handful of discharges, the Enfield's barrel heats up so much that water sizzles upon contact. Once during a battle, John "died" on top of his musket and, not wanting to break the illusion of looking dead, burned an imprint of the barrel on his hand. "That did not feel good," he said.

By the time we marched back onto the field for our first battle a few hours later, I'd taken in so much information about marching and muzzleloading that my brain throbbed. I couldn't tell my "right face" from my "pinched nipple" and feared so badly for my safety that I considered penning Wendy one of those "By the time you read this letter" letters.

• • • • • • • •

There are two battles at the Brooksville Raid, one on Saturday and another on Sunday. They're planned eleven months in advance by a committee of fifteen men and women and include cavalry, artillery and infantry demonstrations. Since its inception, reenactors have come from every state except Hawaii and as far away as Germany. And, despite the raid's actual historical outcome, both sides come out as winners: on Saturday the Union troops win, but on Sunday it's the Confederates' turn, because, as one reenactor told me, the event's coordinator, Robert Hardy, a Baptist preacher, "wants the Confederates to win on the Lord's day."

This revisionism didn't escape the eye of Dan DeWitt, a columnist for the *St. Petersburg Times*. That Sunday he wrote an article titled "Brooksville Raid Is Fun, but It Isn't a Lesson in History." He called the raid "romanticism, pure and simple" and juxtaposed its large-scale, Gettysburg-like battles to its modest historical truth. "This is how it really was: A Union raiding force of 240, more interested in killing the Confederacy's cattle than its soldiers, was confronted by a handful of boys and old men in civvies. These Confederate irregulars suffered their only fatality when one squad of them mistakenly ambushed another."

At the end of his article, DeWitt professed that he'd like to see the raid "die from lack of interest" but acknowledged that it wouldn't happen because it's popular and raises money for the local historical society, even if "[they] obviously [don't] care about accuracy." (Eight thousand people attended the year I was there.)

He also suggested rescheduling the raid to July, when the actual event took place. Then there was the issue of slavery, which DeWitt says the reenactment sweeps under the rug. "Explain its brutality; own up to it . . . that way, all the children I saw walking around waving miniature battle flags will know what they really stood for."

A few days later, Ralph Epifanio, a Confederate reenactor and former New York schoolteacher, responded with a letter to the editor. The newspaper printed an excerpt, but Colonel Bob published it in its entirety on his website, Florida Reenactors Online News Magazine. Epifanio suggested that reenacting be viewed "for what it is . . . not true history, but rather an interpretation," and that if they were to pursue "historical fact we could forgo the entire battle, dress a couple hundred felons in blue, and follow them in cars as they pillage and burn their way through Hernando . . . County. There would be a great deal of arson, and no chicken would be safe." As for moving the raid to July: "Go for it," Epifanio says. "I'll even loan you my wool uniform and provide a can of 'Off.' As for me, I'll be alternating between my air conditioned house and my screened in, solar heated pool."

"I hate to see this subject brought up time and time again," Colonel Bob wrote wearily in a post. "One side sees it one way and the other side the opposite way. Neither will give an inch."

. . . .

Our Saturday battle went much like our drills—Bad News Bears–ish—so we all agreed to shape up for the Sunday skirmish. That morning when I showed up at formation I learned that many of the other Yankee units had left. Some quit because they didn't want to lose Sunday's battle; others fled after an overnight rainstorm saturated the campsite. Our company's number had shrunk too, from twelve to seven. Gary, a diabetic, got KO'd after eating a doughnut, and Bill McIntyre, the company's second-oldest member, tweaked his leg during the Saturday battle.

Colonel Bob, ever-present cigarillo clamped between his teeth, inspected our uniforms. I feared that he'd notice I was wearing a "CSA" belt buckle instead of a "US" one. If he did I'd concocted a backstory. "I pilfered it off a dead rebel, sir," I'd say. But when he got to me he didn't mention it. He just looked me up and down.

"Charlie?" he asked.

"Yes, sir." (Answering "Yes, sir" comes really easily when you wear a uniform.)

"You enjoyin' yourself?"

"Yes, sir."

He looked down at my shoes. My pant legs were tucked into them, revealing my farby Campers.

"We're gonna have to get you some boots," he said, looking quizzically at my shoes.

"Yes, sir."

He paused for a bit then continued. "Did your tent leak last night?"

"Yes, sir." This made him laugh.

"Well, well," he said, taking a beat. He considered my Ted Kaczynski beard. "You look like you been here a hundred years."

"Thank you, sir."

I tried to stifle a smile, but one crept out anyway. I don't know why I was so flattered, but I was. I guess I liked that he recognized how much effort I put into looking "authentic." All those ingrown facial hairs, all the itching, all of Wendy's "When in the world are you going to shave that thing?" had been worth it.

"You're the only newbie who stuck around for the second day," he continued. "That means a lot to me."

"Thank you, sir." As he continued to examine our troops' outfits, I stared ahead solemnly but smiled widely inside.

· · · · · · · · ·

A schedule of the weekend's events had been written on a whiteboard near our unit's campfire. Now and then I'd check it so I knew where I was going. At 9:55 a.m. that Sunday, I stood in front of it. Checking to see when I'd next be needed, I noticed that five minutes from then a church service was going to be held.

I hurried over to a large blue-and-white-striped tent that'd been erected off Sutler Row and took a seat in the second row of folding chairs. In front of me two women were dressed like Louisa May Alcott. On a riser near the minister's podium, a folksy quintet sang catchy songs and strummed a bass, mandolin and autoharp. The three women and two men seemed to have materialized from a 1970s PBS special, in their wire-rimmed glasses and earth-toned vests. Looking at the empty seat beside me, I noticed a hymnal and picked it up. It read, "Re-Enactors Mission for Jesus Christ."

After a few songs, a man with short dark hair and a snow-white ZZ Top–length beard walked up to a podium. He addressed the congregation of about fifty people, nearly all of whom were dressed in period garb.

Chaplain Alan Farley wore a beige waistcoat and a pair of wire-rimmed glasses that slid down to the tip of his nose. I'd later learn he was a former reenactor himself, and that he'd left his company after becoming disillusioned with the political infighting that plagues many groups. Since then he's pursued a higher calling, "Ministering," as his website announces, "to the Civil War Re-enacting Community Since 1984." From his home base in Lynchburg, Virginia, he crisscrosses the country, tacking on thirty-five thousand miles a year, to preach at twenty different Civil War reenactments.

During the Civil War, 3,694 chaplains ministered to soldiers; most were Methodist. They spent their time preparing soldiers for battle and, as only 25 percent of combatants belonged to a church, proselytizing. Farley's a Baptist and he's continuing the chaplain's evangelical tradition. According to a short YouTube video profile of him titled *Whose Side Was God On in the Civil War?*, he's distributed over a million replica gospel tracts to reenactors and spectators during his nearly three decades of "spiritual outreach." During the service I went to, he spent much of his sermon railing against Catholicism, labeling its tenets as unsuitable qualifications for admission into heaven. As a very lapsed Catholic I wasn't offended, but instead, I found myself captivated by his bombastic fire-and-brimstone delivery. He acted like how I imagine one of those traveling preachers did during America's Second

Great Awakening, like a pre-televangelist evangelist. Despite having to reach only a few rows, Farley didn't preach so much as shout. He was so loud, his voice could have carried to the back rows of the Rose Bowl. He got so excited, in fact, that he frequently had to wipe his nose and mouth with a white handkerchief. Some of the parish ate it up, reciprocating his revivalist temperament by bubbling into a small frenzy. The two women in front of me often responded with an "Amen" or "Amen to that one" whenever Farley said something that struck a chord. It was mesmerizing and one of the best performances I'd seen in years.

Although I've lived in two of America's most secular cities for the last sixteen years, I grew up in a religiously conservative corner of America, so I couldn't help but feel as though I'd traveled back in time, not to 1864, but to the 1980s when school friends would invite me to weekend religious retreats. I never knew how to respond to preachers then, and I wasn't sure how to respond now. I guess, when it came down to it, I was captivated by Farley's histrionics the same way I am when I see any sincere theatrical performance. It didn't take much imagination to see how, as the narrator in the YouTube video says, Farley has "seen over 1,800 people come to the Lord through this unique avenue of service."

Toward the end of his sermon, Farley asked us all to bow our heads and close our eyes. I did so and listened intently while he read four commandments and asked us to raise our hands if we'd broken any of them. Before he could even utter the words "Thou shalt not" I began to raise my hand in anticipation of what was about to come.

"How many of you have told a lie?" he asked.

I raised my hand. (Too many to mention. Mostly little white ones.)

"How many of you have ever stolen anything?"

I raised my hand again. (During college. Vitamins. Shaw's Supermarket. Auburn, Maine.)

"How many married men have ever lusted after another woman?" By now I figured I should just keep my hand up. (I would never cheat on Wendy, but I'm a guy. Lust is practically in my DNA. Still, even I can't explain the women on my fantasy list: Emma Thompson, Helen Mirren, *Jane Pauley*.)

"Then you're an adulterer," Farley said.

Really? But before I could protest, Farley was asking us another question.

"How many of you have ever felt hatred so strong in your heart that you wanted to hurt someone?" Four for four. I was batting 1.000. (At work. After my company downsized, I got booted out of an office with an ocean view and into a utility closet. I wanted to pummel the guy who stole my chair during the move, but that's another story for another time.)

"Then you're a murderer."

I wanted to jump up and shout in protest, but according to Farley, the Bible says I'm a murderer and adulterer even if all I have are mean and lascivious thoughts. And all this time I thought having mean and lascivious thoughts meant that I was a human being.

To this day, I still don't know how I ended up in front of the congregation, off to the side, while everyone else, heads bowed and eyes still closed, remained at their seats. One of the women who'd been sitting in front of me turned out to be Chaplain Farley's wife, Faith, and she rose out of her seat and approached me with a small black leather Bible. In a soothing and peaceful manner she opened it to Romans, where she'd underlined a few passages. I'd come to Brooksville for a bit of playacting, but things were starting to get very real.

"If you wanted this Bible, what would you have to do?" she whispered.

"I'm sorry?" I asked. I had a hard time hearing her over Farley's preaching.

"If you wanted this Bible, what would you do?"

"Um, I'd ask for it?"

"No, you'd take it," she said.

I was surprised to hear her say this. Frankly it seemed rude. I wouldn't just steal it from her, even though five minutes earlier I'd admitted that I had once—okay, maybe twice—stolen. (Again, college. This time Vivarin. Same grocery store.)

"That's all you have to do," she continued, "is *take* Jesus's word." I was still a little confused, so she flipped through Romans and pointed to the underlined passages and read them aloud, like at the end of *The Usual Suspects*, when Chazz Palminteri connects the dots and figures out that Kevin Spacey is really Keyser Söze. She was "proving" to me that the only way I was ever going to make it to heaven was to accept Jesus Christ as my one and only savior.

It's altogether possible that she and Farley were thinking that I'd be their 1,801st convert, but they couldn't have imagined how seasoned a pro I was. On all the religious retreats I went to as a kid I'd developed a patented defense system devised solely to evade conversion. "Can I think about it?" I asked, assuming that, like so many times before, my delay tactic would work, and that I'd escape a heathen. But she was a pro too. She'd heard that one before.

"If you get into a car accident later today and die, it's too late." She had a point, and as much as I wanted to boast about my unblemished driving record and extol the advancements in automobile safety, I couldn't manage a comeback better than "Touché."

She tried a couple more times, but couldn't penetrate my waffling, so finally she gave up on me and suggested I speak with Chaplain Farley, who was wrapping up the service.

Faith locked her hand tightly around my arm and escorted me toward the makeshift dais, but before we arrived I was nearly tackled by an elderly woman, also dressed like Louisa May Alcott, who bear-hugged me and yelped, "Welcome to the church!" I felt so bad that she'd just buried her nose in my unwashed armpit, that I said, "Yeaaah!" and squeezed her right back.

After a brief conversation with Chaplain Farley, I finally came clean with him. I told him that accepting Jesus as my one and only savior wasn't in my heart, and to say that it was would be the worst lie of all. "Besides, my wife is a Buddhist," I said. Though, in retrospect, what that had to do with anything I don't know. He looked deeply into my eyes and I into his and he thanked me for being such an honest person.

"Can I pray for you?" he asked.

"Of course," I said. It was nice to leave things on a good note. I turned to walk away. But I didn't get far before he grabbed my shoulder and bowed his head. I didn't know what to do, but bowing my head seemed apropos, so I did the same. "Dear God," he said, "thank you for bringing Charlie here today and for his *honesty*, a quality that's all too rare in today's society."

For a moment I considered telling him that Wendy isn't really a Buddhist, she's lapsed like me, but I didn't want to go there. And as I walked away it dawned on me that telling him she was a Buddhist in the first place was technically another lie.

. . . .

When we marched onto the field for Sunday's battle, an emcee introduced our company. *"This is the 7th Michigan Company,"* he said in a slight southern twang over the crackly PA system. *"This is exactly how they marched. Each man stood side by side, two to a row."*

Rows of spectators, in some places ten deep, lined two sides of the expansive field. The wind blew so strong I had to hold on to my hat so it didn't fly off. To keep step I focused on the soldier's shoes in front of me. It felt good to wear blue—although, if I'm being honest, I didn't really feel all that different from the day before when I wore gray. I was, just like in Colorado, simply soldiering.

"By files left!" Jack yelled and we switched formation.

Two rather spherical company members, who I secretly nicknamed Roseanne Barr and John Goodman, showed up at the last minute for the battle. Roseanne was new to the hobby, and the wet, black gunpowder that streaked her face let everyone know it. This little bit of hazing, called "Fresh Fish," served two purposes: it was a rite of passage for virgin soldiers and it let all the other reenactors know that there was a newbie on the battlefield and—look out!—*anything* could happen around them.

"Looks like the Confederate forces are advancing quickly."

After we marched past the crowd, we hurried toward the center of the field where other units engaged a very hard-to-kill line of Confederates in a small skirmish.

Our company maneuvered well. All the complicated "pinwheels" and "right dresses" and "by files left" that tripped us up during the first battle now went off like clockwork. We obeyed our battalion commander and leaned into a breastwork, waiting patiently to fire several volleys toward the Rebs. When it was finally our time to fire, I remembered all the steps without a hitch, biting off my paper cartridge of black powder, sticking the percussion cap on the musket's nipple, waiting until I heard the "F" in "Fire" to pull the trigger. What's best is that I never heard one gun go off by itself, only a simultaneous explosion that was the end product of a perfectly synchronized group. We were one with our guns. Damn, we Yankees were good.

There was something oddly rewarding—dare I say, meditative—about going through all the steps of loading my old-fashioned musket and firing it in unison with my battalion. It'd been a long time since I was part of a team and it felt good to sacrifice my own selfish needs for the betterment of a larger group. I also really liked firing an old gun.

For some reason all the thought and effort that went into a carefully considered explosion felt like an accomplishment, that the machine couldn't work without a man behind it, like the winding of a clock or the cranking of an old car.

Roseanne was glued to my left side, Chang to my Eng, and was enjoying herself too, although her shots didn't "boom" quite like mine. In fact, they barely "popped." John eventually recognized that something was amiss. Caked dirt on her Enfield's nipple prevented the cap from sparking and the powder from igniting.

He grabbed her musket and scraped off the residue with his thumb. "All set," he said and gave it back to her. She smiled and poured a packet of gunpowder down her barrel. I did the same. I couldn't wait to hear the boom and see the cloud of smoke and breathe in the acrid air. In less than thirty-six hours the memory of my brother's terrible accident had quite literally gone up in smoke.

Our battalion commander, a wiry man with a dark goatee and silver glasses, bellowed our next set of orders as long and loud as he could, pausing in between each word for maximum effect. *"Baaataaa-liooon. . . Reeeaaadyyy . . . Aaaiiim . . . Fiiire!"*

I pulled my trigger on the "F" in "Fire," just like we were taught—so did Roseanne Barr—but this time her rifle didn't "pop," it KABOOMED. A large flash of fire shot out of her barrel, and the deafening sound, like a Manny Pacquiao jab to my left ear, knocked me and the four soldiers to my right off balance. We all winced and grabbed our ears.

"What the hell?" a chorus of soldiers screamed.

"I can't hear anything! I can't hear anything!" Rich yelled, holding his left ear. It felt like someone had rammed an ice pick into my ear.

"This is how they really fought at this time, folks."

Apparently, when Roseanne's rifle didn't fire a few times before, the gunpowder didn't ignite. But she wasn't aware of this. So after each discharge she continued to fill it up with more powder. But after John cleaned the gun's nipple, he forgot to dump out the excess gunpowder. When Roseanne finally got off a good shot, her rifle had anywhere between *three and five times* the suggested amount of powder. In other words, she shot off a small cannon just inches from my ear and in my attempt to "man up" for this reenactment, I wasn't wearing any earplugs.

I staggered backward from our line, holding my ear and trying to regain focus. If I had my wits about me I would have recalled how prescient other reenactors had been when they told me to be careful, but all I could think about was trying to find a place to die. So the next time I heard a line of Confederates fire, I took a hit. I bent over as if I'd gotten shot in the back and inspected the ground for red ants and cactuses, wishing to God I'd corked my ear with wax. While I staggered I spotted a young chaplain, dressed in black and carrying a Bible. He was reaching out to help me.

"Do you want to die or are you just going to play injured and come back to life?" he asked.

"I want to die," I said, shouting over the nearby gunshots. "Just looking for a place to do it." Faith had been right after all. I was going to die that day without accepting Jesus.

"After the battle be sure to support some of our merchants on Sutler Row."

I placed my burning-hot gun on the ground and faced away from the crowd so I could watch the battle. Nearby, a Confederate soldier wearing one of those small Civil War caps called a kepi crawled along the ground, breathing heavily and moaning. Watching his Brando-esque turn I wished I'd put a little more effort into my death.

About fifteen feet to my left—out of sight and unbeknownst to me—a line of Confederates loaded their muskets and prepared to shoot a volley in my direction. When they finally did, the explosion was so great the air shook—like lightning striking the back of my neck.

"Here comes the Gatling gun!"

I didn't care if I looked dead anymore. I stuck my fingers in my ears and curled up in a ball, wishing the battle would stop. I was nearly thirty-eight years old, semideaf and very concerned that my ghetto health insurance wouldn't cover a cochlear implant.

Rat-a-tat-tat! Rat-a-tat-tat! Rat-a-tat-tat! Rat-a-tat-tat!

The Gatling gun mowed down the remaining Union soldiers like they were fish in a barrel. The spectators cheered loudly. The Confederates had triumphed.

"Gentlemen, this would be a good time to take off your hats."

At the emcee's request the crowd quieted down. A couple buglers played taps in harmony. I pulled my fingers out of my ears and searched the battleground for signs of life, but all I could see were dead bodies in blue—some facedown, others twisted into weird shapes with their arms splayed out.

Ahead of me a line of Confederates bowed their heads and clasped their hats against their sides. The wind calmed down, the battle flags drooped. Even Mother Nature knows good drama when she sees it.

Later I'd find out that the small explosion from Roseanne's rifle had burst my left eardrum. It took two weeks to heal. But at the moment, lying there on the ground, I could still hear well enough to listen to the drawn-out notes of taps. They hung in the air an achingly long time, so long that, to my surprise, a tear rolled down my cheek. Not from the pain, but because when you combine "dead" bodies on a battlefield, taps and the hushed, reverential silence of four thousand people it doesn't so much pull on your heartstrings as it yanks on them.

Then, after a barely audible click, the emcee breathed into his microphone and intoned:

"Resurrect."

CHAPTER THREE

I, Carolus

I got the call when I was in Legion VI's command tent, jerry-rigging a belt to my chest armor. Earlier that morning, during one of our drills, the leather strap kept unhooking from the steel plates and falling off. When it went, so did my sword. Now I was trying desperately to fix it.

"Carolus, we need you *now*!" Flavius hollered.

I peered out into the fort's courtyard and spotted Flavius—a fifty-three-year-old rare coin dealer who goes by David Michaels when he's not dressed as a Roman legionnaire. He was flanked by two men: a Goliath of a Roman soldier who was dressed in a black tunic, gold helmet and gold chain mail, and a scrawny, shirtless Celt who wore a pair of green sweatpants. "Shrekius," as I called the giant, held one end of a rope. The other end was tied around the young blond prisoner's neck. The kid's arms arced behind him over a pointy wooden stake and he cast his eyes toward the ground and frowned.

"Hurry up, Carolus, we have to guard the tribune," David as Flavius said.

"Coming as fast as I can," I replied, hastily tying my helmet's leather chinstrap. I plodded outside into the courtyard. The twenty-five-pound segmented armor—*lorica segmentata*, as it's known in Roman reenacting circles—reduced me to a sluggish waddle.

David, Shrekius, and Celt Boy exited without inspection through the fort's tall southern gate, but the sentry stopped me.

"Where do you think you're going?" he asked.

"I'm with them. I was told that they needed my help protecting the tribune."

"All right. Do you know what the password is so you can get back in?"

"Yeah. You say 'Sol,' then I say 'Invictus.' To the sun god or something, right?"

"Close. The unconquered sun."

"Right, the unconquered sun."

He started to roll a fat log away from the tall wooden gate, then stopped. "Oh, and one other thing. It's pronounced 'In*wic*tus,' not 'In*vic*tus.'"

"Heh?"

"In*wic*tus."

"In*wic*tus?"

"Very good."

"Thanks. Sorry about that. Don't know much Latin. My bad."

"Mea culpa."

"Heh?"

"It's Latin for 'My bad.'"

"Right. Sorry. *Mea culpa.*"

"No worries. It's a Latin thing. Lots of people struggle with it. Have a good time at the crucifixion!"

He creaked the gate open just wide enough for me to squeeze through. I lumbered out to a field of patchy grass. About a hundred feet to my right a birch tree had been trimmed down to a six-foot post. It abutted a field of swaying golden wheat. I caught up to David, Shrekius and Celt Boy and together we greeted the tribune, a stocky twenty-something from Bakersfield, California, named Brandon "Brutus" Barnes. He wore a gold helmet adorned with red feathers, like a Roman rooster. "Hail, Brutus!" I said.

"Hey, Carolus, what's up?" he replied. Shrekius tugged on Celt Boy's rope, pulling him closer to the stake.

Crucifixions predate the Roman Empire by many years. The Persians, Macedonians and Carthaginians all loved to tie or nail people to stakes and kill them. To limit any unnecessary suffering—or messy cleanup—they typically ended their victims' lives by either stabbing them in the heart or asphyxiating them with lung-clogging smoke from a fire burning just below. Inspecting the area around the post I didn't see any charcoal or nails. There wasn't even a horizontal beam fixed to it, so stigmata was definitely out of the question. We were all carrying heavy steel swords so if worse came to worst we could still stab Celt Boy in the heart, and a shot to the sternum from Shrekius would surely bust a bone or two. But I kind of doubted it'd ever come to that.

While I was meditating on the differences between twenty-first-century crucifixions and ancient ones, however, something totally unexpected happened. Shrekius just inexplicably got tangled up in the rope. It wrapped around his legs and arms like he was prepping for a bad escape-artist routine. While he tried to figure out how to free himself, Celt Boy saw an opportunity. He reached into one of his socks and pulled out a pair of scissors. When Shrekius spotted the anachronistic tool, he was so stunned that he did something even more inexplicable. He let go of the rope and it fell to the ground. Celt Boy couldn't believe his luck. For a moment he hopped around a bit, not knowing what to do, and then, realizing that freedom was just a few paces away, he took off, sprinting toward the wheat field with one of the most unusual gaits I've ever seen, like a meerkat who'd just injected a triple-shot mochaccino into his kneecaps. It was pointless to pursue him. There was no way any of us could catch him. That kid galloped faster than Mercury.

"Way to go, guys!" Brutus said, throwing his arms up in the air.

Watching Celt Boy escape gave me an idea. So I trudged back to the front gate.

"Sol," the guard said in a deep tough-guy tone.

"Invictus," I replied, eager to get inside. But he didn't open the door. "Invictus," I said impatiently.

"In*vic*tus?"

"Oh, right, sorry. I meant 'In*wic*tus.'" He perked up.

"All right then, come on in. How'd the crucifixion go?"

"Epicus failus," I said.

He rolled the log away and let me in.

I jogged through the fort as fast as someone saddled with a few dozen pounds of scrap metal can. My eight-pound helmet crunched down on my vertebrae like floors of a building collapsing on top of one another; my armor's shoulder protection ground the bones of my upper back. I trotted by a dozen or so brown leather tents and the red-roofed longhouse, trying not to notice the weary Roman soldiers seated on tree stumps with their legs spread far too wide for this underwear-optional hobby. Campfire pits smoked; an older, bearded guy cooked a cauldron of soup over an open flame; somebody's wolflike dog (or maybe it even was a wolf) eyed me like I was a juicy piece of steak. It took forever to travel the 175 feet to the north gate and when I finally reached it the left side of my body had gone completely numb.

"Where are you going?" another guard asked.

"Crucifixion . . . Celt . . . escape," I said, huffing.

"That's cool," he said, giving off a more laid-back vibe than that other uptight Rent-a-Sentry. "You know the password, right?"

"Yeah, yeah," I said, eager to get out. "Sol Inwictus. Open up, the clock is ticking."

"Okay," he said, inching open the wooden slab. Then he stopped and became deadly serious. "Hey," he said, looking intensely into my eyes, "don't get caught alone out there."

It was the first time I'd been on this side of the fort and didn't know what to expect. The Celts lived in a newly constructed round house just over a nearby hill, through a dense forest of pine trees, and I was warned that they wouldn't hesitate to kill a vulnerable Roman. I surveyed the horizon for any signs of life. *Chunk!* The gate shut behind me. *Thump!* The barrier locked me out. I was alone.

An asterisk of stakes, enveloped in concertina wire, lined the murky waters of the fort's four-foot-wide moat, itself an outer protection to the structure's rampart and ten-foot-high walls. The wheat field, swishing like kelp on the seafloor, extended in front of me until it dead-ended at a wooded hillside.

I hung a left and lumbered around the side, where I found Celt Boy and Brutus facing off like two ancient gunslingers. Brutus inched toward the other man, extending his hand in diplomacy; Celt Boy inched away in fear. I advanced slowly, but whenever I so much as sighed, these long metal studded straps hanging down in front of my crotch jingled, so I held my breath and put one sandal in front of the other.

I grabbed my sword's handle and pulled, but it didn't budge. I pulled again. Still nothing. Something wasn't right. Either it was too big or my *vagina* too tight. I gave it one last mighty tug and finally yanked it out, raising it over my head, like Russell Crowe in *Gladiator*. Then I charged toward Celt Boy and screamed, "Ahhhhhh!" In Latin.

For a moment Celt Boy darted back and forth, not knowing what to do. He looked at Brutus and me, me and Brutus. Then reality set in. No matter how fast I charged, he could escape. Truth be told, he could have crawled headfirst inside a burlap sack and hopped faster on one arm than I could have run. And with that little grain of knowledge, he sprinted off into the chin-high wheat, his arms in front of him like a circus dog who's just missed his cue.

Brutus and I shrugged at each other and walked back to our respective gates. When I got to mine—a tired and dejected Roman legionnaire—I rapped on the door. The guard opened it a crack and peered out.

"How'd it go?" he asked.

"Not well," I replied. "Can I come in?"

"What's the password?"

"Oh, bite me."

. . . .

Sixteen hours earlier, while still very much a part of the twenty-first century, I drove past a road sign that said, "Lafe, Pop. 385." It'd taken me two hours to get to this tiny northeastern Arkansas town from Memphis International Airport, and as I drove my rental car down the two-lane Crowley's Ridge Parkway I was struck by how quickly the town passed me by.

Lafe is located in the middle of Crowley's Ridge, a 150-mile geological scar in the otherwise flat Mississippi Embayment, but the town itself lies at the bottom of a shallow bowl framed on one end by a gas station and on the other by a redbrick Lutheran church. In fact, if you keep your speedometer set at the designated 40 mph speed limit, it takes exactly a minute to drive from one end of town to the other. Turn off the parkway and it takes all of five minutes to traverse its backstreets, a mixture of homes with opaque plastic sheets affixed to windows to keep out the cold and cars parked on lawns. Now and then, though, you'll see flickers of hope rising, sometimes literally, out of rubble: a lighted baseball field inches from the ruins of an old gymnasium, a modern gas station a few hundred yards from an old paint-flaked one. But for the most part Lafe feels stuck in time. It has a tiny, unmanned, one-room post office and on the adjoining abandoned grocery store the words "America's Turning 7up" are now barely readable on its side. It's the last place on earth you'd expect to find a twenty-six-thousand-square-foot replica Roman auxiliary fort. And yet there is one, tucked well off the parkway behind tall trees where no motorists can see it.

Toward the north end of town, just at the base of the hill that leads up to the church, I spotted a sandwich board painted with the profile of a Roman helmet, the words "AD 43" and a *gladius*. The sword's tip pointed down a long paved driveway. I followed it for half a mile until it turned to dirt, then followed it some more. Behind a cluster of trees I came to a makeshift parking lot and pulled in next to David "Flavius" Michaels and Lorie Ann "Pompeia" Hambly, two members of Legion VI Historical Foundation, a twenty-person Southern California–based Roman reenactment group that I'd been working with for the past few months. They were unpacking some items from the U-Haul that a few members had towed two thousand miles to the reenactment site. "Well timed," David joked. "We just finished setting up camp."

David was dressed in his Roman citizenry clothing: an overcoat, scarf, tunic, calf-length trousers, open-toe leather sandals and workman's hat. Lorie Ann, an attractive brunette with bee-stung lips—and a master's degree in military history—wore modern clothing.

In the weeks leading up to the weekend-long AD 43 reenactment—named for the year Rome's conquest of Britain commenced—I somehow managed to convince Wendy to construct ancient Roman clothing for me: two red tunics and a scarf called a *focale*. A local tailor hemmed a pair of red Lands' End sweatpants into calf-length *braccae*. Now I stuffed them into a burlap bag and hiked with David and Lorie Ann farther down the dirt road. The next morning when the event began, all modern items, save the suggested "big mouth Gatorade jar"—for handy nighttime peeing—had to be stowed out of sight. As the AD 43 website advised, "Never drink yellow Gatorade at an event."

The three of us walked over a bridge that spanned a small stream and arrived at a shower and bathroom house, where a couple shirtless men in *braccae* milled about. A bit farther on we came to a simple red and white cinder-block building that housed Drusilla's Popina, the compound's kitchen. An older woman in a long purple dress stood behind the counter and served grapes, summer sausage and cheeses to weary-looking Roman reenactors. "Over there, that's the Black Scorpion," David said, diverting my attention from the countertop buffet to a small white utilitarian building. "It's a pub. They encourage us to graffiti its walls in Latin." Behind us, a guy in a tunic filled up a gold canteen with water that flowed out of a lion-mouth fountain.

I'd known about Fort Lafe—or *Castra* Lafe, as the reenactors call it—for over half a year. I'd seen photos and videos online, but despite all the "You won't believe your eyes" reviews I heard, I always pictured it as a solo structure. I never thought it would be a Roman *compound*. We advanced another few feet to the north and that's when I saw it, the pièce de résistance. The property opened into a wide, expansive field that was framed on all sides by a mixture of tall coniferous and deciduous trees.

"There it is," David said. "Carl and Mark have been building it for ten years, can you believe that?" A path of long grass had been mowed between us and the wooden fort's south gate and it seemed for a moment that it unfurled before us like a red carpet.

"Oh, my God," I said. "It's huge." And it was: 175 feet by 150 feet, with ten-foot-high walls. Atop the two southern watchtowers, torches flickered in the late afternoon sky. "Yowsa," I said, unable to call up an appropriate Latin exclamation. "That's remarkable."

. . . .

I first met David and the rest of Legion VI at Old Fort MacArthur Days, the timeline event I attended back in July 2009 that ignited my interest in reenacting. At the time he and other members were encamped for the weekend and educating the public about many things Roman: engineering, warfare, cooking, even blacksmithing at a temporary forge that they'd constructed onsite.

Wendy and I first spotted him demonstrating how the group's arrow-shooting ballista worked to a group of wide-eyed boys. "*Wah, Ho regal,*" Wendy said in the baby-talk Chinglish we sometimes speak. "He looks like Simba." As one of the group's leaders, he wore his centurion uniform: a helmet with a plume of red and black feathers that fanned from ear to ear, a red cloak that draped over his back and chain mail covered with silver military award discs that Wendy mistook for pots and pans. When you blended his somewhat feline facial features—wide mouth, catlike eyes—with his kingly garments, it yielded a trimmer, less menacing Ron Perlman meets *The Lion King.*

After I told him that I was a writer he mentioned the group's annual spring pilgrimage to Fort Lafe. "I'd love to have an embedded reporter on the next trip," he said. A Roman fort in Arkansas? By Hercules, I practically booked my plane reservations that day.

In December we reconnected at the legion's monthly drill in L.A.'s Griffith Park. About fifteen soldiers and a few women gathered that pleasant Saturday morning at a picnic area across the street from the Greek Theater. While the men drilled and marched in Roman regalia through the nearby hills, the women prepared food for the group's Saturnalia party, an annual celebration in praise of the god Saturn.

In January I suited up for the first time in some of the company's loaner gear, this time in Valencia, a 1960s planned community about forty miles north of L.A. that's advertised on L.A. buses as "Awesome-land," though given its uncanny resemblance to *The Truman Show*, I'm not sure what's so awesome about it. About six other members and I drilled Roman military formations on a community soccer field, a few feet away from a group of South Asian cricketers. We followed David's commands to *transforma* (about face), *ad scutum, clina* (turn to the shield side) and *silentium* (shut our pieholes). I learned lots of wonderful factoids that day: that the word "sinister" is derived from the Latin *sinister*, meaning the unlucky or left side, that *dexter* refers to the right side and that Caligula was the nickname of the Roman emperor Gaius Julius Caesar Augustus Germanicus and that his handle meant "Little Boot," because as a kid he accompanied his father on lots of military campaigns. I even got a Roman name that day, Carolus, which David said was the closest Latin equivalent to Charlie.

After drilling we hiked about a mile—nineteen fewer than a typical soldier marched in a day—on the community's bike paths, or "Roman roads," as David called them. The short walk felt ten times as long given that the shields we carried weighed only slightly less than a car door. We stayed in step by chanting *sin* (left), *dex* (right), *sin, dex*, and David kept our spirits up by bellowing a call-and-response.

> *Yonder comes the bearded wanderer*
> *Round the Empire he did go*
> *Gallic fens and German forests*
> *Spanish deserts, alpine snow*
> *Round the Empire he did go*
> *And where he wanders, we follow*
> *Sin, dex, sin, dex,* sin, dex, sin!

He wandered to the northern ocean

Crossed the channel, crossed the Thames

Marched on up to North Britannia

Told Legio Sexta, "Here you'll stay!

And build a wall here, by the way!"

Legionary, rue the day

Your Caesar said, "Now here you'll stay!"

Sin, dex, sin, dex, sin, dex, sin!

So now we're stuck in cold Britannia

Watching over sheep and hogs

Keeping down the Britonculi

Getting stuck in Scottish bogs

Legionary, chop those logs!

Keep a watch for Pictish dogs!

Sin, dex, sin, dex, sin, dex, sin!

Sunday morning joggers stared at us. Kids smiled and pointed. Some folks assumed we worked for USC—the school's mascot is a Greek Trojan—while others thought that we were jousters even though no one was riding a horse or carrying a lance. Once a man approached us, eager to share a story about a Roman road that cuts through one of his relative's properties in eastern Europe. It takes a lot of *colei* (balls) to dress up as a Roman soldier and hang out in public parks and it's a much better icebreaker than walking your dog. Trust me.

After the January drill in Valencia I went to the group's annual meeting at David's nearby suburban home. About twenty members were in attendance and many of them were wearing the group's customized maroon T-shirt with a wreath on its front. While people snacked on hors d'oeuvres, the movie *Hero of Rome* played on the flat-screen. Its DVD jacket promised "Classic pec-flexing action from Italy" and from the few frames I saw of the glistening muscleman Gordon Scott, it didn't disappoint. After a brief grazing period, David stood up and addressed his fellow Romanophiles. "For years I thought I was the only one interested in dressing up like a Roman," he said. Others—women and men who ranged from college age to senior citizen—spread out on bar stools, living room furniture and the floor, nodded their heads in agreement. It was the first time I'd seen David without his battle gear on and he seemed smaller, more vulnerable, a man speaking from his unarmored heart.

Like many of the other people who reenact ancient Rome, David first got hooked on the time period after seeing a movie. "I saw *Cleopatra* when I was a kid," he told the group. "And it stayed with me." At first he dressed up as a Roman soldier on Halloween. "Then, one day, I realized that what I was doing was reenacting," he said. "At root, reenactors like to play dress-up. We want to look cool, and nothing looks as cool as a Roman." More nods from the audience.

After David finished speaking, he turned the floor over to the legion president, Arik Greenberg, an earnest and impassioned thirty-nine-year-old with curly dark hair. When not running the group and lecturing on New Testament theology at Loyola Marymount University, Arik curates the Museum of the Ancient Roman Soldier, or MARS. The project, which is dedicated to restoring ancient Roman artifacts from a private collection, has earned him invitations to collaborate on exhibits and events at the Getty Museum. But at the meeting, Arik, who wore a replica eighteenth-century sailor's jacket, devoted most of his speech to reiterating, or perhaps reinforcing, the group's autodidactic mission, what reenactors like to call "experimental archaeology."

"We portray life to learn about the era," he said, standing in front of the now darkened TV. "Why the sword is on the right side, why they cooked the food the way they did. We do it to educate ourselves." I sat in the kitchen on a bar stool, nibbling on a baby carrot and feeling a little bit like I did at Old Fort MacArthur Days, as though I'd been transported back to college, at least when I decided to show up for class. "The word 'history' comes from the Greek word *historia*," Arik continued. "Which means to learn or know by inquiry. And by teaching ourselves, we learn about history." As he wrapped up his ten-minute speech, he encouraged the members to draw their research from first or second sources and not to rely on Wikipedia—a challenge for hobbyists studying an ancient culture.

Unlike my short "Stalingrad" and Brooksville experiences, I got to spend a few months with Legion VI, getting to know the inner workings of the group. Unlike the organizers of the Brooksville Raid, the members didn't want to rewrite history, and unlike the Nazi reenactors who didn't address the Third Reich's racism, Legion VI was a group of nonpolitical amateur historians with a deep fascination for an extinct culture. Their thirst for knowledge went beyond martial fascination and revisionism. They had me at *ave*.

That day I became a legion member paying thirty-five dollars in annual dues that covered my participation for the year and earned me a sweet little *caligae* key chain to boot. It also gave me access to their Yahoo! group so that I could follow their online conversations in between drills and workshops, or, as they called them, *fabricas*.

Typically they discussed upcoming events, brainstormed how to increase membership and shared links to videos, eBay items and news stories about recent archaeological finds. Now and then they debated historical claims, sometimes quite argumentatively. Their messages were composed with bursts of Latin interjected here and there. E-mails sent to the entire group opened with the salutation *avete omnes*, Latin for "hello, everyone," while messages directed toward two people were addressed "Brutus *et* Dio" or some such derivation. Members always signed off with their Latin name—"Vibria," "L. Vitellius Robigius," "M.VAL.BRUTUS"—and the words *vale* ("farewell") or *gratius* ("thanks"). Me, I mostly sat back and observed, rather than engaged. The one time I did e-mail Arik privately, I signed off *dale*, not *vale*. Clearly I had a lot to learn.

. . . .

Growing up, I never understood why people got so into Rome. To me it always seemed so long ago, so foreign, so . . . *ancient*. Sure I saw *Gladiator*, but I certainly didn't feel compelled to go out and buy any armor afterward. For most of my life, my knowledge of the ancient empire was limited to the Mel Brooks movie *History of the World—Part I*, and all I learned from that was that someone could smoke out a charging chariot with a massive "mighty joint."

So I was surprised at just how into Rome I got. In particular how advanced the Romans were and how after the empire's collapse it took nearly a millennium to recoup much of their knowledge. Consider that their formula for concrete was lost for over a thousand years. *How does something like that happen?* I wondered. *How can societies grow and develop and then just crumble? Why can't they sustain themselves?* It was a fortuitous time for me to be immersed in their history, a thousand-year-long tidal wave that washed over Europe and left its residue on the continent and, by default, ours too. Everyday drives through L.A. revealed ghostly images of our own troubled "empire": shuttered libraries, foreclosed homes, potholed roads that went unfilled because of budget shortfalls. *Is this how Rome started to crumble too?* I wondered. *Is this the beginning of our end?*

On a less fatalistic note, I became completely obsessed with Latin and its role in how it helped shape the English language. Consider my hometown of Lancaster, which was named after the English city and originally called Loncastre. *Castre* means "fort" in Latin. *Lon* is a Celtic word that means "clean" or "pure." The clean, pure river that runs through the English town is called the River Lune. Hence *Loncastre* means "Roman Fort on the River Lune." That's also why the Fort Lafe guys call their structure Castra Lafe. If your town ends in -chesire, -caster or -chester, then it also was—in the Old World, at least— originally named after a Roman fort.

Reading books, magazines and newspapers became less about content and more about spotting Latin prefixes and suffixes, and words that we've borrowed directly from the ancient language: *agenda, caveat, natural, verbatim, bona fide.* Latin engravings chiseled above church entranceways became translation puzzles I tried to solve. During lulls at work I played Latin word-match games on my computer. Did you know that the abbreviation for pound, "lb.," is a derivation of the Latin word *libra*?

But of course, the empire didn't just spread Latin, architecture and infrastructure. It also, with a big assist from the emperor Constantine, helped spread Christianity. In fact, if it wasn't for the Roman Empire, nearly one-third of the world wouldn't have been exposed to the religion, countries wouldn't be called Romania and we wouldn't have a Senate. As John Cleese says in the movie *Life of Brian*, "apart from the sanitation, medicine, education, wine, public order, irrigation, roads, a fresh water system and public health, what have the Romans ever done for us?" It, along with ancient Greece, is the very foundation of Western culture; and what had, only a couple weeks earlier, felt untouchable, inaccessible, distant and mysterious had in a short time and with the help of my Legion VI *amici* started to feel practically contemporary. *When you think of it like this,* I thought, *it feels like the American Revolution just happened.* And, when you consider that the earth is 4.54 billion years old, it really just did.

One of the biggest surprises, however, was learning that the

Romans, who excelled at both staging lavish spectacles and waging wars, were the first reenactors. In ancient Rome, gladiators would dress like some of Rome's conquered enemies—Samnites, Thracians and Mirmillones—and fight one another in the appropriate style . . . *to the death.* As the empire expanded, so did the demand for larger, bloodier spectacles, like elaborate naval combat reenactments, called Naumachia. If gladiator fights were Rome's silent movies, then Naumachias were the ancient world's digitally projected 3-D IMAX blockbusters—that were literally drenched in blood. Held either in lakes, flooded basins or, more amazingly, flooded amphitheaters, like the fifty-thousand-seat Colosseum, thousands of prisoners of war would construct ships and fight to the death, bloodying the water in the process.

As the Castra Lafe reenactment approached, I sincerely hoped that its organizers weren't going to schedule any Naumachias over the weekend.

· · · · · · · ·

While Legion VI strives to re-create a well-rounded portrait of ancient Rome, the annual two-day Castra Lafe reenactment is all about kicking butt ancient style and immersing oneself in the day-to-day life of the world's first professional soldiers. To prepare for such nostalgic brutality, the event's scenario deviser, a red-haired tank of a guy named Rusty "Justus Rustius Longinus" Myers, had produced a bunch of MP3s in Latin to help all the attendees learn their commands. On one track Rusty played different calls on his bugle so we'd know when to do lots of important things like "fall in" and "change rank." I tried listening to the recordings on my way to work, but found it impossible to study a three-thousand-year-old language while negotiating L.A.'s rush-hour traffic. By the end of my commute I couldn't have told you if *tela!* meant "charge!" or "incoming missile!"

In 2010, the year I was there, the plan was to reenact Rome's invasion of Britannia, in AD 43. This gave Rustius the chance to create a dramatic, intense scenario that would pit the cohesive Roman "mincing machine" against a ragtag group of wild and crazy Celts. Without being privy to any of this information heading into the reenactment, however, I was lost for most of the time I was there.

After I arrived and got acclimated, the other eight Legion VI members and I went out for a final twenty-first-century meal. When we got back I went to bed, sleeping on the floor of David's leather tent, which he'd erected inside the fort walls. In yet another botched attempt to "man up," I made the tragic mistake of trying to tough it out on the cold, wet ground.

"I didn brin a sleepin bag," I told David, shivering atop a sheepskin rug. I'd wrapped myself in a couple wool blankets but they couldn't keep me warm in the damp, forty-degree March air.

"That's very noble of you to be authentic, Carolus," he said from the comfort of his rope bed. "But totally not necessary." It was the first time in my life I envied someone for lying on a bed whose "box spring" was woven rope.

Sometime during the night I abandoned the tent for the front seat of my rental car, but despite warming up I didn't sleep any better. When the sun rose I stumbled outside and wandered the parking lot amazed at how far some legionnaires had traveled: New York, Texas, Pennsylvania, Canada and even California. *Wait a minute,* I thought, rubbing my eyes, *I'm from California.*

I hoofed it over to Drusilla's Popina, the onsite cantina, for some breakfast. A spread of eggs, bread, oatmeal and honey and sausages had been laid out for the fifty or so Romans. I scooped some oatmeal into a wooden bowl, but didn't have a spoon, so I lapped it up like a dog. I was learning very quickly that suspending decorum and embracing filth, germs and funk were part of what made reenactments "fun."

While I was gnawing away on a black sausage, a couple loud horn blasts rang out from the fort. Evidently the number of toots signified that it was time for me to cease smearing food all over my face and gather for formation. I hurried back to the courtyard and retrieved my armor from inside David's tent. Piling on my gear—leather vest, armor, belt, *gladius*, canteen—required the assistance of a couple other soldiers. I felt like I was backstage at Fashion Week, modeling Jean Paul Gaultier's latest homoerotic line. If I had any muscles whatsoever I'd have made a pretty hot stripper.

I joined the other soldiers outside the fort, not far from where the hitherto-mentioned "Escape of the Celt Boy" would later take place. When I arrived, holding on to the belt that would soon cause me all sorts of wardrobis malfunctionis, I thought that I'd accidentally stumbled onto a performance of *The Lion King*. Among the four dozen armored and chain-mailed legionnaires were four *signifers*, each of whom wore a different type of long animal hide—bear, wolf, lion—on his head. If that wasn't bizarre enough, another *signifer* wore an expressionless silver face mask, straight out of *Eyes Wide Shut*. It wasn't until later that I learned that *signifers* were the bravest of the legionnaires, the ones who stood in the front of the cohort or century and carried the legion's emblem. (I recognize that Rome's auxiliary structure can be wicked confusing, so very quickly: a legion consisted of anywhere between three thousand and six thousand men, a cohort three hundred to six hundred men and a century one hundred men.)

Rustius, who wore chain mail and a golden helmet with a fan of red feathers, strode by to inspect our uniforms. After he moved on, the legionnaire in front of me broke rank, leaned over and started fondling another soldier's shoulder fabric.

"Man, that is *really* nice cloth," he said, rubbing it between his fingers like a *Project Runway* judge.

"Thanks," the guy said. "It took me a year to make it."

Shortly thereafter, a group of Canadians loudly debated Lady

Gaga's gender. (For what it's worth they concluded that she was a man with a four-inch clitoris.) Another Canadian openly fantasized about being manhandled by a pugilistic Madonna. But the most flagrant distractions emanated from the back door of a tall, Edward Herrmann look-alike who I'll call Flatulus. Often, and without any warning, he'd blast so much hot air out of his butt that he could lift a small dirigible off the ground. Unlike most men, who take great pride in the volume, pitch and odor of their farts, he never owned up to his dirty bombs. He didn't even change expression as he released them. It was as if his ass had Tourette's syndrome. It would just go off without warning, while he remained a silent—but deadly—bystander.

I tried to lie low—and upwind of Flatulus—by surreptitiously jotting down notes in a leather-bound notebook. I didn't want to call too much attention to myself after I'd heard that one of our commanders, a meaty bulldog of a guy named Edge, didn't think too highly of NPR. "They should call it National Communist Radio," he grumbled when David told him I contributed stories to it. *Well, then, no Carl Kasell on your home answering machine,* I thought.

Toward the end of our morning drill, Rustius told us that there'd be lots of "fun stuff" over the next two days, and a little cruelty too. "If we're mean to you," he said, "it's not because we're jerks. It's because we want you to have a great experience." His speech sounded just like the one Randy Beard gave us before "Stalingrad," except Rustius had a thick southern accent.

Just as we were about to be dismissed, he placed his hands behind his back and launched into a story about a Roman soldier who once built a bridge across a river "to show the Germans he could. He could have built a boat, but he didn't; he built a bridge. And he crossed the river, had his way with a German woman, then crossed back over the bridge and destroyed it. Why? So he could build it again in ten days' time. This was inconceivable to the Germans. It drove them crazy."

He paced back and forth in front of us for a bit, not saying anything, then turned and with great zeal cried, "That was Caesar's army! That was Rome! We are relentless! We are Rome!" All around me soldiers grabbed their swords and thrust them into the air and started to chant in unison, "Roma! Roma! Roma!"

"Dismissed!" Rustius cried and as I started marching back toward the fort, Flatulus totally ripped one.

· · · · · · · ·

I didn't see any combat the first day. Mostly I performed grunt work: gathering firewood, standing guard in one of the fort's four towers and marching with the rest of the troops through the thick surrounding woods. I helped with the aforementioned botched crucifixion and joined my fellow Romans to rehearse a defensive posture called a *testudo*, or tortoise, in which soldiers create an impenetrable mobile shell with their shields. I wasn't sure exactly how or when the real action would take place, but now and then Rustius introduced plot points that contributed to the event's larger scenario. For example, during one of our drills I learned that there was a traitor among us.

At one point during the day I turned to see Rustius escorting two shirtless, pasty men with beer guts through the fort. He poked them with a gnarled staff and barked orders in English and southern-accented Latin. Upon further inspection I noticed that their groins and feet were crudely wrapped in unbleached cotton.

"Who are those guys?" I asked David.

"Slaves."

"I hope they're wearing sunscreen," I said.

Later, while helping to erect one of our commander's large leather tents, I reached out to the younger slave, a handlebar-mustachioed thirty-something named Joel. "So how'd you get caught?" I asked.

He looked at me quizzically. "Uh, we didn't. We're *slaves.*" He patted my armor condescendingly.

Upset that he wasn't adhering to the historical hierarchy, I snapped back. "Hey, you're a slave," I said. "Stop doing that."

"*Si, dominus, si, dominus,*" he replied, bowing down to me.

"That's more like it," I said.

At Lafe, random improvisations like this happened all the time, often when no one was around. Once while standing outside David's tent, I witnessed an exchange between a Roman soldier and Rustius. The soldier told him that he'd just killed a Celt, then laid the man's clothes at his feet and relayed some information integral to a larger plot point that I was completely unaware of. They both took it very seriously and yet only three out of the seventy total reenactors there saw it. I caught it by accident, because I was ten feet away. Perhaps these episodes happened because the reenactors were pining for a "period rush," the sensation that you've traveled back in time. Or maybe it was a chance for the guys—nonactors—to live out a fantasy, not just of reenacting Rome but of "acting in a movie," to experience what it's like, if only for a moment, to be Kirk Douglas or Russell Crowe. Whatever the reason, usually when people "act" or put on a show, it's done with the intention of entertaining an audience. But at Lafe, I quickly realized that we weren't just "actors," we were our own audience too.

At the end of the day, everyone—even the twenty enemy Celts—gathered in the fort. As the sun set behind us, all the Roman legionnaires filed by a table to collect our "pay"—intricately reproduced Roman coins—and to collect a letter from "home." After receiving mine, I returned to my rank, unrolled my missive and discovered that it'd been painstakingly written in Latin on a piece of papyrus. I can only imagine what it said. Probably something like, "Hi, this is your wife. I just wanted to let you know that while you're off roughing up a bunch of barbarians, I'm hooking up every night with Lucius. Remember him? The *notarius* in the upstairs apartment? He's really great in the sack. Unlike you. Gotta run. Have a good time with the boys, loser."

Before we were dismissed, a man dressed in a maroon tunic and ornate helmet topped with red ostrich feathers stood before us. In real life his name was Julius Feigelson, a former TV producer, but his Roman persona, he told me, was a general. He jokingly referred to himself as "Julius Geezer" because at sixty-nine, he's one of the hobby's oldest participants. By now I realized that I was never going to figure out everything that was going on so I dialed down my inner dramaturg and accepted that he was a big deal and had come to deliver important information. He told us that he'd come to our fort as a representative from the Senate and as he paced back and forth in front of us, I could tell something had gone terribly wrong.

"It seems that there is equipment missing out of this camp," he said solemnly, drawing out the vowels of each word. "Not just any equipment. *Gladii, pila*, enough to start an insurrection." I tried to recall if I'd seen any suspicious activity that day—if some sticky-fingered Celts had stuffed some of our weapons down their pajama bottoms—but I didn't. Geezer continued. "I was asked to come here, to investigate and ferret out the conspirators, and that's exactly what I intend to do. I will be looking at the situation with a very critical eye and I must tell you, when I look at a man and question him I can look right into his very soul." The air was tense, the mood somber. The guy next to me gulped.

But the quiet tension didn't last long. Suddenly a wild-haired Celt who'd been seated to the left of the legion spontaneously started to scream, "A pox on you, Romana! *Romana morte!*" We may have been the world's greatest army, but at that moment we were so shocked that some guy popped up and started screaming in Latin that we froze. Nobody lifted a *digitus*, nobody drew his *gladius*. Except Rustius. He'd been standing behind Julius Geezer, twenty feet away from the Celt. He dashed over, drew his sword and quickly slayed the young man. It was a rash move that infuriated the senator.

"No! No! Rustius, we act! We don't *react!*" Geezer screamed. "Keep your cool! Legions get destroyed reacting!"

"But—," Rustius started to say.

"No buts. What am I going to tell the emperor if this erupts into a war? If we start a war, every one of you will die by the sword of the emperor!"

I may not have had a clue what was going on, but I didn't care. It was totally insane and very entertaining.

. . . .

That night I ate dinner with Dan "Prefectus Petersonis" Peterson at the Black Scorpion tavern, outside the fort walls. When we arrived, I took notice of the pub's interior, which had been tagged here and there in Latin. I wrote some of the phrases down, but wasn't sure I spelled them correctly because many were written in archaic fonts. Later I could only translate one: *Ave classiarii milite*, which meant "Hail, marine soldiers."

Dan is a tall, wide-faced and boyish-looking man with messy brown hair and had changed out of his *lorica musculata*, the buff chest armor he wore earlier in the day that was designed to look like the Situation's torso. Now he wore a red cape. His welcoming smile and gee-whiz disposition belied his eccentric reputation as a "very odd bird," as one reenactor put it. Consider that when he was stationed in Germany, Dan kept a Komodo dragon as a pet and that he's currently building a twenty-two-foot-long *T. rex* that he'll somehow mount onto the back of his jeep, as an art-car homage to *Jurassic Park*.

The two of us sat at a long wooden table that was illuminated by flickering votives in an overhead chandelier. Two thick black sausages lay uneaten in a wooden bowl in front of me; while we talked Dan ladled grub out of an aluminum-foil-lined pot with a long wooden spoon.

Dan now lives in Kentucky, where he curates the 101st Airborne Museum at Fort Campbell, but he's best known, at least in reenacting circles, as the inventor of Roman reenacting. For nearly forty years he's been consumed with bringing Roman soldiers back to life. Unlike, say, the well-documented and heavily photographed Civil War soldier (and all soldiers since then) it's been a lot harder to know exactly what a Roman soldier looked like. "There's just so little data available," Dan told me in between spoonfuls of food. It's hard to believe, but it wasn't until 1975 that the layman knew what a typical legionnaire looked like. That year the British military researcher H. Russell Robinson published a book called *The Armour of Imperial Rome*, which refuted what had previously passed for "authentic." Remember all those 1960s Roman gladiator movies? They wouldn't pass the smell test now.

Robinson's findings inspired Dan to fulfill a fantasy he'd had since he first gravitated to toy Roman soldiers in the third grade. Dan told me that he wanted to take Robinson's archaeological research and see if he could translate it into three dimensions, to know firsthand what it was like "to wear the same cool clothes [he] saw in movies." At the time, while stationed in Germany, he started to experiment by kitting up with other U.S. soldiers. He wrote a book, *The Roman Legions Recreated in Colour Photographs*, which documented his then-Europe-based reenactment group's re-creation of a Roman legion.

Today Dan consults with Sam Agarwal, a Virginia-based telecommunications engineer turned manufacturer of Roman militaria. Agarwal's company, Deepeeka, based in Meerut, India, is one of two businesses that manufacture replica Roman soldier gear. Moving production to India has slashed the cost of Roman armor by 80 percent. Helmets that once cost a thousand dollars now ring up at two hundred, one reason why the hobby has grown in the last twenty years. "In the early nineties there were two legions in the U.S.," Dan told me. Today there are over thirty. Still, there are fewer than five hundred Roman reenactors in the States.

Dan also developed the needlefelt style of combat that we'd use during the next day's climactic battle. Encasing the blades of swords and javelins in automotive-grade felt would ensure that all the Russell Crowe wannabes could bash their *gladii* into one another and not get hurt. As Dan put it, "Half the guys are here this weekend because of that movie. It renewed interest in ancient Rome."

But he also told me that movies aren't the only cultural force that drives people to suit up as *legionnaires, optios* and *centurions.* "Roman soldiers are in the Bible," Dan said. "That's a big connection for a lot of people in the U.S." The world's first Roman reenactment group, the London-based Ermine Street Guard, got its start putting on passion plays in pubs. Rustius's South Carolina–based Soul of the Warrior Productions has been "presenting biblical first person characters for 10 years" to church groups. One of his websites, Confessionofjustus.com, advertises their role-playing services: "Imagine your church being taken over by a legion of Romans," it says above the fold. While some church groups welcome the "enemy" into their fold for passion plays, other Christians are less tolerant. As David once told me, "Every now and then at public events you'll get people who come up to you and say, 'You're the ones who killed Jesus.'"

Whatever the reason, the hobby has taken off, just as some people have started to notice parallels between the U.S. and the Roman Empire. And perhaps one piece of evidence that we are like our ancient ancestors is that people have the means to build replica auxiliary forts and spend their downtime dressing up as Romans.

Shortly after I ended my chat with Dan, I met Mark Saddler, one of the two men who'd built Fort Lafe. By now it was dark outside and in the faint glow of the candlelight I could just make out his face; he resembled John Candy, minus fifty pounds or so. He wore a dark cloak and looked—not surprisingly—a bit spent from the long first day.

At first Mark didn't want to talk about the fort. It's located on private property, tucked well behind the house of his building partner, Carl Steyer. Considering there's a website for the event with a link that gives directions to the site, I was surprised that he was so reticent. "We prefer it 'down in the weeds' of the Internet," he said, "so it's hard to find." Yet if anyone were to google "AD 43," a popular search, given that it's the year Rome's conquest of Britannia began, the reenactment's site would be the first result. Later I'd learn that the fort had once been vandalized by some local kids and I can only assume that Mark felt hesitant divulging its coordinates to a writer.

The story of how two men decided to build arguably the world's coolest backyard fort started more than ten years ago when Mark and Carl attended a timeline event in Mississippi called Gulf Wars. The reenactment covered lots of different eras and, to Mark's dismay, a wide variety of reenacting styles. "We saw all the time and effort some people put into being authentic, only to be encamped right next to a reenactor with a modern tent who wore sunglasses." Why, they wondered, did some reenactors cut corners when others strove for authenticity? Wouldn't it be that much more impressive to create something *totally* legit? Inspired by the hard-core purists they saw, the two men got to work researching Roman auxiliary forts. They drafted a blueprint and took it out to the large field behind Carl's house. Fortunately for the men, Carl possesses a technical prowess on par with MacGyver. According to Mark, Carl can figure anything out, so tackling such a large and complex project wasn't a pipe dream; it was just a matter of time, money and effort.

For the past ten years the pair has spent nearly every weekend between November and March building and improving the fort and its surrounding buildings, adding on new additions with each flip of the calendar. The only weekends they don't work on it are during the hot spring and summer months, when ticks, mosquitoes and snakes add a level of danger and discomfort that even these hardiest of men would rather avoid. Come fall, however, when Mark's not using the watchtowers to hunt deer, they're back at it. While the two men have invested a lot of their own money, Mark told me that they couldn't have done it without the financial and physical support they've gotten from others.

The year I attended, a handsome round Celtic house, perched on a nearby hill and unseen from the fort, had just been erected. Its final piece, a tall door, was constructed in Michigan and driven down by another reenactor. Although to my eyes the complex looked pretty spectacular, Mark and Carl aren't content. In the future they hope to include shops, a couple apartments, a granary and a bathhouse. A "city block," as Mark put it.

As the Black Scorpion started to empty out and the exhausted, sunburned Romans retreated back to the fort for some much-needed shut-eye, I had time for one more question. At first I didn't even think to ask it. After all, the men were so infatuated with Rome and its early history that I just assumed they'd visited the city, to walk among the ruins, to set foot in the Colosseum, to marvel at the Pantheon. But to my surprise Mark told me that they hadn't been. Well, then at least Europe, where an auxiliary fort like the one they'd constructed would have been built to protect soldiers on campaign? But again, no, they hadn't. As a very tired-looking Mark put it, "There's not enough time."

. . . .

That night I slept in the fort's longhouse on a creaky rope bed topped with a hay-stuffed mattress. After I had gone thirty-six hours without any sleep, the clumpy, brittle padding felt like a California King fitted with Egyptian cotton. I was sleeping with the gods.

At formation the next morning, Rustius unveiled the battle's rules of engagement. "Don't get too carried away. Fight at only sixty to seventy percent of your capacity," he ordered. "You will get pulled out of combat if you swing your *gladius* like a baseball bat. So keep your emotions in check." Apparently he spoke from real-life experience. At one point he told us about a time that he was in a tense police line and was about to hit a family member in the head when he took a breath, checked himself and walked away. As he recalled the incident he assured us that we "can do the same."

Moving on to less antagonistic matters, he promised that today's scenario would be top-notch. After all, he told us, he wrote it, and since he was a "Roman," it therefore had to be good. (I only *think* he was joking.) In closing he gave us a short pep talk that celebrated the phenomenon that was Rome, how it grew from its humble beginnings as a city on the Tiber River to eventually rule much of Europe. He compared it to its ancient Mediterranean cousin, which he claimed was not as fated for glory as Rome. "We're not Greeks who have no greater vision of their destiny. Our driving destiny is to rule the world!" Then he thrust his sword in the air, and with that all fifty soldiers chanted, "Roma! Roma! Roma!" Except Flatulus. But you can probably guess by now how he celebrated.

About an hour later, ten of us were called to escort a heavy wooden wagon outside the fort into position for our forthcoming attack on the Celtic house. Aside from the plastic safety glasses we wore and our bulging twenty-first-century bellies, we must have looked pretty authentic trudging toward the forested hillside. As we lugged the wagon out of the north gate, I realized then that I'd forgotten to slip on my protective cup. Earlier Brutus had told me that the family jewels were off-limits. *I hope he was right,* I thought. *I hope no Celts will target my nuts.*

I stood next to Jim "Secundus" Pieper, a short L.A. city bus driver and fellow Legion VI member. David was one pace ahead of us, behind our two commanders, the *optio* and tribune, two men dressed in the finest Roman armor.

From the start it was clear that something wasn't right. Only ten soldiers to wheel precious cargo into no-man's-land? The same dangerous area that the sentry warned me about the day before, when I was in hot pursuit of Celt Boy? Nobody talked. I felt like we were headed into an ambush. *Could the traitor,* I wondered, *be among us?*

Perhaps no one was as worried as David, who, about fifty feet in, turned around and muttered under his breath, "Keep your eye on the *optio*." He raised his foam-tipped javelin and aimed it at the back of the guy's head, just in case something out of the ordinary happened.

Flatulus and Shrekius, the two largest soldiers, pulled the wagon. Its wheels creaked as it slowly rolled through the field. Wind pushed through the tall golden grass, creating a whooshing sound. The sun was bright, the temperature perfect. Jim looked at me nervously.

"Are we going to die?" he asked.

"I don't know," I said, slowly raising my javelin and pointing it at the *optio* too. It was quiet. Too quiet. Still I felt reassured knowing that the tribune, Brutus, was someone we knew and could trust. The Legion VI member was a former nuclear power plant SWAT team member who'd once been shot in the gut by a crazed scientist. I knew that his experience in crises would shine. But I shouldn't have been so trusting. Without warning he drew his *gladius* and slit the *optio*'s throat, then ran away with remarkable agility for a stout guy in armor. He was so fast and his assault so surprising that none of us had time to throw our *pilas* at him. We'd identified the traitor and he was one of us, a fellow Southern Californian, a fellow Legion VI member.

Suddenly about a dozen blue-faced Celts with swirls painted on their chests poured out of the woods and crept toward us. *Let the battle begin.* "Guard the wagon! Don't let them take it!" Jim cried. We quickly broke rank and encircled it, facing out. I drew my sword and my belt fell down around my ankles. The Celts spread out across the wheat field, so that it looked like only their severed heads floated above the tall grass.

I raised my shield to block any incoming rocks—Hacky Sacks painted blue—from hitting me. Jim drew his sword. Behind us fighting had commenced. I could hear grunts and blows and thuds of needlefelt whacking armor. It sounded a lot clumsier than the movies, but a lot more real, even if the weaponry was encased in felt. A spiky-haired blond kid approached us, drawing Jim away from the wagon and into a wild swordfight. I bided my time until the Celt lowered his shield, then, ignoring Rustius's command to dial it down, flung my javelin as hard as I could and struck the Celt right in his *nvts*. He threw his arms up, laughed a little and fell to the ground.

I turned my attention back to the cart just in time to see Joel, the slave from the day before, now painted with swirls on his chest, ram his javelin hard into a Roman's eye. The soldier fell to his knees, convulsing and groaning with the same sorrow Oedipus expressed when he discovered he'd slept with his mom. David, who'd been dead on the ground, quickly came back to life, broke character and yelled, "Medic! Medic!" All fighting ceased. Joel knelt down to inspect the Roman's eye. "Oh, man, I'm really sorry," he said, looking at the gash created when the Roman's glasses had collapsed into his cheek. "There's a contusion there," David said. People started muttering about how lucky he was to have been wearing glasses. Someone went so far as to say that without them the Roman may have lost his eye.

After a brief medical time-out, fighting resumed. Even the Roman, visibly shaken by the accident, rose to his feet to battle some more. But it wasn't the same. I soon got hit in the back with a javelin and gladly died, shaken too from what had just happened. When all was said and done it took two minutes for the ragtag group of Celts to defeat history's greatest army. With their victory went the traitor, Brutus, and the wagon too, slowly creaking its way up the hill and disappearing into the woods.

. . . .

An hour later our entire "century" marched up through the dense forest and arrived at the Celtic house. No one was home. While some soldiers searched inside, about a half dozen of us hitched up our tunics and peed on their lawn. It seemed like fitting retribution.

After the last soldier finished, Rustius called us to attention. He had shocking news. While searching the house, a soldier had found a letter with Julius Geezer's seal on it. The men gasped. There wasn't *a* traitor. There were *two*. And Julius Geezer, the very Roman senator who could look into a man's soul, was one of them.

As quickly as you can say "dramatic climax," another soldier approached Rustius with even more bad news: while we were fertilizing the Celts' lawn, they'd taken control of the fort. "We must stop the rebellion now and arrest Julius!" Rustius cried. "We must take back Castra Lafe!" The plot had thickened—and mercifully been clarified. It was now our job to take back the fort.

We divided our century in half and marched back down a dirt path cut between a cluster of evergreen trees, until we were back in the wheat field, spread out and facing the fort. It must have looked pretty cool from atop the watchtowers, seeing all those men in shiny armor and red tunics, but to me it felt like hell. I couldn't wait for somebody to kill me. Somewhere along the line I'd picked up a shield that weighed twice as much as the one I'd been using earlier. My left arm had gone numb and, to make matters worse, whenever I took a step I stirred up a swarm of gnats that sought refuge up my nose.

I could make out the Celts' silhouettes atop the watchtowers, against the backdrop of the bright sky. Some drew back their bows; others manned the ballistas, itching to fire their foam-tipped arrows in our direction. In the center platform above the north gate I could make out the profiles of Brutus, Julius Geezer and even Dan Peterson. Was there no end to the duplicity? I mean, betrayed by the ultimate Roman reenactor? What a slap in the face.

"Movete!" Rustius barked and we all started to march. It didn't take long for my shield to get tangled in the grass and I quickly fell behind.

"Celerate!" Rustius shouted at me. *"Celerate!"*

Another Roman translated his command. "That means 'Speed it up.'"

"Oh, you mean like 'accelerate'?" I asked.

"Yes," he said. "Now hurry it up."

"That is so cool," I said. "I love Latin!"

I heaved my shield with both hands and double-timed it. Okay, I time-and-a-halfed it.

Chahunkthwap! I looked toward the fort and the origin of the strange sound to see a missile that'd been fired from the ballista. It wobbled through the air and landed short of our front line. It would have been the perfect time for me to yell "Incoming missile!" in Latin if I could have remembered how in the world to say it.

Up top in the watchtowers, the Celts reloaded. Seeing this, Rustius bellowed, *"State!"* and we all stopped in our tracks just out of range. *"Ad contum oblique,"* he said. We marched again, coming together just as the sky started to drizzle arrows. I hoisted my shield. *"Ad testudinem!"* Our two flanks started to form a testudo, the shell-like defensive posture we'd practiced the day before. We advanced forward and sideways until we stood about 150 feet from the fort.

A tennis ball whizzed by my head. The front four men of our century raised their shields in front of them like riot police at a WTO protest. Then each man in the four rows behind him lifted his shield over his head. Or at least tried to. I stood behind a towering Kiwi named Wayne who measured a good seven inches taller than me. I could barely lift the shield over my head, let alone keep it aloft over his Kareem Abdul-Jabbar–like frame. But there was no time to complain. I dead-lifted it so high that my segmented armor dug into my shoulders. We advanced slowly and chanted, "Roma, Roma, Roma." Arrows, Hacky Sacks and tennis balls shot from the ballista rained down on us. I heard a projectile hit my shield. One more blow and by the rules, I'd be dead. All around me soldiers starting falling to the ground. There was just too much enemy fire for our testudo to stay together. It cracked and splintered and disintegrated, leaving me vulnerable to more artillery fire. I lowered my shield, as if to say, "Please, somebody just kill me." And somebody did. A Hacky Sack nailed me square in the chest. I eased myself down onto a dirt path, once again dying the world's most nondramatic death.

As I lay in the dirt, watching my compatriots storm the fort, a handful of Celts and Roman traitors dropped thirty-pound bales of hay onto the intruders from atop the north gate. The controversial and highly dangerous tactic later became a heated topic of conversation among the participants on Lafe's Yahoo! message board.

After thirty seconds I came back to life—as per the rules—and snuck up under the gate where David and Wayne were hanging out. All around us people were ignoring Rustius's advice, hammering away on each other with every weapon imaginable. Another hay bale smothered an unsuspecting Roman a few feet away from us. "You want to kill Brutus?" David asked.

"*Si, Flavius, si, Flavius,*" Wayne and I replied.

We peered into the fort's courtyard where Brutus was chatting casually with one of his new Celt BFFs.

"Okay, stay behind me," David said. There was a small skirmish going on just to our right, but if we were quick and agile enough we could sneak by it and kill the traitor. We drew our swords and hunched over to protect ourselves. David held up his left hand and counted down, "Three . . . two . . . one," dropping a finger with each number. We charged ahead, swords raised, three bloodthirsty Russell Crowes out for revenge. "Ahhhhhh!!!"

"Die, traitor!" I yelled.

"*Et tu, Brute?*" David yelled.

Damn, I wish I'd thought of that!

I thrust my sword into his ribs, Wayne sliced at his knees and David slit his throat. But Brutus didn't fall.

"Uh, hello? I'm already dead, guys!" he said.

"What do you mean?" Wayne asked, climbing to his feet.

"Didn't you guys pay attention to the rules? Once you've been killed you can't come back to life."

"What about the thirty-second rule?" I asked. At both reenactments I'd been to before, there was a thirty-second rule stating that once you died, you had to wait thirty seconds before resurrecting and reenacting again.

"There is no thirty-second rule."

"Nobody told us that," David said.

Chapter Four

Wings of the Shire

A psychologist friend of mine likes to say, "What you feed attention, grows." That is, whatever you pay attention to will flourish. This can be a good thing: the more you train yourself in a new skill the better chance you'll have of finding employment in it. And it can be a bad thing: if your dog just died and that's all you think about, you'll probably spiral into a depression, eat lots of cookies and turn into a fat, mopey slob.

For the past six months I'd been feeding a lot of attention to history and my knowledge was growing. Really growing. But to be perfectly honest I was worried. I was getting so into it I was having a hard time thinking about anything else. I was becoming what you might call crazy stupid obsessed.

When I started my journey, I didn't think that I'd become *so* enamored with the past, so hooked by its stories, so interested in its characters. I'd even devised a plan so I wouldn't get bored. One week I'd read a historical book and the next week I'd read something contemporary and so on. This may have worked for a little while—I'd read *April 1865:*

The Month That Saved America, then *White Tiger*, a novel set in modern-day India—but soon I found myself unable to get past the first chapter of *any* book that wasn't about some great historical event. As the months went on, a pile of dog-eared novels accumulated by my bedside, swapped out for historical fare like *The Portable Enlightenment Reader*, *An Edible History of Humanity* and even *The Oxford Dictionary of World History*. (Okay, so I skimmed that one.) In the car I eschewed NPR for history-themed podcasts like the BBC's fantastic "A History of the World in 100 Objects" and the audiobook version of *The Autobiography of Benjamin Franklin*. At home I erased recorded episodes of *The Daily Show* to make room for old movies like *Once Upon a Time in the West* and TV shows like the History Channel's *America: The Story of Us*, a series reenactors universally deplored for the filmmakers' sartorial inaccuracy. What's worse is that I became so obsessed I started ostracizing my friends. While many of them were going on about sports and movies, I was oblivious to virtually every current event. Once, at a party, I barraged them with a bunch of unsolicited historical facts: "Did you know that Andersonville was the fifth largest city in the CSA? But it wasn't a city, *it was a prison*." "Did you know that the Romans made it a policy to limit their expansion to the Rhine? That's why Germanic languages survived." "Did you know that it was the railroad industry that persuaded Congress to create time zones because their timetables were a mess?" I was starting to sound a lot like that annoying little kid from *Jerry Maguire* who kept telling Tom Cruise that the human head weighs eight pounds. It's no wonder my friends stopped talking to me. Fortunately Wendy couldn't have been more supportive. She recorded TV shows and bought books for me, e-mailed me links to history websites and even started geeking out on history herself. At night in bed whenever I'd read an interesting historical fact and mutter, "Huh!" she'd ask, "What is it? What is it? Tell me! Tell me!" I felt like our two minds were working as one, and that we were both growing together and understanding the world a little more. The only difference was that she wasn't spending her weekends dressed in uncomfortable clothing, sleeping on cold ground and getting shot at.

Our historical simpatico was likely one of the reasons why I spent a great deal of time at work browsing real estate listings in Philadelphia and Boston—*two cities I don't even want to live in*—just so I could envision the two of us happily ensconced in a narrow redbrick Colonial home. I guess the thought of us in a house with creaky floors felt unapologetically romantic. She could play Dolley Madison and I could be James and we'd live by candlelight and write with quills. Or something.

Something else happened too. The more history I absorbed, the more I felt like a detective. Everywhere I looked, I examined things not for the way they are, but for the way they *were*, for the way they came about. Layer upon layer of buildings, people, roads, belief systems, art . . . everything looked like geologic strata. Everything had a historical precedent. Popping an aspirin recalled the myriad maladies that plagued people only a century ago; pulling out a dollar bill and looking at the "Eye of Providence" seal brought to mind the founding fathers' deft compromises about religious freedom; the heated debate around the Arizona immigration bill dredged up old tensions between states and the federal government (not to mention the many anti-immigration protests since our nation's founding). Becoming a history junkie, I discovered, is a lot like learning about that negative-space arrow thingy in the FedEx logo—between the "E" and the "X." Once you know it's there, that's all you can see.

And yet, with summer—the busiest time for reenactments—fast approaching, I felt like I needed to take a time-out, at least from the battlefield. In three reenactments I'd nearly frozen to death, lost my hearing and been flattened by a bale of hay. Wasn't there a way to dress up in itchy clothing and learn about the past *without* getting hurt?

Yes, I found out, there was. But it would involve me confronting one of my biggest childhood fears.

. . . .

Here's what I used to know about Poland: World War II started when Germany invaded it in 1939, *Time* magazine named union organizer Lech Walesa Man of the Year when I was a kid and it takes ten Poles—I won't say "Polacks"—to screw in a lightbulb. One to screw in the bulb, nine to turn the ladder. *Hysterical.*

That was until I came across Suligowski's Regiment, a group of seventeenth-century Polish Winged Hussar reenactors headed by Rik Suligowski Fox, a man who's haunted my dreams for the past twenty-five years.

Perhaps I should explain.

In the mid-'80s, Rik played bass in a bunch of heavy metal bands with scary names like Sin, Hellion and, most famously, W.A.S.P. My brother, Rob, loved heavy metal music and whenever my parents were out of the house he cranked W.A.S.P.'s song "Animal (Fuck Like a Beast)" up to eleven. As a twelve-year-old who wanted nothing more than to be the lead singer of Depeche Mode, I covered my ears and shut my bedroom door whenever I heard the band's lead singer, Blackie Lawless, scream.

If W.A.S.P.'s bloodcurdling racket wasn't enough to send me cowering under my sheets, the band's cover art was. Consider the "Animal" single. It featured a tight shot of a man's lower abdomen with a buzz saw sticking out of a tiger-print codpiece. Its message was loud and clear. Actually it wasn't. At the time, I had no idea what it meant, other than maybe, "If you have a two-by-four that needs cutting, my crotch is the man for the job."

Despite all the trauma I suffered at the hands of Rik's old band, I was curious about what exactly a Winged Hussar was and why a former heavy metal dude was spending his weekends dressed as one, so I decided to pay him a visit.

Rik lives in Lake View Terrace, about twenty-five miles north of Los Angeles. It's a relatively rural part of Los Angeles County and popular with horse owners for its many ranches and paddocks. During the dry summer months, the sun bakes this inland foothill region and sears the grass and shrubs, turning it brittle—and flammable. In 2009, parts of the area nearly burned to the ground during a massive wildfire that engulfed 160,000 acres of nearby forest.

Before we met, Rik e-mailed me directions to "Dom Suligowskiego," the rented house he shares with his wife, Tarrah. "Look for Old Glory out front," he wrote. *Yeah,* I thought, *and the pentagram burned into your front yard.*

I arrived at the beige, single-story dwelling on a temperate Sunday morning in April. It was ringed by a chain-link fence and I nervously reached over an iron gate to let myself in to his driveway. The nearby 210 Freeway buzzed so little at that hour that a neighboring rooster drowned out any sounds of traffic. Peering around a large tree that dominated the front yard, I spotted a sign in the living room window that said, "Smile, you're on hidden security cameras." The doorbell was broken so I called through the screen door. "Rik?" I said, my voice cracking a bit.

After a moment he came to the door. He wore a red T-shirt with the words "Kielbasy Power" encircling a muscle-flexing sausage. "Nice to meet you!" he said.

The whites of his eyes were bloodred. *Now would be a good time to run,* I thought, *before he grabs me, throws me down the well like that guy in* Silence of the Lambs *and yells,* "Put the fucking lotion in the basket!"

"Sorry, I just put my contacts in," he said, swinging open the door a bit further and adjusting his vision.

I shook his meaty hand. To my relief he didn't throw me down a well or request that I slather myself in lotion.

Although he's been out of the rock 'n' roll business for more than twenty years, vestiges of his metal days remain: long jet-black hair, a dagger tattoo on the left side of his neck, two fang marks on his right side from the vampire stage he went through. But it was clear from walking around his busy house that he's moved on. Or rather moved *back*.

Nearly all the decorations in Dom Suligowskiego reflect his love affair with Renaissance Poland. A poster of *Ogniem i Mieczem (With Fire and Sword)*, a movie set in the seventeenth-century Polish-Lithuanian Commonwealth, features prominently in the living room, pointy high-back chairs surround the kitchen table, wallpaper designed to look like castle walls lines the dining area. There are tapestries on the walls, chain mail and helmets in the living room, a coat of arms over the fireplace and even Moroccan lanterns—"trappings" Rik wrote in an e-mail, "as might actually be found in the home of a 17th century Polish nobleman." Even his appearance—thick goatee and curly mustache—give him a decidedly chivalric Tim Curry look, although he's rounder now at fifty-four than he was in his svelte hair metal days.

As we made our way to a narrow hallway that he calls the "Wall of Shame," we sidestepped a few of the couple's many cats. There, plastering the two walls, he showed me framed letters of recognition from Polish American leaders and newspaper articles that detailed his efforts to promote this overlooked era of Polish history. Any fears of Rik branding the number of the beast onto my forehead quickly subsided.

After leaving the music business in 1988 ("When grunge music happened, I knew it was time to get out," he said), Rik bounced around, doing odd jobs, working as a property master on films, doing extra work and even joining the California State Military Reserve for five years, tucking his raven locks under his helmet. "I'm obsessed with everything about war," he said. "Except attrition." Turned off by the acting grind, he rediscovered his passion for "larger-than-life" performance when he joined a local Renaissance faire. "I fancied myself the swashbuckler type, you know, Errol Flynn, Tyrone Power," Rik told me in the faintest hint of a Brooklyn accent left over from his Greenpoint youth.

At first he played a pirate, then he joined a Spanish court. As his interest in western Europe grew, so did his curiosity about Poland, a region of the world excluded from most Anglocentric Renaissance faires. So he asked his father, Leonard Suligowski, a former director of heraldry for the Polish Nobility Association Foundation, what was going on in Poland at the time. Turned out it was the largest empire in central Europe.

Rik walked around the corner, back into his living room, and pointed to a small model of a Polish Winged Hussar on top of a bookshelf. When he was a kid his dad had fashioned it out of an old Lone Ranger model rearing up on Silver. After learning about the dashing cavalrymen, Rik remembered the model. "It sparked a memory," he said. The memory of his youth, when he played with toy knights and built castles out of discarded Marlboro Red boxes. The youth he suppressed while seeking fame and fortune in rock.

Not long after he became acquainted with the era, a traveling exhibit called Land of the Winged Horsemen: Art in Poland, 1572–1764 came to the San Diego Museum of Art. His dad had seen it in Baltimore and told Rik that included among its many artifacts was the armor worn by the winged Polish cavalry. Patrons, naturally, weren't allowed to touch it, but when security wasn't looking his dad did.

"And?" Rik asked his father.

"I felt something," his dad replied.

Rik called the museum. The exhibit was in its last week so he raced to San Diego. As soon as he arrived he asked a security guard to take him to the armor. He entered through the exit, against traffic, blowing by all the other artifacts—the portrait of General Stefan Czarniecki in his red robes, the silver spoon a nobleman carried in his boot to prove his high status—and arrived at a huge arched doorway. "There were spotlights shining down on the armor," he told me, then suddenly stopped midstory. I looked up from my notebook to see his eyes fill with tears. He pointed to the hair on his arms. It stuck straight up. "This happens every time I tell this story." His voice cracked a bit. Finally the man whose music Tipper Gore once labeled as "savage" gathered himself and returned to his memories, continuing on in a slow, deliberate voice. "I stood in the doorway. There was no rock music, no amps, no guitars, no bands. It was like I touched a current and it went through my body. And I heard this voice that said, 'I'm home.'" He paused again, wiping a tear from his eye. "And I said, 'I have to tell America about this.'"

• • • • • • • •

Rik never became a household name like some other metal musicians. You know, Ozzy Osbourne, Gene Simmons, Bret Michaels. "I had this penchant for joining sinking ships," he told me while the two of us hung out in his office. A few old band photos decorated the walls, and a couple dusty bass cases leaned up against one another in the corner. He'd just shown me a photo of him with Spinal Tap and Mick Fleetwood. "So many bands had promise and potential and they all went down. I tell people, 'I've been on the merry-go-round, I'm reaching for the brass ring and just as I'm about to grab it, somebody pulls the plug out. I can touch it but it's not mine.'" When I met Rik he'd been unemployed for a while. He didn't offer up a lot more than that, and I didn't pry. His story isn't unusual. L.A. is filled with people who almost had it, who almost grabbed the brass ring. That's how we're raised in America, to believe that we can have it all: fame, fortune, immortality even.

Out back, he introduced me to his and Tarrah's eight horses— mostly rescues, some named for Greek gods. The sun burned off whatever bit of marine layer had made it this far inland. The neighboring rooster had piped down and the sound of passing cars drifted over from the freeway. As we strolled along the paddock, petting his horses, he explained how the Winged Hussars, Poland's light cavalry, attached wings made of eagle feathers onto the saddles or soldiers' backs to terrify their enemies, so the horses looked as if they were flying into battle. "They looked like a strange fantastic beast, like God's angels coming out of heaven," he said. And with the wind whipping through their feathers and the horse hooves stomping the ground, they made a ferocious sound, like horsemen of the apocalypse. Later, a member of Suligowski's Regiment would tell me that "a Pole without a horse is like a man without a soul."

Because there are only three Polish Winged Hussar reenactment groups in the United States, there aren't enough people to hold battle reenactments. So in the beginning Rik took his impression to some of the less Anglocentric Renaissance faires because they provided high visibility for his troupe. At first he didn't wear the wings, just a fur hat, tunic and boots, but that caused confusion. Nobody could figure out who he was. People mistook him for a Cossack or Vlad the Impaler, otherwise known as Dracula. "I would get mad," he said. "I couldn't understand why people didn't know about this. Something had to be done. To make people aware so they don't make these mistakes."

Rik's initial online forays didn't go much better. His passion for the subject on message boards rubbed Renaissance faire webizens the wrong way. "I came off as an arrogant, belligerent, self-serving loose cannon," he said, baffled that all people cared about was Queen Elizabeth and Henry VIII.

At night he slaved away on the floor of his old apartment trying to reconstruct the Winged Hussar uniform, banging, shaping and bending steel into the right dimensions. Finally after much trial and error he'd created a replica uniform that he was proud to wear. He attached a Mohawk of painted turkey feathers to the armor. Now he figured he could show up at faires and strut with pride. He could say that he hadn't just dressed up as a Winged Hussar, he'd built a uniform . . . with his own two hands.

He toned down his approach too. He printed business cards with his website and handed them out to faire attendees. From there he graduated to Southern California timeline events like Old Fort MacArthur Days and Marching Thru History, as well as Polish commemorations like the annual Polish Harvest Festival in Yorba Linda, California, and the 2002 Pulaski Day Parade in New York, when Rik, high atop a horse, rode down Fifth Avenue in full Hussar kit. He called it "shock and awe, but in a positive way. Like my days in rock, being on stage in front of thousands of screaming people." Still, most Renaissance faires resisted Rik's impression, especially after he appeared in full Hussar uniform. "You come into somebody else's sandbox wearing these wings," he said, "and they can interpret that as a territorial stealing of their thunder."

Getting under the skin of make-believe Elizabethans was one thing, but ruffling the feathers of the other U.S.-based Winged Hussar groups has been another. Rik's relationship with the other units has often been contentious. As Rik tells it, he's the pioneer of Winged Hussar reenacting in America. In fact, he was so excited to share his knowledge with the world that he uploaded images of hussars from Polish periodicals and pictures of his and his father's models and paintings to the Web. But soon, he told me, those images started popping up elsewhere online without him getting the proper credit. To this day Rik is still pissed about it and says he never got his props from the other Polish reenactors. Not only did he first publicize the idea of reenacting the Winged Hussars, he figured out how to build the armor and uploaded information online, only to have other groups "steal" his ideas and not credit him as the "inventor." During the year I got to know Rik, I saw just how much it irked him. When the East Coast group Boleslav Orlicki's Light Artillery started identifying themselves as "The *Original* Polish Living History—*First* to portray *accurate* Hussars, Pancerni, and Infantry" (my italics), Rik went off. "It wasn't until our group's independently researched and published documentation stated that Suligowski's Regiment is 'The first 'officially recognized' portrayal of the winged hussars and Polish military nobility in the U.S.A.' that a few 'other' like-minded living history groups . . . had to . . . suddenly amend their own websites to reflect their overly healthy competitiveness and grudge-bearing." To make sure everyone knows that he's the first Winged Hussar reenactor in the country, he aggressively promotes himself as "America's first 17th century living history re-enactment group of Polish Winged Hussar knights and military nobility of the mighty Polish-Lithuanian Commonwealth," which was something, he told me, that the other two groups consider unnecessarily self-serving.

> They say "We don't give a flying fuck who did it first, just that it's being done." Well, everything important in history has a point of origin. Do you think that when Chuck Yeager broke the sound barrier in the X-15 the other guys in the program were like "Fuck him?" In the reenactment community, that stuff happens. I'm like the Johnny Appleseed of this. I did it first and I'm spreading the seeds of what I've done, but the people who pick up and eat the fruit, throw it at me.

Obviously Rik does care—deeply—about who reenacted the Winged Hussars first. And he's not about to back down. He told me he's using all of his heavy metal aggression to publicize himself and Poland's history. When I first got to know him, he sent me more than one hundred pages of publicity documents. His reenactor résumé alone totals a whopping eleven pages. As he once said, "If you don't market yourself, you're dead."

At times I couldn't tell if Rik was more interested in promoting Polish history, his pioneering spirit or himself. But his agro approach has undoubtedly raised the profile of an obscure historical group. Go online today, and you'll find ample evidence of Rik's impact on the hobby and on the memory of this striking group of horsemen. Still, with all the mudslinging going on, I often wondered why people dedicated to the preservation of Polish chivalry didn't ever sit down and just settle things courteously.

• • • • • • • •

There are so many Renaissance faires in the United States that when I called *Renaissance* magazine to ask for the exact number, a man had to put me on hold for a couple minutes to tally them up. When he finally came back he said, "Sorry, there are just too many to count." "Over a hundred?" I asked. "Oh, yeah," he replied.

The Renaissance Pleasure Faire, where I'd join Rik for a day, welcomes 200,000 visitors a year, which makes it the country's highest attended faire. Most festivals put on what Rik calls the "Liz and Hank Show" (Elizabeth I and Henry VIII), in pseudo English villages that overflow with the obligatory bawdiness and pageantry one would expect from Tudor England. But the Pleasure Faire and its make-believe town of Port Deptford, while plenty bawdy, resembles a famous American port more than an authentic Renaissance-era town. "It's the Ellis Island of England," Rik put it as we loaded a heavy trunk of armor into his black SUV (license plate: HUSSAR). The all-inclusive vibe employs lotus flower dancers from "Siam", *danse macabre* and Afro-Brazilian martial artists, to name a few. The festival, which started off modestly in someone's backyard, is the country's oldest faire and for the past five years has been held at the Sante Fe Dam Recreational Area in Irwindale. The small industrial town lies twenty miles east of Los Angeles and is better known for its NASCAR track and massive Miller Brewery than any resemblance it may have to Tudor England.

Bruce Willis (not that one) and Josh Wojda, two other members of Suligowski's Regiment, joined Rik, Tarrah and me for the day. Our plan was simple. As invited guests we'd have the chance to walk Deptford's streets, mingle with the crowd and pass out informational flyers about the group and Polish history.

As we unpacked Rik's truck in the parking lot, an elderly man in a baseball cap shuffled by. "Who are you?" he asked, taking in the flamboyantly dressed posse.

Bruce turned to look at him, a long wooden Ukrainian pipe drooping out of his mouth. "Seventeenth-century Winged Hussars from the Polish-Lithuanian Commonwealth. We defeated the Turks in the Battle of Vienna and saved Christendom."

"Way to go!" the old man said, continuing on. "We need more of you guys today."

It'd be hard to find a more colorful uniform than that of the Polish Winged Hussar: yellow calf-high boots, electric blue velour pants, neon pink tunic, silver breastplate and neck armor, leopard skin cloak, saber, Wonder Woman–like forearm armor, silver helmet with a nose guard that made me go cross-eyed and Mohawk of eagle feathers—painted turkey feathers in this case—that ran the entire length of my spine, peaking eighteen inches over my head. "It created the impression that there were multiple riders," Josh said. "Horses are prey animals. They tend to run away when they see something they don't know. It was psychological warfare."

While our wings may originally have been meant to terrify enemy horses, they had the opposite effect on humans. After an awkward entrance into the fairgrounds in which Rik and I had to limbo our way backward under an arching gate, we were met by a mad rush of patrons who wanted their picture taken with us. "You're going to be a rock star for a day," Rik said, noting the throngs of young women sucked in by our outfits. It wasn't exactly the Beatles at Shea, but a sort of twenty-first-century fame, with promises of imminent and widespread Facebook exposure. (*Winged Hussar was tagged in a photo.*) I was happy to comply with all the photo requests, beaming a toothy grin for anybody with a point-and-shoot, until Josh suggested that I "adopt a stern look." I complied. "That's better," he said. "But don't look into the camera. That'd be stepping out of character."

After fifteen minutes of politician-like photo ops, we took off to cruise Port Deptford's dusty mazelike streets. We strolled past merchants called Ye Bag Wench and Olde Soles, watched people play games in which the objective was to hit someone in the face with a tomato and even passed an outdoor stage where two "Washing Well Wenches" were coaxing an audience member to remove his tightie-whities and slip them over his jeans. By now the mercury had hit eighty, and the bright sun heated me up so much that I could have fired pottery inside my armor. The striking uniforms frequently caused people to stop us and ask if we were "real." Questions like this opened the door for one of the group members to deliver an impromptu history lesson. "We're the most famous cavalry in Europe. We chased the Turks out of Europe and saved Christendom. Here's a flyer." "We're the most famous cavalry in Europe. We chased the Turks out of Europe and saved Christendom. Here's a flyer." "We're the most famous cavalry in Europe . . ."

It was easy to see why people thought we were fictitious. Unlike the nonanachronistic Renaissance faire that I worked at a long time ago, the Pleasure Faire's anything-goes inclusiveness attracts visitors dressed as everything from bumblebees with Viking horns to fang-toothed trolls to who knows what. At one point Josh leaned over and said, "I haven't seen any Stormtroopers here today, but they'll be here eventually." He sounded disappointed. "This is entertainment. People come here for turkey legges and beer."

When people weren't questioning our validity, they cracked jokes at our expense. Rik had warned me in an e-mail about potential confrontations.

[K]eep a weather eye out for any funny condescending or askance glances . . . from any of the other "nobles" there . . . they can tend to get or be "snooty" because, I guess, we do tend to attract a lot of attention and perhaps they feel territorially "threatened" or maybe that we steal their thunder . . . just something to keep your "spider sense" open to.

The year before, someone had falsely accused a hussar of telling him to "go fuck [him]self," but there'd be no such allegations today. Most of the comments hurled at us struck me as innocuous and cheeky, the kind of bad puns you'd expect to hear at a Renaissance faire. We heard a lot of "Huzzars!" and "You look very aerodynamic" and, because of our uncanny resemblance to Hawkman from *Flash Gordon*, "Have you seen Master Flash today?" The most original little dig came from some detached voice that yelled, "Is he your wingman?" But people were generally perplexed and of the "I'd like to say you're Spaniards, but I'm not sure. What the fuck are you?" variety.

I thought we'd managed to avoid any real confrontation when we rounded a corner and caught the attention of a shirtless Justin Bieber look-alike. He had a black eye and looked us up and down. I, on the other hand, only looked him down. As he approached us, I noticed that he'd either stuffed the crotch of his brown tights with half an avocado or was smuggling a small turtle into the shire.

"And exactly what do you guys do?" he asked cockily.

"We look good," Rik replied, trying to defuse any tension. When that didn't elicit a response from Bieber, he caved and said rather flatly, "Polish Winged Hussars."

"Huh?" Bieber said.

"Polish cavalry."

"Yeah, well, what do you have all that armor for?" I felt like I was back in school on the playground and a heavy metal kid was picking a fight with me. Except in this case, a total dweeb was picking on a heavy metal guy.

"To our enemies we're angels of death," Rik said. "Normally we'd be on horses."

A friend of Bieber's, taller than him by a head, backed him up. "It's very flashy, but what good does it do you in battle?" I couldn't believe a couple fifteen-year-olds were picking on us.

"It scares the hell out of the enemy," Rik said.

"Yeah, you are kind of scary," Bieber said. Then he turned his attention to Bruce Willis, who wasn't wearing feathers or armor. "Where's your armor? Did you lose a bet?"

"I'm a dragoon," Bruce replied. "We don't wear armor."

"You have a gun," Bieber said. "*He* doesn't have a gun"—pointing to Rik and his sword—"I feel like a gun would be better than *that*."

"That's why I'm a dragoon," Bruce said.

Rik had asked me to keep my spider sense open, but what he really should have told me was not to turn into the Hulk. I'd had enough of Bieber. I needed to stick up for my fellow hussars. So I swooped down on him like a strange fantastic beast, like one of God's angels descending from heaven.

"Who are *you*?" I asked. "What's *your* outfit?"

"My outfit? I'm a slave. I ran away."

"Uh-huh," I said, taking notes. This unnerved him.

"Are you writing me down?"

His friend tapped him on the shoulder and muttered, "Let's get out of here." Then they noticed that I had a voice recorder hidden under my notebook. "Are you a police officer?"

"What happened here?" I asked, pointing to his black eye.

"I got hit running away," he said quietly.

"Who are you running away from? Who is your master?" I felt like such a tool for playing along with whatever made-up master-servant world Bieber had concocted.

"I'd rather not say."

"What's this?" I asked, pointing to a swirly silver pendant around his neck.

"It means soul friend. My friend has an identical one." Bieber fanned his beautiful blond bangs away from his eyes and looked at his friend, who nodded that it was time for them to go.

"Nice to meet you, sir," Bieber said and the two boys hurried away.

I adjusted my helmet so that its strip of metal lined up perfectly with my nose and hitched my leopard cape so it covered my shoulders. Bruce put his pipe back in his mouth, adjusted his big fur hat and looked at me. "There are a lot of weirdos here," he said. And with that we continued to strut down the street.

· · · · · · · ·

During my research I'd met a bunch of reenactors who told me why they'd made the leap from history junkie to history participant. Some grew up playing with miniature toy soldiers and now, as grown-ups, got to, in essence, be that toy; some played video games and wanted to inhabit the soldiers on the screen; others did it because it connected them to their heritage; some liked the camaraderie and the chance to be outdoors among like-minded guys. F. L. Watkins, a Viking reenactor I met at Reenactor Fest, a sort of Comic-Con for reenactors, told me that a visit to Iceland triggered his interest. When he was there he looked in a phone book and noticed that people were listed by their given names, not their surnames. This was so different from what he knew that he wanted to know more about Nordic traditions. One thing led to another and he ended up becoming a Viking. Another time I spoke to a woman who reenacts the fur trade. When I asked her what was so appealing about "yesterday," she said, "I guess, the faster you hurdle into the future, the more you want to cling to the past."

At first I thought that Rik's Polish heritage was what compelled him to dress up and spread the word about Winged Hussars, but later I realized there was something else going on, something more spiritual, more mystifying.

After the faire I went back to his place. It was late afternoon and we were tired from a long day of meeting and greeting. We were standing in his living room, saying our good-byes, when Rik said, "I think there's something in the genetic DNA memory." I'd heard a couple other reenactors use similar language, so I quickly retrieved my voice recorder. "There's a code back there as to why this stuff feels so natural to me," he said. I gingerly offered up that some reenactors I'd met believed that they'd been reincarnated. "Do you believe in reincarnation?" I asked.

Rather than answering me directly, Rik told a story. One day, when he was twenty-four and still living in New York, he met an astrologer, a big Nordic guy who looked like Dolph Lundgren. At one point, the astrologer put his hands on either side of Rik and said, "You strike me as somebody from the Napoleonic era. I see you being cut to pieces." Rik wasn't sure what to make of this. At the time he didn't really have a connection to his heritage or an interest in military history. Or at least it wasn't on his radar. He was still chasing the brass ring of rock 'n' roll.

But what Dolph said stuck with him. It was such a vivid, ghastly vision—being cut to pieces. Later when he told his father about the experience his dad asked him if he'd ever heard of the Polish nobleman Jozef Sulkowski. Rik hadn't. Turned out that Sulkowski was one of Rik's ancestors and served as one of Napoleon's adjutants. He was ambushed in Cairo, cut up and literally left for the dogs. "It was at that moment that I experienced an icy cold feeling in my solar plexus, a cylindrical sensation of coldness," Rik told me. "I can't explain why, but the words just came to my head. 'Could I be the reincarnation of this ancestor?'"

Rik will never know for sure if that's the case but he did tell me that he believes there's a "higher purpose" to what he's doing and that by reenacting he's connecting to his ancestors. Standing there, he told me his relatives were among the knights who charged the Turks at Vienna. "To be able to reach through that wormhole and touch that part of your ancestry, that DNA genetic marker perhaps, and make that connection . . ." He trailed off for a bit, then continued. "Why are we so attracted to a specific point in history, or that particular battle, or that particular type of soldier or that particular type of weapon? *Why am I drawn to this? Why?* I don't know, but to me it's just there, it feels natural."

I think, more than any of the reeenactors in this book, I best understand where Rik is coming from. Like me, we both need to be onstage, any stage. For him, when his dream of rock stardom faded, he transitioned to acting and when that faded, he replaced it with reenacting, which allowed him to "perform" in eye-catching clothing *and* promote his heritage. A twofer, if you will. For me, when my acting dream faded, I transitioned to the airwaves telling stories on NPR, and now I'm writing this book, which is about entertaining and educating you, as well as me, about the past. Even though I might not feel much connection to my German heritage, I do feel a very strong pull toward

British culture. So I ask a lot of the same questions Rik rhetorically asked me that day after the faire. *Why? What is it about British culture that appeals to me?* Why am I drawn to Shakespeare, Peter Sellers, Noël Coward, Madchester music and *Blackadder*? I don't know, but to me, it just feels natural.

Whatever the explanation for Rik's strong link, he may not have grabbed the brass ring when he wore spandex and played metal, but he's found it now wearing a uniform of feathers and armor. And by the looks of things he isn't just grabbing the ring with his hands, he's biting it so hard he's leaving teeth marks.

CHAPTER FIVE

Their American Life

For the first thirty-nine years of her life, my wife, Wendy, lived in Hong Kong, and for most of that time Great Britain ruled the region—what the writer Jan Morris once called the "pimple on the body of China." During those colonial years, Hong Kongers didn't have the right to vote. Rather, the British government appointed governors to run the colony.

Since China took back Hong Kong in 1997, democracy has, not surprisingly, been slow to spread. Today, as citizens of a "special administrative region," Hong Kongers are only permitted to vote for half of the sixty seats in its legislative assembly. Choosing the region's chief executive is the domain of eight hundred people who've been appointed to an election committee. If you're one of the other 7,060,400 citizens you have no say. And simply don't vote.

When Wendy moved to the United States in 2004, she told me that she wanted to become a citizen so she could finally vote, not just because she hadn't been able to do that for most of her life, but because she thought it was her duty. She didn't want to take advantage of what America has to offer and "chuck away the rest."

Three years after getting her green card she applied for citizenship. But, contrary to popular opinion, the U.S. government doesn't just hand them out. They make candidates suffer through a ten-question quiz. Answer six correctly and you're an American. That's right, to become a U.S. citizen, all you have to be is just one point better than half right (or the equivalent of a D student).

One evening in early 2009, she summoned me to our living room, where she was cramming for her upcoming test. Flash cards, notebooks and highlighters surrounded her on our couch. She handed me a thin, glossy booklet. The words "Learn About the United States: Quick Civics Lessons for the New Naturalization Test" were printed on the bottom half of it. On the top half were photographs of the U.S. flag, Mt. Rushmore and the yellowed Declaration of Independence. For the past month she'd been studying the one hundred potential test questions that lay inside.

I flipped through the booklet, picked a question at random and silently read it to myself: *How many amendments does the Constitution have?* I took a long, deep breath and thought for a few seconds, then quickly flipped through to another question. *What is one thing Benjamin Franklin is famous for?* Okay, that was an easy one. He discovered electricity. Everybody knows that. Then I read the five answers:

U.S. diplomat
Oldest member of the Constitutional Convention
First Postmaster General of the United States
Writer of "Poor Richard's Almanac"
Started the first free libraries

They left out the bit about him discovering electricity, I thought. I grabbed my laptop and googled, "Ben Franklin, discover electricity," just to be sure I was right. Long story short, I wasn't. He didn't discover it. The ancient Egyptians and Greeks wrote about it thousands of years before Franklin. Ben, however, did correctly surmise that lightning was a form of electricity. He proved this one overcast day when a bolt struck the kite he and his son were flying. Somehow Franklin survived the incident and lived long enough to write his autobiography that was later turned into an audiobook that I listened to in the car and that was voiced by a guy who was so annoying Wendy wanted to shove a *Poor Richard's Almanac* down his throat.

I skipped to another question: *The Federalist Papers supported the passage of the U.S. Constitution. Name one of the writers.* Droplets of sweat started to form on my brow. My heart began to race. *OMG,* I thought, *I'm a thirty-seven-year-old American and I don't know jack about my country!* Wendy had asked me to help her study, but I was the one who needed help.

Lots of it.

Around the same time, the Tea Party movement was galvanizing across the country, organizing reenactments of the Boston Tea Party. Dressed in colonial garb, middle-aged white people in tricorns, upset by government spending and the spate of recent corporate bailouts, dumped perfectly good Lipton into Boston Harbor. Their acts of defiance or sedition or whatever seemed to imply a couple things:

a. That if you didn't side with them you weren't somehow truly "American."
b. That the current political climate mirrored the conditions leading up to the actual Boston Tea Party of 1773 and that in protesting the government bailouts they embodied the revolutionary spirit that helped shape our country.

The Tea Partiers' rage could be attributed to a few people, including Bob Basso, a septuagenarian former TV reporter with a knack for attention-grabbing media stunts (he once reported a story from atop a pile of manure). In March 2009, he uploaded a YouTube video called *We the People Stimulus Package*, in which he dressed up as founding father Thomas Paine, stood in front of an old '76 flag and an enlarged version of the U.S. Constitution and unleashed a motivational speech with so much fury that he nearly extinguished the tall candle that flickered before him. At one point, while ranting about how apathetic the general public has become, he bellowed, "You're sucking at the hind tit of a dead cow!" His video became so popular he made another. And another. Each time reiterating his political platform: make English the official language, reinstate God into public life and tell Congress to go eff itself. (Okay, my words, not his.) In a little over a year, 13.3 million people watched his six "Paine" videos, earning him an appearance on *Glenn Beck* and the praise of YouTube users like SystematicChaos6 and Anarchist4U.

At the end of the *We the People* video Basso encouraged viewers to mail a tea bag to their congressman and warned, "If you decide to do nothing . . . then buy a gun. You'll need it." People obeyed. They sent tea bags. Which, in retrospect, proved to be a lot more dangerous than purchasing a gun. The bulky, suspicious-looking envelopes stuffed with Celestial Seasonings rekindled the anthrax scare and prompted evacuations at some congressional offices.

I was curious to learn if everyone who wore a tricorn was a Tea Partier, so on one perfectly lovely spring Saturday, Wendy and I headed to Riley's Farm, a working orchard and quasi-colonial New England village seventy-five miles east of Los Angeles. Perched five thousand feet above sea level, Riley's welcomes school groups and folks like us who want to experience what life was like in Revolutionary-era America.

After ordering some magma-hot chicken pot pie at the Hawk's Head Public House, I invited the village's John Adams impersonator to our table to chat about his experiences as a living historian. Faster than you can say "Anarchist4U," he was regaling us with an incident that took place shortly after President Obama's health-care overhaul passed. With a rapt fifth-grade audience glued to his every word, our country's second president cautioned the eleven-year-olds that "socialism was rearing its ugly head." Mr. Adams's stump speech didn't exactly bowl over the students' teacher, who yanked the kids away from the anachronistic founding father. (For starters, the word "socialism" wasn't even coined until the 1830s, nearly ten years after Adams died.) I wasn't sure how to respond to Adams's anecdote so I did the only thing I could do: shovel some smoldering-hot pot pie in my mouth, which seared the outer layer of my soft palate. Fortunately, as a result of the newly passed Patient Protection and Affordable Care Act, I later got it taken care of.

Not much was going on at Riley's so we left after a couple hours. When I got home I was curious to know more about the standards the farm sets for its historical interpreters, so I ventured onto its website and read its "Farm Journal" blog, which turned out to be a platform for its proprietor, Jim Riley, to rant about everything from "abortuaries" (family planning clinics) to the "medical fascism" of "Obamacare." *And schools pay these guys to educate children about the founding of our country?* I thought, mentally crossing Riley's Farm off my list of future places to pick apples.

I may not see eye to eye with "John Adams," but I had to admit that my own grasp of American history was still flimsy at best. Over the years, I've tended, like many people, to elevate our founding fathers into one-dimensional demigods, probably because I always see their faces on dollar bills and only know fragments of what really happened at places like Lexington, Yorktown and, yes, Boston Harbor.

So I decided that it might not be a bad thing to find out more about my country. And I figured there was no better place to look for it than America's heartland.

. . . .

On February 23, 1779, nearly three years after America declared independence from Great Britain, twenty-six-year-old George Rogers Clark, commander of the Continental Army's Virginia Regiment, captured the British-held Fort Sackville in what's now Vincennes, Indiana. It only took three days for his volunteer force of approximately 170 men to take the fort, but his victory proved significant to the American cause. It helped to double the size of the original thirteen colonies, thus ensuring that expansion-happy colonists could finally move west into what would later become the Northwest Territory and the states of Michigan, Ohio, Indiana and Illinois. But despite the magnitude of Clark's contribution, you'd have a hard time finding a man on the street today who's heard of him.

Theories abound as to why his legend never grew: the printing press didn't make it to the frontier, so his triumphs couldn't be easily documented and distributed, and his three-day victory wasn't all that sensational. Consider that because of his clever tactics, he didn't kill a whole lot of enemy troops, and even more remarkably, not one of his soldiers died, despite battling through wet, wintry conditions, and, um, being at war.

After his swift, heroic victory at the Battle of Vincennes, the rest of Clark's life wasn't so great. In fact, it was downright awful. The U.S. government never reimbursed him for his war expenses, which he paid for with borrowed money. He grew bitter and drank—*a lot*. One night, either drunk or the victim of a seizure, he tumbled into a fire at his Indiana cabin and burned his leg so badly it had to be amputated. With the discovery of ether still another thirty-seven years away, the only "anesthesia" administered to him during the two-hour surgery came from just outside the door, where fifers and drummers played music to lift his spirits. Nine years later he suffered another stroke while living with his sister near Louisville, Kentucky, the city he'd founded forty years earlier. He died shortly thereafter.

Though in most of the country George Rogers Clark remains largely unknown—barely remembered by some as the older brother of William Clark (of Lewis and Clark)—in the Wabash Valley of Illinois and Indiana, the guy's pretty much a rock star. After spending much of my trip from the St. Louis Airport driving on the two-lane George Rogers Clark Memorial Highway, I arrived in Vincennes after dark, crossing the Wabash River into Indiana. While on the Lincoln Memorial Bridge, I looked to the right and spotted a dramatically lit George Rogers Clark Memorial. It was a humid Friday on Memorial Day weekend, and with my windows rolled down I could just make out a handful of words that ringed the top of it: THE CONQUEST OF THE WEST.

After pulling into the George Rogers Clark National Historical Park, on the site of the now razed Fort Sackville, I reconnected with Jane Whitehead, an animated and freckly retired children's librarian who I'd met three months earlier at Reenactor Fest. The fifty-six-year-old Whitehead is the adjutant of the Northwest Territory Alliance (NWTA), a Midwest reenactment company that's spent the last thirty-seven years educating ding-dongs like me that the Revolutionary War didn't just take place on the eastern seaboard.

Whiteside had kindly erected a four-foot-wide canvas wedge tent for me under a large maple tree and near a makeshift parking lot. "I brought you lots of clothing options," she said, shining a flashlight inside my tent. I peered inside and saw a large bulging white paper bag overflowing with period clothing and three different colonial hats. "I brought a towel too, in case you want to take a shower."

"Wow. Thanks!" I said, realizing that I'd probably just met the world's nicest person. Or as one of my friends called her, a "typical Midwesterner."

Vincennes was my fifth reenactment and, aside from the fabric I bought for my Roman tunic, I'd yet to pay for one article of clothing. While most reenactment groups have loaner gear for prospective members, I never thought they'd be *so* generous with me. In our "me first" age of iThis and YouThat, reenactors' magnanimity and enthusiasm for sharing is, indeed, quite rare. Jane excused herself for a bit and I flicked on my Maglite. I held out a black tricorn and looked at it from all angles. Then I stepped back and asked myself, "If a stranger randomly contacted *me* would I let them wear *my* clothes for the weekend?"

"Come join us for Gatorade and bagels," Jane said. I fumbled my way outside into the dark toward a canvas dining fly, where she and her nineteen-year-old son, Robert, sat in the warm glow of candlelight.

A history minor in college, Jane started reenacting twenty-five years ago, and even though her husband never took to it, she introduced Robert to the hobby while he was still in diapers. Growing up part of the time "in the eighteenth century," Robert, a wiry, bespectacled first-year student at DePaul University, soaked up a lot of history, placing him in the awkward position of often knowing more about the American Revolution than his instructors. Once, after one of his high school teachers showed the movie *April Morning*, about the beginnings of the American Revolution, and laid out a few incorrect reasons why America won the war, Robert could barely hold his tongue. "I wanted to say, 'Uh, no, it's because the British were far from home and couldn't resupply their troops,'" he said, munching on a bagel. But of course he didn't. After all, he's a good Midwestern young man, and good Midwestern young men don't do those types of things.

Before I turned in I told Jane and Robert a story I'd heard at Reenactor Fest. As the story goes, the child of two "British" reenactors once refused to say the Pledge of Allegiance on his first day of kindergarten. When his teacher asked him why he remained seated, he pointed at the flag and said, "I'm not going to salute that rebel rag." Jane and Robert cracked up, but I could tell they'd heard similar stories before.

. . . .

I rarely slept more than a couple hours the first night of any reenact-ment, because of jet lag, my inability to acclimate to hard ground and the general giddiness that came with the new experience. So when I emerged from my tent on that humid Saturday morning having caught only a few winks, I thought my mind was playing tricks on me. The park's broad lawn had been transformed into a miniature village of pup tents, and campsites buzzed with family activity. Young "colonial" and "British" kids—from babies to young adults—ate breakfast with their parents, tossed around period leather lacrosse balls and dealt old, un-marked cards at picnic tables. All this was a bit strange. So far the reen-actments I'd been to had been chances for mostly guys to go off and do guy things. Sure, I saw a smattering of women here and there, but by and large I'd started to think of reenacting as a guys-by-the-fire-beating-their-fists-against-their-chests sort of weekend getaway. I certainly didn't expect to see what looked like a massive family reunion. The ages even ran the gamut. While I waited in line to use a Porta-Potty, an elderly Revo-lutionary gentleman whizzed by in an electric wheelchair. Behind me a woman coddled a baby outfitted in a lace cap.

I hurried back to my tent and slipped into my garb: white knee breeches, a plain white cotton shirt that hung down to my knees ('twas the fashion), black tricorn, a pair of thigh-high yellow leggings that conjured up images of Malvolio from *Twelfth Night* and a farby pair of old black J.Crew shoes. As Jane said when I showed them to her, "They have a top seam and laces but they'll pass for the weekend."

I greeted her in my new outfit, eager to find out which unit I'd fall in with, but to my dismay she just looked at me with a shrug and said, "None."

"Heh?" I replied.

"I'm so sorry, but our insurance won't cover it."

At all the other battle reenactments I'd participated in I had to pay an entrance fee that went toward an insurance policy, so I couldn't understand why Vincennes would be any different. It was the first time I'd been told I couldn't fight, and for a moment I wasn't sure what to do. I'd flown nearly two thousand miles to St. Louis, rented a car and driven three hours to George Rogers Clarkland but I couldn't stand in a line and hold a musket? There were four military demonstrations planned for the two-day event. I couldn't participate in *one* of them? Even as a target? Apparently not. Isn't it funny how some reenactment groups think it's a liability to let a complete stranger handle a dangerous weapon?

As Saturday's events got under way, I felt a little aimless and lonely, like Michael Stipe in the "Everybody Hurts" video, so I walked around the park—picture a much smaller Washington, DC, mall—and poked my head in different encampments. Under one canvas dining fly, I spotted a man dressed as a Jesuit priest—covered head to toe in black, like Father Guido Sarducci—but sporting a salt-and-pepper beard.

Until now, the reenactments I'd participated in were opportunities for mostly middle-aged men to act like soldiers, wield replica weapons and "kill" each other, but the military and its hierarchical structure didn't jive with this "Jesuit," "Father" Craig McGirr. Spending the weekend getting barked at by "George Washington" just wasn't his cup of tea. Still, the Michigan consulting manager loved history and the idea of dressing up and educating the public. So, he told me, with the faintest hint of a Midwestern accent, that he went about creating a historically important figure "who could read and write and demand the respect of everybody." Finding that someone was a breeze. As early as the 1680s, French Jesuits established a mission at Fort St. Joseph in Niles, Michigan. They sent letters that detailed their life and work in the New World back to their superiors in France, which were then published to raise money for the Catholic Church. Letters that Craig read to develop his character. "It was like getting a subscription to *Time* magazine," he said, struggling to slip off his wedding ring in the early morning heat, the last step to fully realizing his eighteenth-century self.

Without performing heroic acts of fantastical courage, I wondered what Craig liked the most about his subdued role. "Ah," he said, digging inside a wooden box and producing a long chain of interlocking metal rings with inward-pointing spikes. *One of Diana Ross's necklaces from her Studio 54 days?* I wondered. He held up the chain-link belt. "Can you believe it? Somebody of the Catholic faith wore one of these!" He dangled the replica *cilice* in front of me. A fragment of one had recently been found at the Fort St. Joseph archaeological site, near Craig's home. "You wore it around an arm or a leg and tightened it with a leather strap," he said, letting me touch the sharp spikes. "As if there wasn't enough pain and suffering on the Midwest frontier in the 1700s, they used these!"

For Craig, simply showing it off to the public didn't effectively convey its function. To get the full effect, he had to demonstrate how it worked. "I will take my pants off and wear this around my leg," he said, scraping it against my arm, a move that—*forgive me, Father*—I kind of enjoyed. Apparently I wasn't his only masochistic audience member. Once a lady screamed, *"Tighter!"* when Craig wrapped it around her leg.

At first I was surprised to meet a "Jesuit" in colonial America. After all, at the time, Protestants loved Catholics about as much as Bill O'Reilly loves Muslims. But then it hit me. I wasn't in "colonial America." I was in "Quebec."

After the French and Indian War, when the Brits seized the mostly French-speaking Quebec territory, they forced its Catholic inhabitants to pledge allegiance to George III, but, surprisingly, *not* to Protestantism. The Quebec Act, as it was called, turned out to be a groundbreaking experiment in religious tolerance, yet it angered many Protestant colonists who were set on moving west into the territory. Not only could they not move west now, but the area was full of a bunch of "papists."

For Craig and other reenactors this religious tension provides lots of fun role-playing opportunities. "The British tolerate me; the Americans fear me," he said. "I'm a papist. I represent the Catholic Church. That's an abomination to colonial Americans." One soldier used to yell, "Bloody papist! Kill the priest!" at Craig to heighten the authenticity for the public. But Craig just blessed him and moved on. Besides, he wielded that *cilice* and if anyone really got out of line he could always wrap it around his or her leg.

Not that there's anything wrong with that.

With the first tactical scheduled to start shortly—off national park property in an adjacent field—the campgrounds would soon empty, so I said good-bye to Craig and hastily searched for an expert historian who could tell me more about the founding of my country. It didn't take long for me to realize that she was "British" and a member of the King's 8th Regiment, because people kept pointing me in the direction of a woman named Angie Potter.

When I arrived at her unit's encampment, a few cute blond kids were playing checkers on a simple wooden board and clean-cut Gen-Xers, dressed as British officers, were finishing their lunch, drinking out of pewter mugs and ladling soup from wooden bowls. When I explained to them that I was looking for Angie, everyone pointed in the direction of a very pregnant woman who sat at a long table, fanning herself.

If the presence of a noncombative "Jesuit" hadn't surprised me enough, meeting Angie did. At the time, the NWTA's thirty-five-year-old commanding officer was eight months pregnant with twins and, even though she was in charge of the entire five-hundred-person organization, she didn't exude the air of someone on a weekend power trip. In fact, she wasn't even dressed like a general. Rather, she was dressed like a British seamstress, in a very long, very hot-looking baby blue dress. She tucked her shoulder-length black hair under a bonnet and wore moccasins because, as she'd soon tell me, "The Crown forces that controlled Fort Sackville didn't get resupplied for two years so they adopted Indian dress."

If there's one common, er, *thread* that unites all reenactors it's that they completely geek out on historical clothing. Most—even the manliest of manly men—obsess about perfecting a historically accurate impression, even if it means broiling in the late May sun. Angie was no different. Before I had the chance to ask her about George Rogers Clark and those three crucial days in 1779, she was describing her clothing to me with the kind of enthusiasm I thought only Isaac Mizrahi could muster.

I typically find women's clothing about as interesting as vampire movies, but I was glued to every word Angie said. All her garments, and those of a typical late eighteenth-century woman, had a purpose that went well beyond mere fashion. These weren't just clothes, they were like a Swiss Army knife that you could wear. She carried firewood and picked up hot pans with her apron. Her long gown enabled her to breastfeed discreetly. Her two white petticoats expanded and contracted to accommodate all those growing babies women were expected to give birth to. She even wore a chatelaine that hung off her waist, an ornament that held all the tools a seamstress would need. "Basically everything was designed for pregnant women, breastfeeding or being a seamstress," she said.

There were clues in her dress that identified her station too. Her two petticoats revealed that she couldn't afford many clothes. On the frontier it was a lot easier to wear one's petticoats than to carry them. During our conversation, Angie told me the story of one well-off woman who wore seventeen petticoats on her wedding night. "Imagine how difficult it was for her husband to get underneath all those layers of clothing!" she said. In addition to advertising one's wealth, wearing lots of petticoats broadcast a woman's wide, childbearing hips, which was just what women needed to lure a husband.

I was so intrigued *I* wanted to become a seamstress right then and there.

She looked around the campground and spotted a young, privileged "French" girl wearing a long orange satin skirt and floral top, brilliant as a peacock.

"She's looking for a husband."

"In real life?" I asked, somewhat confused.

"No, that's her impression. She's a 'young available woman.' Notice how the French wore brighter colors?"

"Uh-huh."

"Americans were drab," Angie said. So drab and "unsophisticated," in fact, that a British soldier named Richard Shuckburgh wrote the song "Yankee Doodle" that poked fun of colonials naïve enough to stick a feather in their cap and call it "macaroni," the Italian word for "fop." *The jerk.*

Within five minutes I'd completely forgotten why I'd come to see Angie in the first place, becoming totally obsessed with her garments. But the more we talked, the more I realized that her clothing wasn't nearly as interesting as her own history-rich life. As a kid, while I was obsessively collecting baseball cards and dreaming of playing in the big leagues, she was falling in love with history. After visiting Colonial Williamsburg at the age of six, she named her dog Revere and successfully lobbied her parents to let her wear colonial clothing to school. "My mom thought that I would be a freak if I wore my reenactor clothes more than one day a week," she told me, and then conceded, "I think that probably was too much." When she wasn't dressing as an eighteenth-century girl, she wore a William and Mary sweatshirt . . . *everywhere.* Later, she studied history at Purdue University, and after grad school at Emory, landed a job with the National Park Service, the country's largest employer of historians.

It seemed like whatever Angie did, wherever she went, history followed. Once, at a history conference in Quebec, a tall, distinguished redcoat reenactor named Bill Potter asked her to go on a walk with him on the Plains of Abraham, the site of many French and Indian War battles. At one point he held her pinky, which protruded out of a cast on her broken right hand. Then they walked to the armory, where he kissed her. "It was childhood romantic," she said. "Like the man rides up on a horse." Later, the couple went on a more formal date in their civvies, this time to Fort Ouiatenon in Illinois. It was freezing cold, ten below zero and windy. They huddled to stay warm. Then it hit them. It was the very same day—well over two hundred years later—that the King's 8th Regiment, *the very unit that they reenact*, had stopped for cannon practice at Fort Ouiatenon en route to Fort Sackville. "I knew at that very moment that this was the man I was going to marry." The next year they eloped. Later, they held a reception at Vincennes, where everyone dressed in "kit."

At reenactments Bill insisted they sleep on straw even though Angie suffers from bad allergies. "He wouldn't compromise on that," she said. "Even though I couldn't breathe."

It occurred to me, during our conversation, that Angie kept referring to Bill in both the past and present tenses. Slowly I started to realize why. The night before, when I registered, I'd picked up a flyer that said, "Bill Potter will miss his first Rendezvous in 34 years." Printed on the sheet of paper were three photos of a redcoat who looked a bit like David Letterman and a page-long synopsis explaining why he wasn't there. The author, an NWTA member, praised Bill's many contributions to the group and the annual rendezvous, and then wrote:

"On April 24, 2010, Bill Potter passed away. Bill had been diagnosed with Creutzfeldt-Jakob Disease [mad cow disease] . . . It is a degenerative neurological disorder and the disease hit hard and fast. From the diagnosis to the inevitable end was mere weeks."

I couldn't have felt worse. Angie and I had talked for half an hour.

She'd been gracious, effusive and generous with her knowledge and time. She eagerly told me all about her love of history and why the subject means so much to her, and yet only five weeks earlier her husband had passed. As I sat there watching her fan herself to stay cool in the overbearing heat, I couldn't help but feel as though, for all the guns and battles and extreme situations some reenactors put themselves in, she was the strongest, bravest one I'd met.

We continued to talk, but the tone of our conversation changed. It was slower, more somber. She told me that after years of working in museums, she recently left the profession. Now she manages a Target near her suburban Chicago home. "It's hard to work in public history," she told me. "They're not-for-profit organizations so the pay isn't very good." Plus, not every town needs a Revolutionary War historian. But, she told me, she doesn't regret the career change. "It allows me to reenact in my free time and doesn't confuse the business end of it. I don't have to worry about ticket sales and sponsors. I get to spend my whole weekend interacting with and educating the public and doing what I love."

The sound of a cannon shot from the distant battlefield interrupted our conversation. "I've got to go battle," she told me, leaning on a wooden chair and slowly rising to her feet. The cute blond kids now played with a Jacob's ladder and the Gen-Xers had left. We never spoke about those three days in 1779, but I didn't mind. I found Angie's life and her spirit—her ability to endure in the toughest of times—more inspiring than anything that happened on a battlefield 231 years earlier.

With the recent tragedy still weighing on her mind, the newly widowed Angie felt somewhat fatalistic about her impending delivery. Like everything else in her life, when she talked about it, she spoke in historical parallels. "My husband was fifty-nine and we are the exact same difference in age as the first couple that got married in Vincennes," she said. "Hopefully life doesn't imitate history in this case, because she died during childbirth." (I'm happy to report that life did *not* imitate history. On July 8, 2010, Angie gave birth to two boys, Hamilton James and Sinclair Mason. As of this writing they've attended more than a dozen reenactments. According to Angie, who I reconnected with via e-mail, "Sinclair loves the cannons, but Hamilton is a bit more afraid.")

· · · · · · · ·

Maybe I've listened to too much Garrison Keillor in my life, but after only a day in Vincennes, I started to feel as though I'd landed in Lake Wobegon. The group's genial Midwestern vibe and the family-friendly colonial "Brigadoon" they've created definitely resembles the fictitious town where "all the women are strong, all the men are good-looking, and all the children are above average."

NWTA members come from a wide variety of backgrounds and professions, including astrophysicists, doctors, factory workers, lawyers, librarians, traffic coordinators and truck drivers. But they assured me that the socioeconomic differences between them disappear when everyone's together and in uniform—that all men and women, are, as it were, created equal.

The college students I met majored in astrophysics, molecular biology, music education, computer game development and, of course, history. They told me they were old-fashioned, that they didn't "tweet" and were "hardly ever on Facebook." They even divulged an affinity for dying traditions like writing thank-you notes.

"I guess that sounds really dorky," Melanie Studzinski, the "French" girl in the fashionable orange dress, told me.

"Not at all," I said. "I think that's really cool." I talked to Melanie and her family while enjoying a turkey legge lunch under their dining fly.

"A lot of kids around here are like that because our parents are a little more grounded. It trickles down."

"There's a lot of opportunity here to interact with people of all different ages," her mom, Andrea Studzinski, a business law professor, said. "And all walks of life that you don't get in school. In our society today we're very stratified. People in their twenties hang with people in their twenties. This is an opportunity to interact with different generations" and for the young to learn from their elders.

Perhaps that's why I found what happened the next morning so moving. I stood at the top of the park's memorial—thirty-three steps from its base—just outside the rotunda where an imposing bronze statue of a caped George Rogers Clark, sword in hand, held court. Leaning against one of the sixteen mighty Greek columns that ring the memorial gave me a perfect bird's-eye view of the group's Memorial Day ceremony. I saw a long line of Revolutionary War–era soldiers in colorful and varied uniforms singing a dirge on the memorial's terrace. When the song ended, the fifers and drummers took off their tricorns. A lone bagpiper played. Everyone bowed their heads.

An octet of colonial musicians dressed in red and yellow coats played a solemn tune on their authentic woodwind instruments. All the color guards from the NWTA units carried their flags and marched west, toward the wide, murky Wabash River. Behind them, three soldiers wearing dark coats and tricorns wheeled a small, creaky cannon over the concrete terrace. "We will be firing rounds from the cannon," a female emcee wearing a wide straw hat told the small but attentive audience seated on the memorial steps. "We suggest that those of you wearing hearing aids consider turning them down." What she didn't reveal—and what Jane had told me earlier—was that, at his request, Bill Potter's ashes were going to be shot out of the cannon.

While the emcee told the visitors about the history of Fort Sackville and George Rogers Clark's triumphs, a group of eight Revolutionary soldiers prepared the cannon. Once they'd positioned the gun on the lawn just shy of some old railroad tracks, a soldier loaded it with an aluminum-foil charge containing black powder and Bill's ashes. I don't think any of the public knew what was going on. But the solemn mood among the NWTA members said it all.

Another soldier lit the fuse.

The crack of the cannon, while startling, wasn't nearly as intense as the reverberation it generated between the nearby steel-girded Lincoln Memorial Bridge and the memorial itself. The thunderous boom echoed back and forth so violently, and the concussion was so intense, that my breeches actually shook. It was like some mythical god had reached down from the heavens and crumpled the air up into a ball. A cloud of smoke drifted toward a handful of swallows who skimmed the river's surface for bugs. Nobody spoke.

A few minutes later, a couple hundred NWTA members assembled in the shade of some cedar trees that bordered a Catholic church's graveyard where numerous (actual) Revolutionary War veterans are buried.

The reenactors fanned out and faced a small group of flag bearers and officers. A tall, older redcoat wearing an auburn wig held sheets of paper—thick as a small-town phone book—that listed the names of every NWTA member who'd passed away since the group's founding. He held a microphone and started to read from it, but all he could muster was the first man's first name, "John." His voice trembled. He shook his head and turned away. A woman in a straw hat comforted him and buried her head into his shoulder. An older Continental Army soldier with a gray wig took the mike and the list and resumed reading the litany of names and their corresponding reenactment units. *Paul Stevens, 8th Regiment of Foot. Bill Bergstrom, 17th Light Dragoons. Lynn Edwards, HRM's Marines.* Members of all ages cried. Many hugged each other.

Suddenly, on either side of me, two elderly men overwhelmed by the heat and emotion fainted. A few men and women rushed to them, hooking their hands under their arms and dragging them backward, away from the crowd. The bearded man on my left recovered quickly, leaning against a tree and drinking water from his silver canteen. A group formed a semicircle around the bald man to my right, fanning his face, cooling his neck with ice and propping up his feet. Jane whipped out her cell and called 911. A few minutes later an ambulance pulled up, driving right through the cemetery. Two EMTs hoisted the reenactor onto a stretcher and drove away. It was a tense five minutes and yet, through it all, the soldier with the microphone never stopped reading the names of the deceased. *Judith Esarove, Lauzun's Legion. Cyndy Vandrush, King's Own, 4th of Foot. Libby Lazdins, Civilian-at-Large.* And on and on and on.

After the soldier read the last name, a priest led the group in the Lord's Prayer. A couple hundred reenactors followed in unison, sounding like a reverent chorus. "Our Father, who art in heaven, hallowed be thy name." Ahead of me, Allison Studzinski, Melanie's sister and a fifer, broke down. Others couldn't make it through either. I didn't know any of the deceased members, but my eyes started to water too. I blinked a dozen times, but it didn't stop the flow. I didn't hear the man read Bill Potter's name, I probably missed it during all the commotion. And I never saw Angie, but I'm sure she remained strong and brave.

. . . .

Throughout the weekend, whenever I bumped into Robert or Jane, I dropped subtle hints to them, like, "Can I fight? *Please, please, please, can I?* I've shot a musket!" Finally, either out of pity or to shut me up, they gave in, allowing me to fight on the colonial side during the weekend's last demonstration.

On Saturday evening I joined Robert, an older reenactor named Al Potyen and a father and son new to reenacting named Chuck and Nick Heinlen near my tent for a quick musket tutorial. Al handed me a Brown Bess musket, the most efficient flintlock firearm of its day and the most technologically advanced "machine" an average person owned. Using a small twig that stood in for a gunpowder charge, he walked us through the loading and firing steps.

Since the Revolutionary War took place nearly one hundred years before the Civil War, the Brown Bess is, obviously, more primitive than the 1862 Enfield I carried at Brooksville. Whereas the Enfield's "lock" hammers a percussion cap and ignites the black powder, a piece of flint rock on the Brown Bess strikes against the "frizzen" (a piece of steel) and produces a spark that ignites powder in the musket's "flash pan."

I figured it out relatively quickly—marveling at how, in a few short months, I'd become well versed in antique weaponry. But it was the etymology lessons that really excited me. Consider the following examples: Robert warned me not to sprinkle gunpowder in the flash pan if any embers remained from a previous discharge, as that would generate a sudden fire or a "flash in the pan." (It'd also, in all likelihood, set my sleeve on fire.) Al cautioned me that cocking the musket into the "half-cock" position didn't prevent the gun from firing, especially if I slammed its butt end on the ground, causing it to "go off half-cocked." (A reenactor once did that and it discharged, singeing the poor guy's eyebrows and blowing his hat two hundred feet in the air.) As we wrapped up, Al reminded us to go over everything that we just learned, or in other words, "Lock, stock and barrel."

The next day I joined the men off park property, past the French Commons, a collection of shops run by local church groups and charitable organizations. We loitered in the shade near the battlefield, sans waistcoats, a garment that the members pronounce "wess-kit." We hoped that by dressing in only our "small clothes" we'd reduce the risk of heat exhaustion and any further fainting.

Before taking the field, Al gave me one last piece of advice. "When you fire your musket, either close your eyes or turn away."

"Why?" I asked.

"Because sparks and thin shards of flint can splinter off and lodge in your eyes."

Suddenly I wasn't so keen on fighting.

An estimated ten thousand spectators attended the Spirit of Vincennes Rendezvous that weekend, and it looked like most of them preferred this half of the reenactment grounds. Very few people visited the part where the reenactors camped out. Over here, off park property, they could shop, eat or sit in the L-shaped bleachers and watch the battles. Give people a choice and they'll take battles and shopping over interactive history lessons any day of the week.

Even though I'd lobbied hard to fight, after the heartfelt memorial service, it seemed like an utterly ridiculous pursuit. I felt as though I hadn't had enough time to process the intense remembrance. Nevertheless, I didn't have much of a choice. Soon Al was waving me into battle. I scurried onto the field. A few broad, leafy trees and a couple fences provided strategic cover, breaking up the otherwise open pasture of long grass. Just like at Brooksville, an emcee narrated the battle. Today, however, it was a woman with a flat Midwestern accent.

"Many of the Indian nations in the colonies formed an alliance with the British during the American Revolution."

We hustled through the gnarly grass, toward a tall, mushrooming tree where some Native Americans—tatted-out white dudes with nose rings and scalp-lock haircuts—loaded their muskets. They'd painted nearly every inch of their skin red, except where it mattered the most, under their loincloths, which revealed rear ends as white as the moon. I fired a shot toward them, turning my head away *and* closing my eyes, just to be extra sure that no shards entered my eyes. When I opened them I saw that none of the natives had fallen.

Within minutes the battleground had filled with white smoke. I couldn't see the British, but they could probably see themselves. That's why the troops wore red coats, so they could stand out through the smoke. Four thousand, four hundred thirty-five Americans were killed in the Revolutionary War, and many more perished from disease. If I really wanted to inflict damage, I was told that I should fix my bayonet, charge the redcoats and stab one of them so he'd die a slow and painful death. After all, the Brown Bess, like the Enfield, wasn't all that accurate—up to a measly thirty-five yards to be exact. That's why the army line fired in unison, so it'd function like a modern-day machine gun or a game of dodgeball in which everyone throws at once. Young Nick Heinlen told me that the difference between the way a round musket ball flies out of a musket and how an elongated bullet flies is equivalent to a lobbed football and a spiraling one.

"At that time the British were the Indians' friends because they were trying to stop the colonists from going westward into Indian territory."

I continued to reload my musket and fire. After a half dozen more rounds, though, the Brown Bess jammed. Rather than trying to fix it, I edged up closer to a tree's inviting shadow and took a hit the next time I heard a shot.

"The natives realized the colonists were much more of a threat to them than the British government."

After a few minutes of smoke and fire and a couple artillery kabooms, both field generals met at the center of the battleground. They chatted for a bit, then in a huff, the Brit, dressed in a kilt, argyle socks and a bear fur helmet, turned around and marched back toward his troops. But he never made it. The American shot him in the back. His arms flew up and he collided with a fence, back flipping over it into a scissor kick that exposed his underwear, much to the delight of the crowd.

The colonists had captured Fort Sackville.

. . . .

Afterward, smelling faintly of gunpowder and the Purell I'd just slathered all over my hands, I joined a handful of reenactors under the same fly where I'd shared Gatorade and bagels with Jane and Robert less than forty-eight hours earlier. For half an hour we engaged in a vigorous back-and-forth about American history. It reminded me a bit of that day at David Michaels's house when he and Arik Greenberg talked so passionately about ancient Rome. I felt like I was in the presence of people who cared so deeply about a subject that they could talk about it for days without any sleep. These were people who not only felt a strong connection to the past but were concerned with how it shaped the present.

The dialogue flew back and forth so fast it was hard to keep up. Everybody kept chiming in with interesting historical facts, some of which, I'd later learn, weren't accurate. As one reenactor had warned me earlier, "Learning history from reenactors is as perilous as learning it from Hollywood or Wikipedia."

Still I loved learning about the *Mayflower*: I never knew, for example, that it was heading for "North Virginia" to set up a plantation around the lower Hudson River, but it was thrown off course and settled by accident in what's now Plymouth. About George Washington and how, at the end of his second term, he voluntarily retired, ensuring that the United States would not be run by a tyrant. And about John Hancock, who at the time of the Revolution was the wealthiest man in New England and a smuggler. In an ironic twist, Hancock bankrolled the Boston Tea Party to protest British taxes. But after the colonists dumped the British tea in Boston Harbor, the Crown reneged their taxes and the tea that Hancock was smuggling ended up costing more.

I'd thought a lot about the state of America over the past few months. Specifically, our icky divisive political landscape, the greed and corruption that led to the economic collapse and the shouting heads on Internet message boards and cable news. I worried that I'd meet a group of hostile, belligerent people in Vincennes who wanted to dump *me* into Boston Harbor, but to my surprise I found the best part of America. The gracious, hospitable, sharing-is-caring side that I thought was extinct.

A couple hours later I was saying good-bye to Jane. I returned her clothing, the knee breeches and oversized shirt, the leggings and the tricorn. I helped her break down her tent and load her car. It felt good to give something back to her after she'd given so much to me.

I'd never felt connected to American history before. If given a choice, I tended to prefer the expanse of British history: Stonehenge, Roman occupation, William the Conqueror, Shakespeare's plays, Victorian fiction, Edwardian clothing, Turner's paintings, Dudley Moore, but after two days in Vincennes I was jonesing for more Americana. I wanted to find out who we were before those first shots were fired in Lexington. When I got home I searched for a group that could help me find it.

CHAPTER SIX

The FOGs of War

It didn't bother me that Maggie weighed two hundred pounds or that she stood only six inches tall. I didn't care that she wasn't exactly supermodel material, so bloated that she had to be wheeled around in a carriage. She was curvy, black and sleek, hourglass shaped and powerful looking, and I thought she was beautiful. That is, until her owner, John Osinski, told me that "she really farts."

To be honest I didn't even hear him at first. I was so mesmerized by Maggie's good looks that I just mumbled an affirmative "Mm-hm." But after a while what he said finally caught up to me. "Uh, I'm sorry, could you clarify something for me?" I asked him. "Did you just say she *farts*?"

John tilted his round black hat up on his forehead and looked at me over a pair of glasses that had slid down his nose. "No," he said, laughing and shaking his head. "She *barks*."

Whew, I thought. I couldn't imagine Maggie doing something so unladylike.

Maggie's what artillery folks call a "two-pounder." That is, she fires a two-pound cannonball—slightly smaller than a tennis ball—

that can knock your block off from up to one thousand feet away. I'd just helped wheel her from John's campsite to a long embrasure of branches and twigs that'd been constructed on the lawn behind the Old Fort Niagara visitors' center. Although it was only 10:00 a.m., sweat trickled down my back, branching out in tiny rivulets and saturating the waist of my knee breeches. The next day was July 4, and for the past few days the eastern seaboard—even way up here in New York State's northwesternmost corner—had been suffering from an oppressive heat wave, and my uniform, while, frankly, really awesome looking, wasn't exactly helping matters.

On a day like today I'd normally wear flip-flops, shorts and maybe a shirt. However, to replicate the look of a French and Indian War cannon crew member, I wore a drab wool overcoat, oversized gingham shirt, white knee breeches, a cut-down black hat, black shoes and a black silk neck scarf that I tied into a cravat. I looked a bit like Yasser Arafat if he'd landed a role in *A Clockwork Orange*. Still, aside from my outfit's thermonuclear conducting properties—and the fluorescent orange earplugs that protruded out of my ears—I actually thought, *Wouldn't it be cool to dress like this all the time?* You know, to look *remarkable?* And yet outside of a Decemberists concert, I couldn't think of one place on earth where I could pull it off without getting the hyperliterate prog-rock folkster beaten out of me.

"Man the gun!" Harvey Alexander, a fit, gray-bearded evolutionary biologist, ordered. All five members of our cannon crew manned our stations. It was my job to light Maggie. I held a three-foot long forked staff, called a "linstock," which held a slow-burning rope. An ash had grown off its tip, barely concealing a red ember. Now and then I blew on it so it didn't extinguish. Sometimes I flicked away the ash with one of my fingernails, slightly burning myself in the process.

It was the first artillery demonstration of a three-day reenactment to commemorate the British seizure of Fort Niagara during the French and Indian War. Maggie and our team, along with two other cannon crews, would be firing really loud blanks toward French reenactors dressed in cream-colored waistcoats. Ah, the French. Always looking spiffy, even in battle.

"Charlie, make sure you keep that slow match hot," Harvey's wife, Harry, said. Harry's real name is Mary Alexander, and she's an effusively warm nursery school teacher from Schenectady. She and the rest of the crew were dressed just like me, except she didn't wear a round hat. She wore a beret with a big red ball on top.

In July 1759, when the British booted the French off this spit of land where the Niagara River flows into Lake Ontario, the cluster of birch trees between the fort and us didn't exist. Neither did the single-story redbrick visitors' center one hundred feet to our left. Ice-cream-licking spectators didn't gather in the redoubts inside the fort walls to watch the spectacle unfold. Women didn't serve in New York's provincial army, either; that's why Mary dressed like a guy and everybody called her Harry. Whatever Mary-Harry said, you did.

Mary-Harry yelled, "Advance cartridge!" So fifteen-year-old Jonathan Pirillo did.

Jonathan, the youngest member of Schuyler's Company—a group that reenacts a unit of New York Provincials from the year 1759—reached into a wooden box and removed a three-ounce charge of gunpowder that'd been packed into a cylinder of aluminum foil about half the size of a Red Bull. On one end of the charge, someone had drawn a smiley face with a black Sharpie. Jonathan passed by me handling it gingerly in both hands, as nervous as an altar boy about to give communion to the pope. I lowered the linstock away from him just in case, by some freak accident, the hot wick made contact with the cartridge and launched him headfirst through the back door of the visitors' center. "Load the cartridge!" Mary-Harry ordered Harvey. He carefully slid it down the barrel, smiley face first.

Historically, cannon crews were an extremely efficient bunch. They could get off seven shots a minute, about twice as fast as the speediest infantryman and his slow-to-load musket. You'd better be fast on the cannon because the job you had was incredibly dangerous. Since cannons obviously did the most damage, they and their crews were enemy number one. The sooner your side got rid of the other side's cannons, the safer your side would be.

Of course, if the enemy didn't kill you, there was always the chance that you'd kill yourself. Accidents happened all the time in real battles. Cannons heated up very fast and if they weren't properly sponged, embers remained inside. When a combustible substance like gunpowder makes contact with embers, well, as you can imagine, "cannon go boom." Fortunately, in the reenactment world, stringent safety regulations at state parks limit how frequently you can fire big guns. Here, at Fort Niagara State Park, we'd have to wait five minutes in between each blast. And while this didn't make for very suspenseful theater, it did afford the cannon time to cool down.

Still, reenactors weren't immune to injuries, which were often gruesome in nature. Consider what happened in April 2010, at a Civil War reenactment in North Carolina. An overzealous reenactor loaded a triple charge of gunpowder down a cannon that contained burning embers from a previous discharge. When the powder made contact with the hot coals, it lit and, even though there wasn't a cannonball inside, it blew the man's hand two hundred feet down the battlefield. They found it, soon thereafter, still inside his protective leather glove. Fortunately for me, the Schuyler's crew stressed safety. Even during rehearsals they sponged Maggie to ensure nothing flammable remained inside.

After Harvey slid the cartridge of powder into Maggie, Mary-Harry stuck a quill down her vent hole. It wasn't an actual goose quill like old-time cannon crews used; instead, it was a red swizzle stick fitted with double-sided tape and coated in gunpowder. But it did the job.

"Set!" Mary-Harry cried. That was my cue. I took a step toward Maggie, hovering the rope a couple feet above the quill. Mary-Harry looked toward an officious redcoat who'd been pacing behind us. He nodded at her. She nodded at me. "Fire!" she screamed.

I missed the quill at first, afraid that Maggie's "bark" would knock me backward, but I quickly recovered, touching the rope's glowing tip to its top. *Whoomph!* A flash of fire shot up from the quill. *I just lit a cannon!* I thought, jumping up and down a little bit inside. But that was it. Nothing more. No boom. No kickback. No *wowie*. Nada.

Maggie had malfunctioned.

A French cannon—an eight-pounder, four times Maggie's size— fired from inside Fort Niagara. It thundered so hard, the ice cream lickers grabbed hold of one another. If this had been a real battle and a large cannonball had hit me, I'd have, at best, lost a limb or two. More than likely, however, I'd have been blown apart in much the same way a watermelon splatters after being dropped off the roof of a ten-story building. Then again, I could have been decapitated, my head snapped clean off my shoulders and launched a couple hundred feet into what's now the fort's archaeology center. As Harvey would later tell me, some people died merely from the concussion of a passing cannonball. Whatever the outcome, it would have totally sucked, and there'd probably have been a big mess to clean up. Instead I just stood there fanning myself, while the rest of the crew tried to figure out what'd gone wrong.

"Five-minute rule," John said, holding up three fingers. That was the joke. For cannon crews, the five-minute rule lasts approximately three minutes. I blew on the rope and awaited orders, melting like a stick of Land O'Lakes in a microwave. Then John approached me. "You know," he said in his easygoing manner, "I think you were right. Maggie does fart."

. . . .

The only thing I remember from history class about the French and Indian War is its name. And if that's all *you* remember, then you probably think the same thing I used to: that it was a war between the French and the Indians. It wasn't. It was a war that pitted the British and their American subjects *against* the French and Indians.

Even though it was the North American theater of the larger Seven Years' War, the French and Indian War lasted for *nine* years, from 1754 to 1763, which begs the question, "Why isn't it called the Nine Years' War?" Beats me.

The Seven Years' War was massive in scale. Battles didn't take place in just America and Europe. They happened all over the world, in places as far away as India, Africa and the Philippines. In fact, it was such a global war that Winston Churchill famously called it the "First World War." If that name had stuck it'd be a lot less confusing, but it didn't because by the time Churchill called it that, World War I had already taken place. Which technically would have made that war World War II, but, oh well, never mind.

At this point in history, a couple decades before American independence, peace was really the exception in the world, especially between England and France. They just plain old hated each other's guts. By the time of the French and Indian War, the two countries had already fought three wars on the North American continent: King William's War, Queen Anne's War and King George's War. At this point, in many ways, the New World was still up for grabs. England's victory in the "F&I," where they seized "New France," ensured that *nous ne parlons pas français aujourd'hui.*

At the time, the New World looked a bit like one of those Walmart Supercenters if Walmart Supercenters stocked beaver pelts (waterproof, used in hat making), indigo ("blue gold," used to dye clothing) and tobacco (addictive, cancerous). But the roads were terrible so merchants had to transport their cargo on rivers and lakes, the "superhighways" of the day. Nothing was more super than the five Great Lakes, which provided swift and convenient access to the North American interior. The French recognized this, so in 1726 they constructed a fortified castle on a strategic peninsula at the mouth of the Niagara River, the waterway that links Lake Ontario and Lake Erie.

Today the castle remains and has the distinction of being the oldest structure on the Great Lakes. The fort that grew up around it, Old Fort Niagara, as it's now known, is one of those rare historic oases in the United States, a beautifully preserved fortification boasting an even more stunning backdrop. If you look north on a clear day you can see the Toronto skyline twenty-five miles across the lake, and if I really laid into one, I could *almost* drive a golf ball across the azure river to the charmingly overpriced Canadian town of Niagara-on-the-Lake. It's so close to the Canadian border, in fact, that I picked up its cell phone service, which leads me to this little bit of advice: If you ever see the word "Bell" in the upper left-hand corner of your cell phone where "AT&T" normally is, don't call anybody. You'll be in debtors' prison for years.

But the real gem remains the fort itself. Once the Erie Canal was completed in 1825 it lost its strategic importance and slowly fell into disrepair, but it has been undergoing extensive restoration since 1924. Now, with its impressive eastern-facing earthworks and a ring of ditches around its exterior, Old Fort Niagara is undoubtedly one of the country's premier historic landmarks. At night it looked—dare I say—*magical*, in particular all the candlelit French reenactors' tents that glowed like massive paper lanterns. One night, while walking toward the purportedly haunted castle, I spotted a specter glowing in its second-floor window only to realize the ghostly visage belonged to a French reenactor checking his cell phone. There aren't many buildings left in America that were built in 1726, and the entrance, a drawbridge over a moat that leads to a cobblestoned walkway under the south redoubt, gives you a rare feeling of having been transported back in time. I imagine it's the closest one can get in America to visiting a medieval castle; that is, unless you consider Medieval Times a historical site, and, for your sake and for the sake of Western civilization, I pray that you don't.

. . . .

A few hours after Maggie malfunctioned, we finally got her to "bark" at the afternoon skirmish. We wheeled her toward the fort, just like the cannon crews of yesteryear, and fired our invisible projectiles toward the redoubts, causing a couple young children to completely freak out from the loud explosions. I probably lit her a good half dozen times and with each detonation the blast propelled me about a foot backward. If there's one truism about men it's that we like to blow stuff up, and if there's one truism about me it's that I *love* to blow stuff up and that I'd been repressing it for far too long.

Afterward I headed inside the fort. Although I was a provincial soldier, I camped inside the French-occupied compound as a guest of the sutler, Donlyn Meyers, the owner of Smoke and Fire. The store sells colonial reenactment supplies and also publishes a monthly newspaper called *Smoke and Fire News*, which is one of the reenactment world's only comprehensive resources. Started in 1985 and based out of Waterville, Ohio, a typical issue features event listings, topical news that affects the hobby (like the New York State budget crisis and subsequent closure of many parks and historical sites), as well as cartoons, period recipes and advertisements for knickknacks like "Cartridge Candy," a powder/gumball concoction wrapped to look like a musket cartridge. I subscribed to it early on and, along with the website Reenactor.net and my trips to Old Fort MacArthur Days and Reenactor Fest, it proved to be one of my most valuable resources.

I hung out with Donlyn and her staff for the rest of the afternoon and helped around her tent store whenever she needed me, which was never.

That evening I left the fort grounds and walked a quarter mile down the park's driveway to the colonial and redcoats' campsite on a shaded lawn opposite some athletic fields. When I arrived, eight Schuyler's members were just sitting down to a traditional July Fourth dinner of boiled pork and sauerkraut.

We all sat in a circle, on wooden trunks and chairs, my square plate resting precariously on my lap. A few members drank Sunkist and Pepsi from stoneware George III mugs. Nearby, a reenactor from another unit chopped wood for his campfire. Across the driveway, civilians in tank tops played volleyball. As minivans packed with families in swimsuits coasted by, the kids gawked at the few hundred reenactors engaged in archaic dining routines: starting fires with flint, ladling grub out of kettles and cleaning plates in washtubs.

In between swigs of beer, I asked John, a sixty-one-year-old hydrologist, why so few Americans are familiar with the war. "It's a British war," he replied, adding that it isn't just the American public who's apathetic about it. Even one of the country's most respected museums hardly acknowledges its existence. "In the Smithsonian's American History museum they literally have one bookshelf devoted to it," he said, shaking his head. Which is pretty shocking when you consider that, as the company told me, if the F&I didn't happen, there wouldn't have been an American Revolution—at least not as quickly. Not only did the Crown spend so much money on the Seven Years' War that it nearly doubled its debt and had to pass the Stamp Act onto tax-weary colonists, but George Washington, a young *colonel* in the Virginia Regiment, was more than a little miffed that he had to serve under a British *lieutenant*. As Harvey told me, "That's one of the main reasons why Washington decided to break away from the Crown."

. . . .

Whenever I interviewed reenactors, I tried to ask big-picture questions about the politics, economics, culture, religion and mores of the day, as well as about the circumstances that led to wars, and which events prompted momentous history-changing power shifts. But, to be honest, when the talk turned to the *unit* of soldiers the men and women portrayed, I got a little sleepy. All the minutiae of a particular company just felt way too obscure and "insidery."

Regardless, I felt like I needed to spend some time learning about a unit, and Schuyler's seemed to be the perfect group to do it with. They were convivial, self-deprecating, witty and curious. I liked them. They have a Yankee spirit that just doesn't exist in L.A.

So who were the real Schuyler's anyway and why are a group of middle-aged twenty-first-century New Yorkers so gung ho about bringing them back to life? To fully understand I need to share a little bit about how the military was structured in colonial America.

The military was divided into two divisions: provincials and regulars. Provincials functioned a bit like the National Guard. Have an emergency? They'll be there. Regulars, on the other hand, were highly skilled fighters, the redcoats, the world's greatest army.

During the French and Indian War, the provincials, poor guys, performed all the grunt work. Two thousand, three hundred eighty provincials fought at the nineteen-day siege of Fort Niagara, including the men of Schuyler's Company, who'd traveled 280 miles west from Schenectady to perform the not so glamorous job of shoveling trenches. Rather than digging one long straight channel that could be easily penetrated by a French cannon, the men dug in a zigzag formation, so the British could advance their cannons closer and closer toward Fort Niagara without getting blown to smithereens. The Schuyler's troops knelt down to avoid enemy fire and sometimes even excavated dirt at night—*in the nude*—to stay cool in the July heat, a historical truth that, if called upon, I'd happily reenact. One of the many placards placed throughout the fort grounds stated that what happened "closely followed siege techniques and conventions that were standard in Europe."

For Kevin Richard-Morrow, a quick-witted, ponytailed data communications specialist, honoring the sacrifices of the local "grunt" is what reenacting is all about. "There's more to America and its history than just the fact that Washington had an idea or Jefferson wrote a document," the fifty-seven-year-old told me. "It's about common guys making it work. To make it happen it took average Joes with average Joe skills. We don't portray the frontline heroes. We don't portray the men of action, we portray the guys who dug holes in the ground, we portray the guys who brought cargo in."

Most Schuyler's reenactors live in the Albany-Schenectady area just like the original men, an area that used to be considered so ridiculously far west in the colonies that Schenectady earned the nickname "Gateway to the West." The men and women don't take their impression lightly either. Before ever kitting up, they spent two years researching the company at local historical museums figuring out exactly what the soldiers wore, perfecting the drab look that they now gleefully embrace. They jokingly refer to themselves as "Men in Drab" and have even created the self-effacing motto, "Bringing a little drab into your otherwise colorful lives." In a nod to their expanding waistlines and thinning hair they also call themselves the "FOGs of war," or rather, the "Fat Old Guys." To achieve the right look of a filthy provincial, John told me that some members throw their new coats in mud puddles as soon as they get them. "They rip them and tear them so they look like they've actually been wearing them for three months."

For the men and women of Schuyler's Company, reenactment is akin to civic duty, a chance to discover new facts about their local history and share that information with each other and the public. Reenact Rome? *As if.* "Maybe if I lived in Britain," Kevin and Harvey both told me.

Informing the public hasn't always yielded the desired results, however. One year the group, whose official name is Albany County Militia 1775, passed out literature at a sportsmen's show, only to find out that a local newspaper had pegged them for a militia trying to recruit new members. Unfortunately the label has stuck and landed them on a number of e-mail lists they'd rather not be on. "We've had to e-mail people a number of times to *please* take us off their list," Harvey told me. "We tell them that *we're not that kind of militia.*"

In early 2010, Kevin and his wife donned Schuyler's Company uniforms at the state capitol to protest New York governor David Patterson's planned closure of state parks, only to be mistaken for Tea Party members, a group that Schuyler's derides for their flimsy grasp of what really happened at Boston Harbor.

Nevertheless the group's attention to detail has earned them affiliations with numerous historical societies and museums in New York State, including Old Fort Niagara. In fact, the fort staff likes them so much that the company has a set of keys to the old castle. This affords them the opportunity to spend a genitalia-shriveling February weekend huddled in front of the fireplace just like the real Schuyler's Company when they were garrisoned there during the winter of 1759/60. The FOGs do draw the line, however, at reenacting the scurvy outbreak that infected the troops. For Tom Quinn, a heavyset fifty-nine-year-old chicken farmer with an uncanny resemblance to John Goodman in *Waiting for Godot*, reenacting hasn't just been about "looking the part." It's about valuing the place he lives. "When I got into this and started to understand more about history it changed my life. It made me really begin to appreciate what it means to be an American and to have the freedoms we have. And it's essential coming generations learn this too."

Hearing how profound the experience has been to Tom made it that much harder to believe that some "elite" reenactors look a little askance at provincials like Schuyler's. If numbers are ever imbalanced between Brits and colonists, the Schuyler's crew galvanizes, dressing as redcoats to level the playing field, something some "regulars" would never do. (Just like the hard-core Confederates at Brooksville who'd never "go blue.")

The sun was slipping out of sight just as a tin of cookies was getting passed around. It wasn't that late, probably 8:30 p.m., but I'd walked so much that day my feet had a heartbeat. I wanted to limp back to the fort and catch the sunset. It was said to be "magical."

"Not before rum call," John said, grabbing a bottle off a trunk.

I lined up with a half dozen members and John poured a couple shots of rum in each of our tin cups. The last time, heck, the *only* time I'd had rum was in a mai tai, and if I recall, the umbrella nearly poked my eye out.

What followed was a sort of eighteenth-century drinking game, in which we all had to drink every time somebody made a toast, which was about once every five seconds. Kevin spoke first, holding up his mug.

"To his majesty, King George III, our monarch!"

"Hip, hip, huzzah!" everyone yelled.

I took a small sip. My nipples straightened. This was no mai tai. The toasts continued down the line.

"To the artillery of Schuyler's Company."

"Huzzah!"

I drank a little more. My esophagus burned.

"To reliable cannon fire!"

"Huzzah!"

Another drink. I started to shiver.

"Here's to Saint Barbara, who protects us."

"Hussazh!"

"To the New York Regiment."

"Who zahsh!"

Eventually it was my turn. I didn't have anything clever to say about provincials or weapons, so I just said what was on my mind.

"To all zhe new hair on my zhest!" Everybody laughed and yelled, "Huzzah!"

It was by no means comedy gold, but at least it elicited a laugh. I liked Schuyler's Company for many reasons, but mostly because they laughed at my lame jokes.

Before I excused myself, Kevin, who tied his thinning blond hair into a ponytail with a black bow, told me that reenacting his local history is a dream come true. As a kid growing up in Albany he watched westerns on TV and always wondered why there were never any "easterns" on. Now, through reenacting, he gets to create his own. Plus, by reenacting regular guys who had regular guy skills, he's learned how to do things most modern Americans can't, like starting a fire with flint and steel. "When I do it," he said, "I go, *I'm not doing anything special.* An eight-year-old from this time period could start a fire with flint and steel. This is the skill set that these men, women and children had at this time period." I swayed back and forth trying to think of all the skills I possess, at least the ones that don't involve pushing a button or drinking 150-proof rum. I couldn't think of any on the spot, but a half hour later after tripping over myself, I finally came up with one: tying my shoes.

. . . .

None of the one thousand reenactors who took part in Old Fort Niagara's 2010 encampment had to worry about tying their shoes. They all wore slip-ons. Although I couldn't tell, the numbers were down from the previous year when 2,300 reenactors commemorated the siege's

250th anniversary. There were fewer visitors too the year I participated. Six thousand to be exact, down from fifteen thousand the previous year. Still, according to curator Jere Brubaker, the fort raised nearly fifty thousand dollars.

Reenactor participation and public interest ebb and flow in "America-based" battle reenactments, or rather, wars that have been fought on what's today U.S. soil: the F&I, the Revolutionary War, the War of 1812 and the Civil War. It basically works like this: interest grows in the lead-up to major anniversaries, like the 1976 Bicentennial and the F&I's 250th. States create commissions and allocate funds, people new to the hobby buy clothing and weapons and join reenactment units and representatives from reenactment groups coordinate with historical sites. As the major anniversaries of colonial reenactments have started to recede, interest is shifting toward upcoming anniversaries of later wars, like the War of 1812's bicentennial and the Civil War's much anticipated 2011–15 sesquicentennial. Nearly every state where a battle was fought has established a Civil War commission. Some, like Michigan, where no battles were actually fought, have as well.

Of course, at Old Fort Niagara, I couldn't tell that the numbers were down or that interest had started to wane, and I didn't care. I fought with Schuyler's cannon crew four times, and each time I learned something new. Like that people wore cuff links because buttons would have cracked when they boiled their shirts. Or that sharpshooters tried to kill the drummers first. Not because they didn't like their music, but because the drummers were actually playing commands. Or that white dudes who reenact as Native Americans are known in some circles as the "Honky Tribe."

The next day I looked at my schedule and realized that this would be the last reenactment I'd go to where there were sutlers—the nomadic merchants who sell their wares at eighteenth- and nineteenth-century reenactments. Even though I'd browsed through their stores at

Brooksville and Vincennes, I'd never had the time to talk to any of them. I was always busy either chatting with reenactors or rehearsing how to load a musket so that I wouldn't set fire to my eyebrows. So I decided I'd spend that Monday inside the fort, window-shopping and chatting to store owners.

Early that morning, I saw two bearded men sitting on a park bench, relaxing and drinking coffee in the shadow of the south redoubt. I'd seen them before—well, at least parts of them. Every morning when I stumbled out of my tent into the fort's courtyard, I nearly tripped over them. Rather than sleeping in tents, they slept under the stars, wrapped in blankets and tarps. "It's as close to God as you can get," the younger of the two, George Neal, told me.

The twenty-seven-year-old and his fifty-four-year-old bench mate, Tony Baker, looked as if they'd just walked out of an old painting. George, a blacksmith, reminded me a bit of a pirate. All his clothing, from his boots to his head scarf, was black. Tattoos swirled on the backs of his hands and up his right arm. Tony, a weaver, looked like a mountain man in his linen shirt, sash, breechcloth, crudely sewn leather shoes and deer leather leggings that had been tanned with fluids from a squirrel's brain. It was, as he called it, a "frontier look that walked the line between savage and white." At one point during our conversation I squatted down to rest my back, only to discover that, in Tony's quest for authenticity, he'd gone commando. *That explains the breechcloth*, I thought, popping back up just as fast as I'd squatted. The pair must have wondered why I spontaneously broke into elementary-school-era calisthenics.

For George and Tony and the other small business owners, the sutler life is one of constant schlepping, driving thirty thousand miles a year, setting up a temporary tent store for two or three days, then tearing it down, driving home, working at the forge or weaving into the wee hours of the morning, then driving to another site at the end of the week. As George put it, "Some reenactors have more money than 'Hey-zeus' and after reenactments they go back to the real world. But for some of us, this is our life. We're still doing this when we go back to the real world. We've taken a vow of poverty for our souls."

I admired the men for devoting their lives to their crafts, but what surprised me the most was the economic dependency that's developed between them and reenactors. Many sutlers told me that 99 percent of their sales are to reenactors. Even more remarkable, though, are the parallels between the economics of colonial and Civil War reenacting and the actual time periods themselves. Since there are fewer colonial reenactors, there's limited demand for goods. Hence, they're all hand-made, just like in colonial days. But for the more popular Civil War reenactment community, items are mass-produced, just like the uni-forms and supplies during the 1860s—albeit today, they're mostly manufactured in Asia. As a result, Donlyn Meyers from Smoke and Fire told me that the two time periods attract different kinds of people. "Civil War reenacting is the easiest time period to walk into," she said. "To do any kind of colonial reenactment you have to be able to do your research because there are no photographs. That makes it more difficult to come up with your impression." To drive the point home she even sells bumper stickers at her store that say, "Friends don't let friends do Civil War."

For colonial reenactors and sutlers, being so dependent upon one another reinforces the small-town atmosphere the community seeks to replicate—a period when, reenactors told me, "one's honor was every-thing." Both George and Tony said they routinely send merchandise to customers to try out for a week, *free of charge*. As a by-product, the close relationship between merchant and customer engenders trust, some-thing that's pretty much extinct in the modern world. In many ways, the nostalgic bubble that reenactors and sutlers create is an idealized version of what America used to be like before the chain stores and strip malls squeezed moms and pops out of business. Musing on my own pitiful relationship with my community—not knowing my neighbors, shopping at big-box stores—I thought, no wonder nobody trusts anybody anymore. It's because *no one knows anyone anymore.*

After I said good-bye to George and Tony, I walked over to a store called Bethlehem Trading Post to peruse its selection of workmen's caps, which I'd been admiring for the past few days. I settled on a nifty reversible orange-and-beige-striped one that I tried on my matted, unwashed hair. While I was in there, a member of the general public wanted to buy a handmade leather notebook. He asked the proprietor, a slender man dressed in a baggy white shirt, if he took credit cards. He didn't.

"I don't have enough cash," the man said.

"That's okay," the proprietor said. "Mail me a check later."

"That's very trusting of you."

"I haven't had any problems yet."

Outside, a rather rotund guy in a Hawaiian shirt lumbered by, pushing one of those Formula One baby carriages down a gravel path. I looked around. The entire courtyard was now buzzing with visitors dressed in bright summer clothes, sandals that Velcroed shut and fanny packs that held cell phones and car keys that can pop the trunk from fifty feet away. They snapped photos and slurped soda out of plastic cups even though it wasn't yet 11:00 a.m.

After three days of traipsing around Old Fort Niagara and hanging out with "colonists," the real world looked a little too much like the movie *WALL-E*, where people too bloated to move rely on machines for every little thing. Of course I've known for years that the sedentary lives of luxury we lead have made us soft, but when you strip away all the remote controls and escalators and La-Z-Boys it really hits home just how cushy our lives really are. As Bill Bryson writes in his book *At Home*, "If you had to summarize it in a sentence, you could say that the history of private life is a history of getting comfortable slowly." And when you stand outside of twenty-first-century life for a few days it looks as though, even with the giant economic downturn, everyone looks quite "comfortable" indeed.

Tired and weary, I sat at a picnic table outside the fort's snack shop. Across from me, a sutler packed up his store, loading tent poles and wooden boxes into his white cargo van. I'd seen him earlier, and it'd struck me how snazzy he looked in his buckled shoes, waistcoat and poofy shirt. Now, seeing him wearing a Tommy Hilfiger T-shirt, jean shorts and flip-flops, I had to do a double take. *Was it the same guy?* I looked closer. *Was it?* Yes, it was. I *think*. He looked just as unremarkable in his civvies as he was remarkable in his colonial garb. I remembered something John Osinski had told me at dinner the night before. "You know when we don't recognize each other?" he asked. "When we're not in kit."

Some reenactors get married in their uniforms, others get buried in them, and it's easy to see why. When you wear them you really do look distinguished, regardless of your social status or what you do in the "real world." (It also gives men a chance to play "dress-up" as a weapon-carrying soldier, a rare instance where no one can challenge their masculinity.) *I don't look very distinguished,* I thought, looking at my reflection in the snack shop window. *I look like hell. I really need a shower.*

Half an hour later I helped Donlyn and her crew tear down the Smoke and Fire store. Tony, George and George's mother and father all helped too. We loaded boxes filled with books, frizzen stalls, flint, flashguards, shirts, canteens, garters, haversacks, leather pouches, gorgets, cuff links, buckles and much more into two white cargo vans. Then we collapsed the tent and squeezed that in too. That night the staff would all stay in a nearby motel, then the next morning start driving the 350 miles back to Ohio. "I'm going to give you a big smelly hug," Donlyn said, wrapping her arms around me. "Right back at ya," I replied, thanking her for her hospitality and the pair of spiffy white knee breeches she gave me. She hopped in her van. I climbed in my rental, sunk into the cushioned seat, lowered all four windows at once and blasted the AC toward my face.

Somewhat regrettably I was once again headed back to the twenty-first century. The sutlers I met would keep one foot firmly in the eighteenth, which, without all the threat of war, religious intolerance, disease, slavery, lack of women's rights, and the constant risk that your house would burn down, you could starve after a bad harvest and that you might not live past the age of five, wasn't such a bad place to be.

I followed Donlyn's van west down a gravel road toward the castle and a blinding sun a few hours from setting. Tents in all stages of breakdown dotted the courtyard as if a windstorm had blown through. I inched my way through a narrow stone gate, careful not to tear off my side-view mirrors. At one point I inched up to her van and could just make out what one of her bumper stickers said. It was from Jamestown and read, "When Surviving Wasn't a Game."

I left Fort Niagara with a lot more than I came with: knee breeches, leggings and John Osinski's neck scarf soiled from three days of sweat. I'd bought a gingham shirt, that workman's cap I so admired and a canteen too. Schuyler's awarded me a St. Barbara's medal—the patron saint of artillery—for my cannon service. I liked the clothing. It was more comfortable than Roman armor and not as itchy as those wool Civil War fatigues. And you know what? I looked remarkable when I wore it. I couldn't wait to wear it again on my next adventure.

CHAPTER SEVEN
The Big Thrill

A little over a week later, I was back with Schuyler's Company. But this time, I wasn't lighting a cannon at an old fort. Instead, I was helping to row a twenty-three-foot wooden bateau down the St. Lawrence River. It was the third day of a four-day living history re-enactment in which six crew members dressed and lived like eighteenth-century bateau-men, and things, at least for me, were not going well.

I can't remember if it was Buddha or Tony Robbins who said that narrowing your focus to a single object helps to take your mind off pain, but quite frankly it doesn't really matter who said it, because he was wrong. No matter how intently I meditated on a small puddle of water that'd collected in the bottom of the *Bobbie G.*, I couldn't stop thinking about the five dozen mosquito bites that pockmarked my body, the lactic acid that'd deadened my arms into lifeless append-ages and the slight headache that marked the beginning stages of dehy-dration.

"Smartly," David Manthey, the *Bobbie G.*'s stout, bespectacled, thirty-nine-year-old captain, ordered. I looked at him blankly. "To row with vigor," he said clarifying his historically accurate command. His sister Reb, who sat in front of me, started to row faster. So did I.

I leaned forward, keeping the handle of the twelve-foot wooden oar in front of my chest, and then leaned back, dropping its blade into the water and pulling the handle toward my neck, but I didn't feel like I'd displaced any water. I'd already rowed a couple hours that morning. The previous day, I rowed for close to five hours—into a *delightful* fifteen-knot headwind. But now, the air was still and we were trying our hardest to make up the ground we'd lost yesterday when we averaged a brutally slow 1.2 miles per hour—about one-third the speed we'd have gone if we'd walked. What little technique I possessed had evaporated a long time ago, and now, because of all the leaning back and forth, the pulling and churning, the oar carving ellipse after ellipse in the air, I was literally falling asleep.

"Everything okay, Charlie?" David asked.

"Mm-hmm," I muttered, staring vacantly at the puddle. But he could tell by my posture—hunched over and defeated—that I was lying.

At the time we were crawling past Boldt Castle, a towering Bavarian-style mansion that looms over the Thousand Islands region, an area of northern New York so reminiscent of Ralph Lauren ads that I swore I could smell Polo cologne. But I didn't bother to take in its fairy-tale-like circular towers for very long; I just continued to stare at the puddle and prayed the pain would go away. After all, Boldt Castle wasn't around in the eighteenth century, when a bateau-man like myself was hauling goods up and down this northern waterway. And I was trying very hard to keep things real. Teetering-on-delirious real.

David blew into a small tin horn, which emitted a high-pitched, kazoo-like quack. A couple hundred feet across the water, Kevin Richard-Morrow, who sat on the *DeSager*'s stern, picked up his horn and quacked right back. "Come to oars," David said. Reb, a forty-four-year-old kennel worker from Maine, stopped rowing. So did I.

For a minute I sat there dazed, elbows resting on thighs, wondering why I'd accepted Kevin's invitation to the Big Row, an annual living history reenactment in which Schuyler's members row these two wooden flat-bottom cargo boats great distances on New York State waterways. "You may find this a more 'immersive' experience than can be had at a large fort based event," Kevin wrote in his e-mail invitation the day before I left for Fort Niagara. "Do keep in mind it is called the Big ROW for a reason—we sail when we can and row when we must. We have, in the past, spent more time rowing than sailing."

You don't say.

I'd never heard of bateau-men or their boats before Kevin's e-mail. To be honest I had no idea who they were or what they did. In fact, I was so ignorant that in the days leading up to the event, I mistakenly told other reenactors that I was going to spend four days rowing a *bateen*, only to find out later that's actually an airport in the United Arab Emirates. Regardless, I was curious to learn what it was like to "be" a bateau-man, to spend ninety-six hours living like someone David called an "eighteenth-century truck driver." Plus, it sounded like a once-in-a-lifetime opportunity. Just what would I learn from this intense *civilian* reenactment that I couldn't learn on a battlefield? Where the only war waged would be between me and Mother Nature?

By the morning of our third day, when I'd entered a narcoleptic, paranoid state in which I'd become convinced that I was infected with West Nile virus, I'd learned a lot of things, but none quite as palpable as the epiphany that I was having now: even if you sit on a really cushy wool blanket, rowing a bateau flattens your keister into something roughly the thickness of Canadian bacon.

"Want some shrub?" Reb asked, snapping me back to reality.

"Please," I muttered, holding out a tin cup like a street urchin. She lifted a glass bottle and poured a bloodred concoction of raspberries, vinegar and sugar into my cup. She and David kept referring to so-called shrub as "eighteenth-century Gatorade," which I gather meant that it replaced one's electrolytes, which I'd lost about ten miles upstream. Frankly I didn't care what it replaced as long as it was freezing cold and in a liquid state. I quickly chugged it down, barely letting it sit in my mouth long enough to notice its delicious Fla-Vor-Ice-like flavor. Then I leaned over the side of the bateau, filled my cut-down black hat with water and poured it on my head. I'm certain that a real bateau-man would have done the same.

Between 1670 and 1830, before the Erie Canal and the railroad eliminated their livelihood, bateau-men transported goods like rum, flour and black powder in wooden barrels up and down America's rivers. We carried barrels too, but ours held provisions like cheese, eggs, potatoes and precooked meats like salted beef, jerky, bacon, sausage and chicken—anything that could survive four days without refrigeration. (I know—chicken, who would have thought?) Wicker baskets concealed our water jugs, burlap bags hid modern "dry bags" protecting our personal items from river spray and our baggy shirts covered our anachronistic—but legally required—personal flotation devices.

David pried open one of the skinny barrels and dug out some cubes of salted beef and a cheese wedge, two foods I'd normally say "I'll pass" to but now practically tore out of his charitable hands. None of us spoke. Even though we'd eaten breakfast only two hours earlier we gorged as if we'd just called off a hunger strike.

Unsatisfied with my makeshift cheeseburger, I dug inside my burlap sack and produced a can of Planters that I'd hid inside a small cloth bag. "Peanuts?" I asked, holding out the can. David and Reb both shook their heads. "Nobody would have eaten them at this time," David said. "They would have literally thrown them to the pigs." *Oh, well*, I thought and tossed a handful into my mouth.

David blew back into his horn. From across the water Kevin, who wore a very wide straw hat, blew into his. Then David yelled, "Rum call!" into a tin speaking trumpet. In addition to their daily wage of seven shillings, bateau-men received meals and eight ounces of rum, which, when mixed with river water, killed bacteria and acted as a sort of precursor to Advil.

After a shot of rum so powerful that it turned my innie into an outie, David asked me if I wanted to captain the *Bobbie G.*

"Yes!" I said rising so fast I nearly capsized the bateau.

I edged my way past him and sat on the boat's stern, a sharp-edged rim that injected all the feeling back into my butt. I grabbed the long wooden steering oar and tilted my hat down so its brim blocked the blinding morning sun. Up ahead, on our starboard side, a large cedar-shingled house dominated a small island. A pair of empty Adirondack chairs faced the river. I inhaled the faintest whiff of Polo cologne, folded a towel half a dozen times, placed it under my butt and fumbled around for the appropriate eighteenth-century command.

"Um, right away?" I asked.

"Give way," David replied.

"Right. Give way!" I cried. David and Reb started to row, while I gazed down a river that stretched as far as my half-closed eyes could see.

· · · · · · · · ·

Before I continue with my Huck Finn–like adventure down the St. Lawrence, I need to hit the proverbial pause button if you will and explain a little more about myself and how I became the type of person who thinks spending a year dressed in ill-fitting clothing is a good way to learn about history.

When I was a teenager, in the mid-'80s, my parents used to take my brother and me to New York City. Sometimes we saw shows; other times we walked around town and looked at things. But I was never all that interested in the cultural sights, the museums and art galleries. What really fascinated me were the skyscrapers, especially at night. I liked to look at the lit offices and imagine hard-working financial analysts poring over documents. *One day,* I thought, *I too will work in an office. One day, I'll be rich.*

Even though I acted in plays during middle school, I stopped during high school when I opted to serve my fellow students as class vice president and student council representative. During the summers I enrolled in Washington Workshops, an urban camp for young Republicans who dreamed of one day ruling the world. I wore seersucker suits, hobnobbed with other preppies and acted like I knew what "arbitrage" was. At home the uncracked autobiography of Lee Iacocca sat on my nightstand; right next to it was an uncracked copy of Donald Trump's *The Art of the Deal.* I once gave my high school girlfriend a BMW matchbox for Christmas. She gave me the same thing.

When I applied to college I wanted to go to Babson College and study business, because that was where rich kids went. But my dad insisted I take the liberal arts route. "You need a well-rounded education," he told me. I was accepted at five of the twelve schools I applied to and enrolled at the one ranked highest by *U.S. News and World Report.* If I'd gotten into another school that was ranked higher, I would have gone there. That's how my mind worked back then.

I started off as a political science major, but after one class I concluded that there was quite possibly nothing more uninteresting on earth to study—except maybe chemistry or biology or, for that matter, biological chemistry, whatever that is. During my freshman year, to help fulfill my arts requirement, I took Theater 101. In a darkened lecture hall we watched videos of Patrick Stewart in *Oedipus Rex* and Zero Mostel in *Waiting for Godot*; we read plays by Brecht and Ionesco and in my slim copy of *Aristotle's Poetics* I underlined phrases like, "Tragedy is an imitation of persons who are above the common level" and wrote "man is sum of actions" in the margin. I didn't have a clue what any of it meant—I still don't—but I loved it. And I realized that, all those years I acted like a young Republican, all those years I dressed like Alex P. Keaton in my sports coats and bow ties, I didn't want to be him. I wanted to be Michael J. Fox. I wanted to be an actor.

Before I knew it I was auditioning for school plays. My first role came in Aristophanes' comedy *The Clouds*. If memory serves I delivered precisely one line—make that one *word*—"Herself." I remember crossing to center stage, and in my best Pee-wee Herman imitation, milking the word until I'd expended the last molecule of air from my lungs: "Herrrrrrrsellllllllllllllllllllllllllllllllllllllllfffffff." To this day it remains my single worst performance and yet for some reason people laughed. "Herself" was a big hit. In one short word—okay, one short word that I'd stretched into an aria—I'd given a large number of people pleasure. And in turn, their laughter, their response, made me feel good. No, it did more than that. It actually made me feel *alive*.

When I graduated college with my theater degree I swore that I'd never lead a "conventional life," that I'd *never* work in an office. I promised myself that I'd continue to pursue my dreams of being a working actor no matter what. I struggled early, like everyone does. I waited tables and lived in a Hell's Kitchen tenement building that was so filthy my mom uttered "Yuck" when she first saw it. At night, after leaving my restaurant job, I folded my tips in half and tucked the cash in my sock lest anyone mug me on the way home. One night, while trudging down West Forty-ninth Street at 2:00 a.m., a homeless person stopped me. My heart raced. *This is it,* I thought. *I'm finally going to get robbed.* But just as I was about to untie my shoe and pull out a wad of sweaty twenties, the man offered *me* money instead. I must have looked pretty destitute in my tattered old sweatshirt, but I didn't care. That was how starving artists looked and I was willing to sacrifice all creature comforts in pursuit of my dreams, and as long as I continued to do so, I was happy.

I started to make my living acting in my midtwenties. I

did everything I could: film, TV, theater, commercials and corporate training industrials. I even played a character on *Sex and the City* named "Mr. Pussy." As for my character's particular skill set, I'll let you use your imagination.

The acting business wasn't like college, though. In college I could play anybody: Akaky Akakievich in *The Overcoat*, ten funny Texans in *Greater Tuna*, even perform in *Pericles*—on a London stage, nonetheless. In the real world, however, as the "leading man's best friend" I always played someone who looked and sounded a lot like me, but never really felt like me at all. As time went on my dream started to fade, the romanticism of working in rat-infested theaters wore off. But I wasn't quite ready to quit. Maybe I would feel better if I made some money.

I never thought I'd move to L.A. New York was a place where real people lived, L.A. was for phonies, *everybody* knew that. In New York people *walked*, they *interacted* with each other; in L.A., people *drove* everywhere and only interacted with other humans from behind the safety of their car windows. What kind of life was that? Certainly not the one I'd worked so hard to have. And yet I went.

After meeting Wendy in Hong Kong and falling in love, somehow we managed over two and a half years to keep up the world's longest-distance long-distance relationship. She moved to the United States in February 2004, and later that year we got married.

I was happy, but my acting career in L.A. quickly stalled. I couldn't muster up the excitement to audition for UPN sitcoms and hair loss commercials. I guess I thought it'd be easier, that someone with so much New York experience would coast right to the top. After all, my friends in New York always said, "You'll do really well in L.A." But I couldn't fake it. I judged all the scripts that I read. To my surprise I liked L.A.—the open skies, the perfect weather, the innovative spirit— but felt lost without my theater community. To stay afloat I worked lots of different jobs: acting, writing for magazines and producing public radio stories. I was growing really tired of not knowing where the next paycheck would come from, of the "hunt." I wanted a steadier, better life for Wendy and me.

When a job opened up at a magazine, I took it. It was twenty-two miles away from our apartment—a seventy-five-minute commute each way—but it was a steady paycheck and the publisher offered health insurance and paid for vacation days. I thought I'd work there for a year or two, until something better came along. I'd been freelancing quite a bit for NPR, telling stories about hobbyists and doing my own silly first-person "Plimptonesque" stories. Maybe I could join the staff of a show, I thought.

But when the economy tanked in 2008, the two public radio shows I contributed to got canceled and the publishing company I work for laid off 20 percent of its staff. We downsized our office space by the same amount. I got booted from my ocean-view office into a utility closet down the hallway, a room so dank it practically has its own weather system. I'd been on the verge of leaving, but now felt lucky to have a job. And yet as I looked out from behind my computer at a fluorescent-lit hallway, listening to the guy outside my office slurp his soup, I realized that I'd become everything I promised myself I wouldn't. I worked in an office. I spent two and a half hours a day stuck in traffic. I certainly didn't feel alive. I felt dead. Deadened. Numb.

So to say this book is solely about me learning about history and the subculture of reenactors would be a lie. This book is also about my adventure, my quest to feel alive again, to, as Teddy Roosevelt once said, "dare a mighty thing." I felt so far away from the joy and excitement I once felt onstage, so distant from the audience, the laughter, that I needed to do something extreme, something completely antithetical to the day-in, day-out grind. And I discovered that I wasn't the only one yearning to be free.

When David Manthey dreamed up the Big Row, he too wanted an adventure, something unpredictable and challenging, something totally different from his day-to-day routine. Plus, he had grown weary of battle reenactments, suspicious of some reenactors' dubious historical claims and so called "reenactorisms," like sitting on a chair in camp instead of the historically accurate barrel. He wanted to do something that no one else was doing, something truthful, something that would give him the feeling of being a kid again, like when he challenged his friends to see who could run to the stop sign first. So he combined his love of boating and local history and got to work, researching bateau-men's lives at the New York State Historical Society in Albany.

Rather than being some dry, academic chore, David found the experience thrilling. Getting buzzed into the high-security vault and slipping on white gloves to handle fragile documents made him feel like Indiana Jones. Poring over old journals and daybooks, deciphering what others might see as mundane facts, brought the bateau-men to life right before his eyes.

> I loved finding out that on one particular day a bateau-man bought six wool hats for his crew. You figure out that it must have been unseasonably cold. Or that, at the end of a captain's shopping list, a storekeeper had scribbled down "three cakes." You can just imagine a "Mrs. Smith" walking into the shop with some of her warm cakes to sell and a bateau-man saying, "Oh, and I'll have three of those, please."

For the metrologist—someone who studies systems of precise measurement—the historical data he found sparked his imagination.

In September 2003, David and three other crew members launched the first Big Row, a three-day, sixty-two-mile trip down New York's Mohawk and Hudson rivers. Since then, the annual event has attracted upward of thirty rowers on six bateaux built by Maritime Academy students in Albany. It's not for the faint of heart or the bashful. Part of the experience includes wearing baggy beige clothing ("slops") and funny hats and not giving a rip what any "civilians" think of you. (But most reenactors I met have no issue with that. They like to stand out, to turn heads. After battle reenactments many stay in their uniforms and visit local restaurants, and others dress up when they visit historical landmarks. The night before the AD 43 reenactment in Arkansas, I ventured out to a Mexican restaurant with eight Legion VI members, half of whom remained dressed in their Roman civilian clothes. Judging from the curious looks we got, I didn't think it was necessary to inform the staff that we all hailed from California.)

Because they wear historical clothing and row wooden boats, most people mistake the Big Row crew for pirates. During our voyage, kids screamed "Arrgh!" and "Ahoy, mateys!" from the shore. A few years ago, after a man on his dock saw the bateaux approaching, he ran inside to his house, fetched a potato gun and returned wearing a paper pirate hat, screaming "Pirates!" while firing a few spuds at the defenseless crew. Sometimes, however, the public's reactions aren't so whimsical.

Take what happened back in 2007, during the crew's four-day, fifty-three-mile row to the Battle of Kingston reenactment. They were the victims of an actual pirate raid. Sort of. One night around 1:00 a.m., while the crew camped along the shores of the Hudson River, an area resident rowed up to the dock where the *DeSager* was tied up. He untied the bateau, tethered its bow to the stern of his boat and started rowing back out into the river. Now, that's pretty crazy, but even more so when you learn that the "pirate," Allan Wikman, was seventy-five years old. The "hectoring nudge" and "political gadfly," as the local paper described him, wasn't just being an elderly prankster. He wanted to teach the crew a lesson. He didn't like the fact that reenactors were going to "celebrate" the time the British burned his adopted hometown. Dressed only in a shirt, shorts and sandals, Wikman rowed furiously into the darkness. The commotion awoke the Big Row's sentry, who spotted the thief and alerted the rest of the crew. David immediately sprung into action, flying out of his tent and bolting for another boat, the *Codpeace*. The fitter thirty-six-year-old quickly closed the gap on the "wingnut" septuagenarian, as Kevin calls him, and managed to set the *DeSager* free. Because it was dark, the crew didn't know at the time how many people were trying to pilfer their boat. Since bateaux are large (and heavy) they assumed it was a group of men attempting to purloin their vessel. It wasn't until a year later, when an article appeared in the local paper by a coconspirator, that Wikman's identity was revealed. As Kevin put it, "He thought that he was going to prove something by stopping us. But the battle is an historic fact. It occurred." Then he added, "We might be a little crazy, but that guy is weird."

During our voyage, nothing nearly as crazy happened, but we did attract suspicious looks from the Department of Homeland Security. Every now and then, stern-looking men in sleek powerboats that had government seals on the side pulled up close to us, presumably because they thought that we were either refugees trying to sneak into the country or terrorists launching the world's lamest-ever attack.

But the crew, particularly David and Kevin, take everything in stride. After all, part of the fun is attempting things that few modern Americans would ever dare, let alone think of. For instance, the two men have competed in historically accurate biathlons in which they don wooden snowshoes and fire replica muskets at the silhouettes of metallic chickens, and they have eaten cracker-fed rats—yes, rats—to replicate a typical meal that sailors would have had in the nineteenth century. "They taste like gamey squirrel," David told me over dinner one night, as we supped on a recipe that, traditionally, called for the little rodents. To my great relief, he'd had to substitute chicken in their place.

• • • • • • • •

During the Big Row, we went to bed when the sun set and woke up when it rose. I slept on the hard ground in a small canvas pup tent, opposite Kevin, my head directly across from his feet—and we didn't go anywhere without Mother Nature's permission. On the first day, she couldn't have been more considerate. With a helpful breeze, we hoisted our square-rig sails and coasted down the river, looking like, what one of my friends would later observe, "Viking types of ships." But on the second day, I learned just how fickle Mother Nature could be. When we woke, the wind had shifted. We were grounded.

When real bateau-men were "wind bound," they went to work, "building or improving their pit stops or working on their boats," David told me over a sausage and egg breakfast. "They'd improve their bathroom instead of just relying on a hole in the ground." We, however, hung out on a shaded, grassy hillside of the marina where we'd camped.

With no TV, Internet, books, magazines, radio or Angry Birds to entertain us, we told stories and played an eighteenth-century dice game called farkle, rolling the dice in our frying pan. I chatted with David and Reb's father, Bill, about his part-time work as a Russian translator and chewed the fat with Rick Russell about his job as a garage owner. Time passed slowly. *Very* slowly.

I probably couldn't have been in a more serene setting with more interesting people, and yet all I could think about was what I was missing in the "real world." Everywhere I looked I wanted to know things: How much was that cute cottage with the For Sale sign in its big bay window? What were the names of those tall windmills on the Canadian side of the river? What was the exact temperature right now—in Los Angeles, California; Lancaster, Pennsylvania; and Hong Kong? I wanted to shoot a video and send it to Wendy, check the news headlines and my e-mail, watch a movie trailer, find out our exact location on Google Earth.

I couldn't remember the last time I'd been *bored*, the last time I didn't have the answer to everything at my fingertips. I'd come to the St. Lawrence River to get away from it all, only to realize that I'd become a virtual slave to the Internet. For most of the time I debated whether or not I should sneak over to my burlap sack, pull out my iPhone and furtively go online. As if seeing my friends' status updates on Facebook would somehow change my life.

Back on the hillside, David routinely rose and checked on a nearby flag to see if the wind had shifted, but it never did. "Fifteen knots," he'd report, somewhat dejected, measuring the speed by observing how vigorously the flag flapped, then he'd sit back down to play some more farkle. Finally, to my relief, at 1:00 p.m. he declared that we had to start rowing—unhelpful wind or not. After all, we had "goods to deliver" and "deadlines to make," or rather campground reservations to keep. In short, just like real bateau-men, we had no choice. We had to row. I sprinted to the dock faster than Usain Bolt.

Five hours and six miles later, we docked the boats and limped into a crowded campground. We were exhausted, hungry, sunburned, slightly disfigured and, judging by the curious looks we got from vacationing campers, likely the strangest-looking group of people to ever erect a tent there. Farkle and Web-disabled grassy hillsides had never looked so attractive.

Unlike public reenactments, where most people gravitate to the battles and avoid talking "to the weirdos," as David put it, the Big Row's "ambush history" approach was practically unavoidable. Everywhere we went, people asked us about our mission. Kevin, David or Reb would talk about the life of a bateau-man and what the region looked like 250 years ago. As Reb put it to one wide-eyed young camper who'd asked us what century we came from, "We're you in 1760. None of this was here, not this campground, not that bridge, none of those powerboats or tankers. All you had was a fort there, a fort there and a fort there." We were like ghosts who'd washed ashore to remind people of who'd come before them.

While we were happy that our surprise history lessons proved a hit with the campers on that second day, after the slow row we needed to make up ground, so to save time we decided to sleep under the stars.

At what must have been 3:00 a.m., while I was deep in the middle of another "I forgot all my lines and am afraid to go onstage" nightmare, I was awakened by a voice—of someone saying, "Excuse me." In my dream I thought it was a stage manager telling me it was my cue, but as I woke up I soon realized that it was somebody real, just a few feet away from me.

"Psst," another voice said.

"Can you please go away?" the first voice said.

The night before, a fleet of mosquitoes had attacked Kevin and me so badly that we had to smother ourselves in suntan lotion infused with insect repellent. Tonight I did the same and to protect myself even further I also wrapped my head in a quasi burka that I'd fashioned out of a scarf and a pair of pants. Now I slowly, *cautiously*, uncovered my head. "Excuse me," the voice said again. I recognized it this time. It was David. "Psst," the other voice said. I realized that the "psst" was from his father, Bill.

For a groggy moment I thought that David was trying to shoo away a homeless person. Then I heard some rustling—clawing actually—like an animal was trying to get into one of our bags.

I started to slowly turn around, but David immediately stopped me. "Don't move, Charlie," he whispered. "There's a skunk right next to your head."

I can think of lots of things I never want to hear. "You've got cancer" is one. "You're being audited" is another, but I've never imagined that on one lovely, starlit summer night I'd awake to find myself an arm's length from a skunk's backside.

"I think we left some food out," David said, indicating Pepé Le Pew, who was swiping away at one of our burlap sacks.

For a moment I considered flinging one of my earplugs at him, but he'd probably spray me and frankly, after a showerless forty-eight hours, I smelled bad enough as it was. There'd been a few times over the past months when I wished that I'd been a Boy Scout—many reenactors once were—but none as much as now. I looked at David and Bill, two cerebral engineers who always had detailed answers for everything, but they both just shrugged.

It occurred to me, as I stared down the barrel of Le Pew's "muzzle," that I hadn't just rewound the clock to the way most people lived in the 1700s, I'd rewound the clock to how people had lived since they first started walking on two feet; that is, in very close—sometimes too close—proximity to nature. Think about these amazing facts for a moment: our hunter-gatherer ancestors started transitioning to farming around 7500 BC. In 1793, when the first American factory opened in Pawtucket, Rhode Island, 90 percent of Americans lived on farms. You could say they hadn't changed all that much from those distant ancestors nearly ten thousand years earlier. But since that factory opened, our entire way of life has been completely revolutionized. Today fewer than 2 percent of all Americans farm. In the span of 220 years, humans and the natural world have separated like oil and water.

But tonight nature and man had rapidly reunited, in the stinkiest of ways. From across the campsite Kevin and Rick lit Le Pew with their tiny Maglites. Initially the light startled him and he wandered off for a bit, but then he doubled back, as if he'd only just realized that he possessed the most dangerous weapon of all: a Weapon of Ass Destruction. He strode up to the sack and swiped at it one more time and then, clearly agitated, slowly backed up, rear end first, toward Kevin and

Rick. When he got about ten feet away from them he flung his tail up in the air like he was giving them the finger. Skunks only carry enough chemicals in their anal glands for five or six sprays over a ten-day period, and you could see Le Pew's wheels turning. *Should I expend some musk on these crazy reenactors or should I conserve it for that stupid porcupine who's always eating my favorite berries?* Then, suddenly, without expending a drop of spray, he lowered his tail, hung a sharp right and waddled away, disappearing into the dark campground and grumbling, *Damn you reenactors!* as he sniffed his way toward his next victims.

. . . .

On day three, about five hours after I started staring at puddles in bateau bottoms and conflating the philosophies of Tony Robbins and Buddha, the sun reached an impossibly cruel angle, as if its beams were being shot through a magnifying lens. The air was deathly still, sweat stung my eyes, my entire body ached. I'd come to the St. Lawrence River to "live" in the 1700s, a period that'd emerged as my favorite for all its radical social changes, human freedoms, artistic flourishes, scientific discoveries and bad wigs, but now I was learning that while lots of really important things may have come out of it, for the most part it totally sucked. *What is the purpose of this?* I thought. If I wanted my hands to blister and my butt to flatten, I could have at least done it on a Bowflex in an air-conditioned gym. I dipped my hat in the river, dumped some more water over my head and said a little prayer to God or Mother Nature or John Lennon—*any deity*—for wind. *Please, whoever you are up there, would you just make the stupid wind blow?*

But it didn't. So I continued to row. For the first time since we launched the boats, everybody was quiet. We'd officially run out of stories to tell.

"Know any songs?" I asked David and Reb.

"Sure," David said from the captain's seat. The sun burned behind him and formed a halo around his head. It was so bright I looked toward my feet, so the only way I knew it was time to start singing was when I heard his mellifluous tenor belt the first few bars of "All for Me Grog."

> *And it's all for me grog, me jolly jolly grog,*
> *All gone for beer and tobacco,*
> *Well, I've spent all me tin with the lasses drinking gin,*
> *And across the western ocean I must wander.*

Around mile twenty-three nobody could muster the strength for another stroke and we were still seven miles from our campground. If the air was just as still tomorrow, or worse, if the wind was in our face, we'd never make it to our destination—the Battle of the Thousand Islands reenactment in Ogdensburg—on time. So, exhausted and somewhat defeated, we stopped and rested. I thought of my long commute, the numbness I get in my arm from holding the steering wheel, the motorists flipping me off, and dreamed of the day when I could do it again. *Can somebody please give me the finger right now?* I thought. I lay across the plank, my hat covering my face.

I'd read so much about this time period, about the seismic shifts in the geopolitical landscape, but I'd never comprehended what it must have been like to be a normal person, an eighteenth-century "truck driver," if you will. His life would have taken place before the steam engine, lightbulb and train were invented. Before typewriters, sewing machines and dishwashers, safety pins, sunglasses, and postage stamps. Before dynamite, batteries and zippers, the theory of evolution, the theory of relativity, the big bang theory, the Hubble telescope, before Sigmund Freud, Van Gogh and Beethoven ever had a thought, before the drinking straw was invented, or raincoats or bicycles, before matches, photographs, phonographs and plastic, before canned food, masking tape and Band-Aids. Universal suffrage was well over a century away, the Emancipation Proclamation another 100 years, Stonewall not for another 209. This guy was living before synthetic rubber, the atom bomb, cameras, before the telegraph, telephone and television, toothpaste, deodorant and even wrenches, before anesthesia, penicillin and antiseptics, before the internal combustion engine ever fired, before toilet paper, for goodness' sake, or even the fountain pen. It's hard to believe but even bras, cash registers and the *Oxford English Dictionary* didn't exist. Neither did our country.

A gentle breeze kissed my cheek. It wasn't anything remarkable, nothing I would have noticed before and nothing I've noticed since, but it had the impact of a gale. David looked to shore and saw a tall American flag on the end of an upscale property flap just the *tiniest* bit. Reb and I eagerly sat up. "Should we—," David started to ask. "Yes," we said, not letting him finish. We quickly hoisted the sail. It fluttered about like a bedsheet on a clothesline. "Let it out one turn on the larboard side," David commanded. By now I knew that "larboard" was the arcane way of saying "port," so I slid across the plank and uncoiled some rope around the winch. The sail filled. *Thank you, John Lennon,* I thought, watching it sputter and whip and thrust, just enough to move us downstream at a slow but steady pace.

. . . .

It took us four days to row sixty-three miles. That's the same amount of time it took me to drive from New York City to Los Angeles (2,795 miles) and nearly the same distance that I commute round-trip each day. We could have walked faster.

Thanks to more pleasant conditions on day four, we arrived in Ogdensburg just in time for the reenactment's first battle. As we rounded a point of land, British redcoats were firing their muskets at a line of French soldiers. Even though I considered our journey an amazing accomplishment, only David's wife, Heather, was on shore to greet us. As we docked the boats and tied them to a tree, colonial reenactors tended their campfires and cleaned their muskets. No one knew what we'd gone through to get there and I didn't see any use in trying to explain.

We hopped in Heather's Hyundai and she took off for Cape Vincent, where we'd launched the bateaux. The plan was to retrieve our vehicles and the two boat trailers and then drive back to the reenactment site, load the bateaux on the trailers and have a celebratory meal in Ogdensburg.

I sat in the backseat, sandwiched between Kevin and Rick. A few minutes later the two men nodded off. For a moment I debated whether or not to take out my phone, and then I did. When I turned it on, the e-mail message icon quickly multiplied: *7, 13, 28, 44, 71*. It finally stopped at 160. At work, "valuable real estate" on our website's home page wasn't being "properly optimized." One of our advertisers had complained that I'd written that their product was made from "rubber" and not "polymer." Kevin stirred. "I think what I like so much about the Big Row is that, in a normal day, you might have one or two surprising or exciting things," he said, "but when you do the Big Row so many things are exciting and surprising."

"Hmm?" I asked, distracted by my messages.

"Never mind," he said. He continued to look out the window. I wondered if my brief reimmersion into the Age of Distraction had ticked him off.

I turned off my phone—and what Kevin said finally hit me. For four days I didn't hear or see or read any stories other than the ones we told. I didn't work by myself, alone in front of a computer. I worked with five other people, together, as a team, to help move us collectively and carefully downstream. Time slowed down to a crawl, which gave us time to talk and collaborate to engender trust. To stay sane we sang songs, we told stories, we conversed and listened. Nobody got distracted by phone calls, e-mails, IMs or texts. I relied on and fought against Mother Nature, I never knew the time, the schedule, and there was no routine. It wasn't until the last day that anybody even mentioned pop culture.

An hour after we'd left, Heather pulled into the boat launch parking lot. Our cars and trucks were exactly where we'd left them, but now they looked like spaceships that'd fallen to earth. The parking lot gravel under the Hyundai's tires stirred Rick, who woke up, looked around and, a bit dazed, said, "Man, that took a long time."

· · · · · · · · ·

A few days later Wendy and I were lying in bed. Since I'd gotten home I'd been distant; part of me was still out on the water. "Is it hard to come back?" she asked. "Mmm," I said distractedly. I hadn't thought about how my time traveling was affecting her. I'd been a neglectful husband. She'd become the Time Traveler's Wife.

When I was reenacting I purposefully didn't call her or use most modern items, because I was trying to stay as immersed as possible. I didn't want to back up once I'd passed through the space-time continuum. But now I was beginning to realize how traumatizing it'd been for her. "When you're gone," she told me, "it's like you're on another planet, in another universe." She started to tear up. I felt terrible. "For the past two weeks it was really hard, not knowing where you were or what you were doing. If you were okay, if you were hurt."

"I'm sorry," I said. "The season's almost over."

One day, while pausing for a rum call, Reb commented that people whose lives are already "reenactorish," like farmers, don't need to reenact. It's the rest of us pencil pushers who do. We're the ones stuck behind a desk, grinding away at our mundane modern lives. For me, the more time I spent away from my desk the less I wanted to return to it. I thought of what I'd written in the margin of my old drama book, "Man is sum of actions." I tallied my daily actions and didn't like a lot of what I saw.

"When are you going away again?" Wendy asked, snapping me back to reality.

"Three weeks," I said. "But it'll be a short one, I promise. In and out, nothing to worry about."

CHAPTER EIGHT

Platoosoon

The summer reenacting season was winding down and I was desperate to squeeze in as many events as possible, so a few weeks after I returned from the Big Row, I jetted off again, this time to southern Virginia and the "jungles of Vietnam." When I landed in Roanoke, however, ears clogged and pretzel crumbs clinging to my shirt, I didn't feel like I was reenacting history anymore, but the movie *Up in the Air* (in which I naturally stood in for George Clooney). Since I first flew to Colorado ten months earlier, I'd logged thirty-five thousand air miles and added another four thousand on the ground, a dubious achievement that would likely earn me a nomination for the Largest Carbon Footprint of the Year award. (If nominated, I plan to argue that I offset my ecological damage by spending two weeks sleeping on tree roots.)

To be honest, I felt anxious about "doing the 'Nam" as reenactors call it. Nothing—well, except reenacting Nazis—had elicited a more impassioned reaction from people than when I told them I was going to reenact the Vietnam War. Most people thought it was in bad taste. "Why would anyone want to relive something so terrible?" they'd ask me. Some reenactors that I spoke to opposed it because of the reactions they'd witnessed at public reenactments—like a timeline event where some "Vietcong" escorted "GI" prisoners off a Huey and vets in the audience openly wept. At another reenactment some young Vietnam reenactors approached veterans and were dismissed as "little twerps" that didn't "get it." It's hard to disagree with one baby boomer who told me, "Reenacting older periods is 'playing history.' But Vietnam isn't history. It's a *reality*."

I met Patrick Hubble, my contact for the reenactment, outside the Roanoke Airport bar. Tall, laid-back and with more than a passing resemblance to the actor Jason Segel, the self-described "time junkie" wore a red tie and an army green cap. On our way to his home in Lynchburg, driving an old Corolla and listening to the Dead Kennedys, the forty-one-year-old mortician told me that his interaction with Vietnam vets has mostly been positive. At living history events and timelines where he dresses as a GI and displays old gear, vets often approach him and tell him how happy they are that he's remembering them. "Most of them think that people don't give a flying rip. It shocks them [that someone does]," he said. In turn, many vets give Patrick their old uniforms and equipment—stuff that'd otherwise be collecting dust. "They know I'm going to keep it, cherish it, love it and bring it out again for folks to see," he said. Plus it gives Patrick the chance to say, "Thank you for your service," something many Americans never did. "I tell them, 'I'm sorry about what happened when you came home,'" that they didn't get a parade and that some people called them "baby killers." "A lot of reenactors think that all the vets need to be dead to reenact a war," he said. "But I don't. I mean, how are you honoring the soldiers if they're dead? I think it's important to do this while these guys are still around."

Like many military reenactors, Patrick was drawn to war since childhood. His family boasts a long lineage of military service. Like mine, both his grandfathers served in World War II, and his father, who died in an industrial accident when Patrick was an infant, was stationed in Germany in the mid-'60s. As a kid in California he sketched Civil War scenes and painted watercolors of World War II, but it wasn't until he was a freshman in high school, when he saw a reenactment of Robert E. Lee's surrender to Ulysses S. Grant at Appomattox Court House, that he discovered reenacting. Soon thereafter, while living in Virginia during high school, he spent a summer at Appomattox Court House National Historical Park working as a costumed interpreter, talking to visitors as if he were a Civil War soldier.

In her book *War Games: Inside the World of 20th Century War Reenactors*, Jenny Thompson estimates that one-third of "modern reenactors" are former military. Patrick trained as a navy combat medic and today suits up once a month for, as he put it, the "*Kameradschaft*" or, rather, the camaraderie between reenactors. As we pulled up to the hillside Victorian house he shares with his wife and twenty-year-old daughter, Patrick said, "When you share a military experience with guys who are in the same boat as you, hundreds or thousands of miles away from home, there's quite the bonding thing that goes on that I don't think civilians can appreciate." I thought of how I bonded with my college classmates: loafing around the dorm lounge trying to catch "Smells Like Teen Spirit" on MTV. But it didn't evoke the same intensity as boot camp or even the Big Row.

• • • • • • • •

An hour or so before we drove to the reenactment site, Patrick and I walked upstairs to his attic. In his green *Polizei* T-shirt, tight black pants, driver's cap and Doc Martens, the devout Christian and Libertarian now looked like a member of an '80s new wave band. The walls of the staircase were covered with old military flags—Soviet naval, French, Japanese—and the stairwell was cluttered with the replica armor of an

English Civil War pikeman and issues of two reenactment magazines, *Skirmish* and *Militaria*.

"One day I'll put my grandchildren through college with all this," Patrick said, unpinning the lock on the attic door. With each step it'd been getting a little hotter, but now as the door swung open, a blast of hot air reeking of old wool rushed out. I stepped inside and saw what can only be described as the "Museum of the Soldier." Hundreds of uniforms spanning the last 350 years of global conflict hung on hangers. Helmets lined shelves, a couple dozen guns were stacked on a rack, canteens, headwear, lanterns and backpacks hung off hooks; on the floor, boots, board games and cavalry swords competed for space. A miniature model of Stalingrad, its buildings collapsed into rubble, dominated the center of the room. "I derive a weird pleasure from the average man's experience during wartime," he said, shuffling toward an interior closet packed with more supplies. It hadn't been my intention to find the ultimate military reenactor, but standing there among it all, I realized that I just had.

"This really belches death," Patrick said, grabbing an AK-47 from inside the closet. "You'll be using that AR-15," he said, pointing to another gun. "Those were the civilian models." I nodded as if I knew what he was talking about, but I couldn't tell the two of them apart. To me all assault rifles look the same, which is to say, they look like they can kill a lot of people in a short amount of time.

"You might want to put a finger in your ear and open your mouth," he said.

"Excuse me?" I asked.

"Otherwise you'll get a concussion headache."

I did as he said. Then he slammed a magazine into the gun's well, pointed the AK at the floor and fired a blank. I wished I'd stuck fingers in both my ears. At any moment I expected his wife to run upstairs to make sure we were okay, but she never did.

"Try these on," he said and laid a pile of fatigues atop Stalingrad. I slipped on some baggy pants and size eleven jungle boots that looked like clown shoes on my feet. But they'd do. After all, we'd only be in 'Nam for thirty hours.

Next, I spread the jacket out on the rubble. The name HUBBLE was stitched on its right breast pocket. He handed me a Sharpie and tore off a strip of brown tape. I wrote SCHROEDER on it and taped it over his name. "Don't pull the pin on this," Patrick said, pointing to an M18 smoke grenade clipped to a harness. "It'll fill up the whole house with smoke." I grabbed the helmet—"Nixon for President" button pinned to it—and tried it on. "Oh, and it's not a good idea to open this," he said, tapping a small bottle of insect repellent secured under its band. "It's a known carcinogen." If there's one thing that separates Vietnam reenacting from all the other time periods, it's the abundant use of *authentic* uniforms and supplies.

I carried all my gear—an entrenching tool, cartridge pouches, a couple canteens, a belt of blanks and more—downstairs to the entrance hallway and followed Patrick to the basement to grab our "C rations." Earlier we'd gone to the grocery store and bought cans of tuna fish and SpaghettiOs. When we got home, Patrick peeled off their labels and spray-painted the cans an olive color.

As a mortician, Patrick has witnessed lots of gruesome deaths, including those of small children and the students killed at the 2007 Virginia Tech shooting. Reenacting battles may seem like a curious way to escape his job, but that's exactly what it provides for him. "I've been involved with death and dying and grief and all that encompasses. Then I go out and reenact something that consumed hundreds if not millions of lives depending on the time period . . . safely. There is no death, especially the way I know it." And yet death—or rather the objects of loss—fills his house. A folded American flag sits in a case on his living room mantelpiece. Behind it is a picture of his handsome young father. Upstairs are weapons of destruction and when we arrived downstairs to pick up our C rations, I was surprised to see two coffins. A plain wooden Russian box leaned upright against the wall, and nearby a Mexican one, designed with a viewing window in its top, provided a base for our recently painted cans of food.

We loaded his Corolla with all our supplies: boxes of blanks, jugs of water, fruit, fatigues and a six-pack of beer, along with the weapons and clothing that made up his Vietcong impression. At private reenactments like the one we were headed to, Patrick plays the enemy. Unlike the 8.7 million men who volunteered for Vietnam or the 2.2 million who were drafted, we'd pay a forty-dollar entry fee for our "service" (or rather, the million-dollar insurance policy).

. . . .

If Vietnam was the baby boomers' war, then it was my generation's "entertainment." While the actual war came into American living rooms every night via the nightly news in the 1960s and '70s, the war's *movies* came into my house via the '80s most revolutionary invention, the VCR. I was too young to see the R-rated features in theaters, but my friends and I somehow procured tapes of *Full Metal Jacket, Apocalypse Now, Rambo: First Blood, Platoon, Casualties of War, The Deer Hunter* and *Born on the Fourth of July*. But that wasn't all. We also watched *Uncommon Valor, Missing in Action, Missing in Action II, Hamburger Hill* and *Good Morning, Vietnam*. It seemed like a new movie came out every week. I remember sitting there, two feet from the screen, hands over my eyes, while the shadowy Vietcong lurked in the steamy, overgrown jungles. Everything looked so foreign and dangerous and all the soldiers looked confused and wild, like they were on the verge of losing their mind. By the time the end credits started to roll I thought, *Now that's somewhere I never want to go.*

The Vietnam War remains an incredibly raw subject, in particular for the generations that lived through it. Some families torn apart by it have never mended. Whenever I talked to baby boomers, it felt like it wouldn't take all that much for them to get into arguments about it today, nearly forty years since it ended. Some fumed that we didn't support our servicemen when they came home; others were still angry at the government for leading us into a war that they knew we couldn't win, a war in which more than fifty-eight thousand Americans and an estimated 2 million Vietnamese died.

More than anything, however, these passionate reactions made me take a harder look at my own generation and our lack of response to the Iraq War. Why didn't we protest more when the coalition forces invaded? Why haven't we held the government accountable for misleading us into an unjustified invasion and occupation? A country that had *nothing to do with 9/11*? Why aren't we raging that, as of this writing, nearly 5,000 American and coalition troops and more than 100,000 Iraqis have died? Why aren't we raging that the government ran up exorbitant budget deficits? But deep down I knew the answer: unlike Vietnam, today an all-volunteer military fights our wars. Today there is no draft.

Although Vietnam is remembered for its unpopular conscription, a higher percentage of men were drafted for World War II (66 percent, compared to Vietnam's 33 percent). But of course the two wars—and the times—weren't the same. One was fighting two powers intent on taking over the world; the second was, well, what was it exactly? That seemed to be one of the biggest problems. A lot of people couldn't have told you what we were fighting for. Many still can't.

The hawks argued that we were trying to stop the spread of communism. They argued what they called "the domino theory": if the communist north defeated the U.S.-backed south, then all of Vietnam would become communist, and it wouldn't be much longer until the rest of Asia "fell." And from there, who knows what region would be next? Lost in all the talk about communism and dominoes, however, was what North Vietnamese leader Ho Chi Minh was trying to do: unify his long-occupied country.

In short, Ho didn't want his country ruled by yet another foreign power (or a foreign-backed power), whether it was the French, who colonized it for nearly one hundred years, the Japanese, who occupied it during World War II, or the government of South Vietnam, backed by the United States. As former secretary of defense Robert McNamara wrote in *In Retrospect*, "We . . . totally underestimated the nationalist aspect of Ho Chi Minh's movement. We saw him first as a Communist and only second as a Vietnamese nationalist. The foundations of our decision making were gravely flawed." So it should come as no surprise that the North Vietnamese and their Vietcong allies in the south were willing to fight for as long as it would take to unify their country. And with an endless supply of weapons coming from China and the Soviet Union, they could. As the North Vietnamese prime minister Pham Van Dong once put it to the *New York Times*'s Harrison Salisbury, "[H]ow long do you Americans want to fight? One year, two years, three years, five years, ten years, twenty years . . . we will be glad to accommodate you."

By 1969, "more bombs had been dropped on Vietnam, North and South, than on all targets in the whole of human history," wrote Stephen Ambrose in his book *To America*. It wasn't for another six years that Saigon eventually fell and Vietnam became a unified, communist country. Today, along with China, Cuba, Laos and North Korea, it's one of the world's five remaining communist nations. As of this writing, communists (China) are our second-largest trading partner and the T-shirt I'm wearing was made in communist Vietnam. On the day I flew to Virginia, thirty-five years after the fall of Saigon, the *Wall Street Journal* led with the story "U.S., Hanoi in Nuclear Talks." In the lead Jay Solomon wrote about the Obama administration's "advanced negotiations to share nuclear fuel and technology with Vietnam in a deal that would allow Hanoi to enrich its own uranium." As I sit here writing this I still have a hard time grasping it all. More than 2 *million* people died fighting a war that should have never happened, a war waged to stop the spread of communism. And yet today China practically owns our country. As the war correspondent Sydney Schanberg once said, "The more you learn about war, the more you understand that at its essence it is insane, bestial and criminal."

. . . .

About an hour and a half after Patrick and I left for the reenactment, we exited the Virginia highway and wound our way along some rolling country roads. Ten minutes later we came to a small yellow sign by the side of the road that said, "V-NAM." A black arrow pointed us down a one-lane dirt road. We passed by a few tucked-away houses and after a mile or so, the area turned densely rural. Oak forest bordered both sides of the road. "Check this out," Patrick said, pointing at a tall brown sign that protruded out of weeds and yellow flowers. It read,

SLOW DOWN

THE LIFE YOU SAVE

MAY BE YOUR

REPLACEMENT'S

After a few hundred more feet, we passed another sign.

BEWARE! YOU ARE ENTERING REDCATCHER TERRITORY

CONVOY SPEED	25 MPH
CATCH UP SPEED	30 MPH
INTERVAL BETWEEN VEHICLES	100 MET

STEEL HELMETS—FLAK JACKETS
WORN AT ALL TIMES
IF FIRED UPON KEEP DRIVING
THE REDCATCHERS WILL PROTECT YOU
ACCIDENTS KILL MORE THAN CHARLIE

Up ahead to our left a couple big, drab general-purpose tents had been erected in a clearing. "Base camp," I said, trying to impress Patrick with my knowledge of military lingo. As we got closer I could make out a small guard shack surrounded by sandbags. An M60 machine gun was propped up on a barrel and real bullets spilled out of its breech. Old, rusted cans hung off a tall, barbed wire fence that ran perpendicular to the road. "It makes noise in case the VC accidentally bump into it," Patrick said. He parked the car just outside the fence and we walked into base camp. Behind the guard shack I spotted a three-hole latrine. Out in front of it a toilet seat lid had been stenciled CHARLIE'S HEAD.

"Come on," Patrick said. "I'll introduce you to Riley."

We hiked over to what looked like a long wooden shed where a couple men in fatigues talked. "This is Schroeder," Patrick said, introducing me to Riley, a midsixties park ranger and the reenactment's organizer. "He's the FNG." I looked at Patrick, confused. "The Fucking New Guy," he clarified. Riley came straight from Central Casting: movie star handsome with a chiseled jaw, sensitive eyes and wide shoulders. After only thirty-six hours in the real Vietnam, his helicopter was shot down. It dropped five hundred feet and crashed, tore his leg apart and earned him a Purple Heart. Now he's finishing his service, reenacting the war in the Virginia woods.

"I'd appreciate it if you kept an eye out for him," Patrick said.

"Sure thing," Riley replied. He looked me up and down. "You'll probably do better in that tent," he said, pointing to the one opposite the latrine. I wasn't sure why, but I agreed.

Only a handful of reenactors were there so I gathered my gear from Patrick's car and set up a sliver of a sleeping space for myself, inflating my bedding, a 1966 air mattress. Then I changed into my fatigues, sat on the ground outside the tent and loaded blanks into a clip. The early August air was so heavy and wet that some guys carried towels to wipe up the sweat.

Slowly people started to materialize—guys younger than me, but older than the majority of Vietnam soldiers, who had an average age of twenty. The close air swelled with testosterone.

"What's up, you choat-lovin' homo?" one guy asked another.

"Not much, faggot," the other replied. The two shoulder-bumped, smacked each other on the back and retired to the other more boisterous tent. As more guys arrived, the quantity of gay jokes rose. So did conversations about the men's time spent in Iraq and Afghanistan.

I felt more at ease camping in the subdued tent, between two civilians, a video game designer from North Carolina and an earnest twenty-seven-year-old who worked on the DC Mall. When I asked the fair-haired park service employee why he'd come he said, "I work at the Vietnam Memorial. I know what happened, but do I *really* know?" I wanted to ask the guys more probing questions, but held back. Before we arrived Patrick advised me to keep a low profile. "Definitely don't mention that you're media," he said. "Some of the guys are a little sensitive to that."

I kept loading blanks, pausing now and then for some watermelon that I scooped off my mess kit's plate. Sixties music blared from the other tent—*How does it feel . . . to be on your own . . . like a rolling stone.* A couple guys tossed a baseball back and forth; others cracked open cans of Schlitz and Old Mud. The video game designer had bought some Armed Forces Radio Service recordings off eBay and uploaded them to an MP3 player that he had wired into the back of an old transistor radio. On the tinny speaker, the broadcaster reported that

Marines had "discovered a large enemy hut, bunker and cave complex" that contained "six new sweatshirts stamped with the word 'Hanoi,' three hundred pounds of salt, fifty pounds of rice, several mosquito nets, twelve ponchos and assorted cooking utensils."

Soon night fell, but the tent stayed bright, illuminated by a portable fluorescent light. I lay on the air mattress, wrapped an old poncho liner around me and covered my eyes with my arm. The Armed Forces Radio Services recordings had been playing for a couple hours now and blended with the louder psychedelic rock. Listening to it all, I felt transported, not necessarily to Vietnam—how could I ever claim to know what that felt like?—but to all those movies I'd smuggled home as a kid, the ones my friends and I watched when we probably should have been learning Latin or memorizing poetry or building a science fair project.

·   ·   ·   ·   ·   ·   ·   ·

The plan was to reenact early January 1968, the days leading up to the Tet Offensive, a military campaign led by the North Vietnamese during the first couple days of the Lunar New Year. By now I'd learned to temper my expectations for what I could learn while "in the action." These "full-immersion tacticals" were more about war games than historical facsimiles of events. In the end, whatever battle we were reenacting didn't really matter. Although Patrick told me we'd be following what the 199th Light Infantry Brigade did, I couldn't have told you anything about the historical events either before or after the event.

Nineteen sixty-eight was a year, as some have observed, when America was on the verge of a nervous breakdown. Aside from the Civil War years and Great Depression, it was arguably the country's most turbulent stretch, our very own annus horribilis. In late February 1968, shortly after Tet, Secretary of Defense Robert McNamara resigned because he didn't think the United States could win the war. On March

31, President Johnson, aware that he couldn't win that November's election, announced that he wouldn't seek the nomination. In April, Martin Luther King, Jr., was killed in Memphis. Two months later, Bobby Kennedy was gunned down in Los Angeles. In August, students rioted at the Democratic National Convention. Every night Americans experienced the war like never before, in their homes, on the nightly news. No year would be as bloody as 1968. In the twelve years the United States had been involved in Vietnam, 19,560 U.S. servicemen had been killed, but in 1968, the number skyrocketed. That year 16,592 died—forty-five a day. That's more than ten times as many casualties suffered per day during the Iraq War's deadliest month and twenty-two times more than the average killed in Afghanistan's deadliest month.

When I woke up the next morning, however, I wasn't thinking about any of that. All I cared about was making it to the woods so I could pee. I slipped off my air mattress, slowly rose to my feet and took one step, when I felt something get caught on my right boot. I looked down and saw a piece of fishing line about four inches off the ground that stretched along the tent's perimeter. I followed it until it terminated at one of those little party popper noisemakers. Overnight, a "Vietcong" had set the trip wire inches from my head. If this was the real war I'd probably have set it off and been blown to bits.

I quickly woke the other forty GIs and, in my best tough-guy voice, told them what had happened. Soon other trip wires were discovered: one tied to a helmet on top of a tent pole, another to the latrine door.

War game on.

The night before, at formation, just as fireflies and cicadas started to materialize, I volunteered to be a radio telephone operator (RTO), thinking that I'd be able to put some of my NPR skills to use. But I soon realized that being an operator involved carrying a twenty-five-pound "brick" on my back. A guy named Buck, who wore a straw fedora and thick black glasses, briefed me on how to operate it. Then he handed me a topographical map with Vietnamese village names on it and an index-card-sized cheat sheet with military codes and squad names like Alpha, Bravo, Charlie, and Bulldog, Hellcat, Foxhound. "There's a strong possibility that the slopes have radios," he told me while demonstrating how to dial in the old unit. "We know the dinks are going to listen." I hadn't heard racial epithets tossed off so casually since John McCain called his Vietnamese prison guards "gooks" during his 2000 presidential campaign. "I hate the gooks," McCain said back then. "I will hate them as long as I live."

"What are my duties?" I asked Buck.

"You're going to hump that thing and be up Sergeant Miller's anus." For a moment I considered all that that would entail—the physics and biology of it—then quickly tried to block it out of my mind. I grabbed one of the radio's shoulder straps and started to pick it up. It barely budged.

Now, after breakfast, with the morning sun so low it hardly penetrated the wooded surroundings, I struggled to walk down the dirt road with the radio strapped to my back. It felt like somebody had stuffed the entire *Encyclopedia Britannica* into a backpack and loaded it on me.

I marched behind Sergeant Miller. About ten other squad members followed me, hugging the road's right side. Another squad marched on the left berm. It reminded me a bit of my Drive on Stalingrad experience except in Colorado I could scan the horizon and see forever. Here all I could see were trees and a long dirt road that stretched a couple hundred yards ahead. I didn't have much time to compare the two experiences, though, because after only a hundred yards, I saw a quick flash of fire at the end of the road, followed by an incredibly loud blast. If Patrick's AK-47 belched death, whatever that gun was had just screamed it. We hung a sharp right into the woods. In the distance, startled dogs howled.

Once we made it into the woods we were safe. Our green fatigues blended into the surrounding deciduous trees. As twigs snapped, leaves crunched and briars scraped, I felt like I was a kid playing cowboys and Indians behind my parents' house. The ground contorted at strange, unpredictable angles just like our wooded hillside. The rotted logs, the fresh leaves, it all smelled the same. I never knew what lay under my foot, if there was a hole or a depression. The years of fallen leaves masked the forest's true terrain.

Still, by now I knew that, barring some terrible accident, I'd make it home to Wendy in one piece, that the bursts of impending fire weren't real, that I'd survive. You get out of battle reenacting what you put into it. You can show up and not learn a thing about history other than maybe an approximation—and appreciation for—what it was like to be a soldier at the time. I mostly tried to remain upright and quiet, to not get my feet tangled on vines. Saddled with over thirty pounds of equipment, I could barely clear fallen trees, and the radio's ten-foot metal antenna often got caught on limbs and bent ninety degrees, thwapping whoever I was near as soon as its tip cleared the limb. Honestly, my biggest concerns were how long it'd take me to unbutton my pants if I had to suddenly go to the bathroom, or if a tick embedded itself in my skin. As Patrick advised me earlier, "When it's over, you might want to check your moist, hairy parts for them."

After about ten minutes of trudging through thick growth we heard an exchange of loud and prolonged gunfire. Another squad was engaging the enemy. Sergeant Miller, who, like Buck, wore thick black glasses, looked at me, pointed two fingers at his eyes, then pointed into the distance and made a "Let your fingers do the walking" gesture. I'd taken a short rest and started to get up, but the radio was so heavy it pulled me back down. I quickly grabbed hold of a tree to stay upright.

A tinny voice from inside my jacket asked, *"What are your coordinates? Over."*

I pulled out the radio receiver and pressed the call button. "This is Charlie," I whispered.

"Did you say Charlie? *Over."*

"Uh," I said, realizing that I'd told him that I was the enemy, the Vietcong, *Victor Charlie.* "This is . . ." I couldn't remember our squad's code name, so I dug out my cheat sheet.

"Rumpunch Two here," I whispered. "Over."

"Rumpunch Two, this is Rumpunch One. What are your coordinates? Over."

I looked around but all I saw were trees, leaves and a handful of aging GIs crouching down to avoid detection. I consulted the topographical map—rings of squiggly circles and elevation points labeled "30, 50, 40"—the likes of which I hadn't seen since my high school geography class.

"I think we're to the right of everybody," I said.

"Rumpunch Two, this is Rumpunch One. Repeat after me: 'Alpha, Delta, niner, Bravo.'"

The guys at base camp were telling me to dial in some secret frequency. I thought of movies I'd seen where people talked to each other in code—*Smokey and the Bandit, Blue Thunder, The Hunt for Red October*—then for some inexplicable reason I uttered, "Roger dodger," like Peter Graves in *Airplane.* I stuffed the handset back inside my jacket.

"Where do they want us to go?" Sergeant Miller asked. I shrugged. He grabbed the receiver and started talking in code.

"The village," he said.

We lumbered ahead a few hundred yards, dropping down into a small depression, then climbing out of it, peaking atop a small hill. Ahead, in a clearing, I saw an older white guy dressed head to toe in black pajamas, wearing a coolie hat and fiddling with a rake outside a hootch. He looked right at us—ten GIs, weapons drawn—but didn't change his expression. Past him, in the "village"—a small cluster of bamboo and wooden hootches—more "Vietnamese villagers" "tilled" the land. I quickly surveyed the area looking for Patrick, but he wasn't there. *"Ba toc kam,"* one villager said in imitation Vietnamese. *"Tuc lum bop,"* another answered. If it was the organizers' intention to give us a "you were there" type of experience, it kind of worked. I mean, I wasn't sure if the villagers were going to be "friendly" or "hostile." But more than anything I felt really uncomfortable, as if I'd just landed in a surreal George Saunders story.

Soon another squad of ten soldiers joined us. "Keep your eyes peeled for any booby traps," their sergeant, a thick thirty-something in rectangular glasses named Ewing said. I lumbered into the village and felt a wave of discomfort wash over me. Part of it was empathy—just what was it like for a twenty-year-old GI from Iowa to be in a mysterious country? Not knowing if that guy over there was a villager or a Vietcong about to kill him? But the other part was just how strange it all was. I mean, white guys acting "Vietnamese"?

"Sarge, this bunker's seriously jacked," one of the GIs said. He was standing next to a small pit. "Permission to blow it."

"Not yet," Ewing ordered.

Another GI rifled through a bamboo hut, searching for weapons. "There's a shit ton of ammo over here, Sarge. Fucking goddamn arsenal!"

"All right, make sure none of them have any weapons," he said.

One grunt, a dead ringer for "Joey" on *Friends,* who I'll call Le-Blanc, quickly rounded up a handful of villagers. Each was probably twice the size of a typical Vietnamese man and acted docile. LeBlanc grabbed their hoes and rakes from them.

"Where are the weapons, gook? Huh, motherfucker?" he shouted. "I asked you, where are all the goddamn weapons?"

"Ba no ba ba bano," a gray-haired "Vietnamese" answered, sticking his hands in his pockets.

"Take your hands out of your pockets, you fucking dink!" Le-Blanc said, but the guy didn't. "Hey, I said take your goddamn hands out of your pockets, you fucking gook!"

"Bo nap na tem."

LeBlanc yanked the villager's hands out of his pockets. "Keep 'em where I can see 'em, motherfucker!" He ordered the villagers to lie on the ground, kicked their feet apart and spread their hands out in front of them.

At Vincennes and Fort Niagara, a few reenactors had asked me to come back next year and bring Wendy with me. I was glad she wasn't with me now.

"Where's Charlie? Where's fucking goddamn Charlie, you fucking zipperhead?" LeBlanc shouted. "Where the fuck is he? Oh, for fuck's sake, Sarge, let me grease this gook!" Watching all this made me feel sick to my stomach, so I withdrew to the village's perimeter, switched my gun to safety and leaned up against a tree. Near me, two GIs chatted. "My dad said they used to put out cigarettes behind guys' ears to get 'em to talk," one of them said, chuckling. I felt like someone had just punched me in the gut.

"Sarge, this gook is wearing GI boots," LeBlanc said, then held up his wrist. "And a GI watch." The villager remained face-first on the ground, expressionless. "You know what we do to gooks that we find wearing GI fatigues?" LeBlanc asked.

Another soldier lifted the villager up by an armpit, walked him toward the opposite end of the village and forced him to his knees. Then he grabbed his hands and placed them behind his head. *"Bap he lam no!"* the villager protested loudly. The GI walked twenty feet away, turned around and, with one hand on his machine gun, mowed down the villager.

Soon all the other prisoners were rounded up. The GIs fitted long bamboo poles under their arms and behind their backs. LeBlanc took charge, sticking his gun against one of the villager's heads. "Whoa!" another GI said. "If you're going to point your weapon at someone's head, please make sure the goddamn safety is on!" Everything swirled and blended, as if I'd landed in a Vietnam reenactment with Abu Ghraib characteristics.

Apparently I wasn't the only one who'd had enough. A tall, lanky prisoner somehow managed to rise to his feet and bolted for the woods. But he only made it about twenty feet before half a dozen GIs opened fire on him. He crumpled to the ground. I'd only been in "Vietnam" for an hour and I'd already witnessed two civilian "murders."

I wanted to quit the reenactment after what happened in the village, but there was nowhere to go, so I hung around, mostly staying silent but playing along for the rest of the morning like a good soldier. While we opened fire on the VC from two sides, during the break when we sat on a dirt hillside and ate our rations, as we walked through waist-high muddy river water holding our weapons over our heads, while we marched back to base camp, singing

> *And it's one, two, three,*
>
> *What are we fighting for?*
>
> *Don't ask me, I don't give a damn,*
>
> *Next stop is Vietnam.*
>
> *And it's five, six, seven,*
>
> *Open up the pearly gates,*
>
> *Well, there ain't no time to wonder why*
>
> *Whoopee! We're all gonna die.*

I played along like a dutiful soldier, all the while thinking to myself, *This is the last twentieth-century war I ever want to reenact.*

. . . .

Sometime after lunch we returned to base camp for some R&R. I couldn't have been happier to take a break, to lie on the air mattress and shut my eyes. LeBlanc's behavior disturbed me so much that I wanted to turn invisible. *If I just close my eyes and act like I'm asleep nobody will bother me,* I thought.

While everything about the physical environment was different from the Drive on Stalingrad, I felt similar to when I lay on the floor of the one-room schoolhouse. Like I wanted to escape and never come back. Not long after DOS I remember calling my brother, Rob, to tell him about the experience. Rob's eighteen months older than me and probably scored a few points higher on his IQ test as well, so I wasn't surprised to hear him make what would turn out to be a very prescient observation. "You know," he said, "you're going off to learn about history, but what you're really going to find is America."

At the time I didn't think much of it. I thought that I knew America pretty well. After all, aside from the eight months I spent studying drama in London, I've lived here my entire life—in both the city and the country. Where I grew up, in rural Pennsylvania, nearly all my high school classmates were white, cows grazed the field next to our house and people waved at each other when they drove down the narrow one-lane roads. Where Wendy and I live now, in L.A.'s San Fernando Valley, 45 percent of the people are foreign born, there aren't any fields and people only wave at you with one finger. That said, on any given night, I can walk fifteen minutes and eat either Thai, Korean, Afghani, Indian, Colombian, Brazilian, Greek, Italian, Chinese, Mexican, Vietnamese, Mongolian, Armenian, Lebanese, Japanese or yes, even "American" food. Where I live now I can see plays, consider the sculptures of Henry Moore and practice Arabic with the local liquor store cashier, all in the same night. I like both "Americas" for different reasons, but at times they both get on my nerves too.

When you've lived in a big metropolis for so long, though, it can be hard to remember what life is like outside of your own little bubble. During the past months while I drove from airport to reenactment and back again, the towns and countryside sometimes looked foreign to me, as if I were in China. Actually, considering that I visit Hong Kong and the mainland about once a year, China has sometimes felt more familiar. Still, I loved discovering new parts of my country. I felt like a tourist in a land where everyone plays by the same rules but interprets them differently.

Now and then I'd pull into a Mayberry-esque village or see a farmhouse sitting atop a lonely little bump of a hill and think, *Wouldn't it be great to give it all up and leave the "hustle" behind?* I'd picture myself sitting behind a big oak desk, looking out on Wendy as she tended her garden, watering the bok choy that the local grocery store didn't carry. How inspirational it would all be, how meditative and quiet. I could almost hear the prose flowing out of my fingertips as I attempted to write the next great American novel, or at least a short story . . . okay, a magazine article. All right, a tweet.

I wish that every town I passed through elicited these feelings, but they didn't. For years I'd read and heard and seen a lot of stories about how industry had up and left many small towns, how Walmart had sucked all the business off of Main Street, but it wasn't until I was in those places, until I drove past the shuttered storefronts, until I saw the Rust Belt's abandoned factories, that I truly understood it. Some towns looked as if the economy had crumbled after the railroad stopped running. Others seemed to be hanging on by a thread, their slow erosion having commenced when the first strip mall popped up—then accelerated after the manufacturing jobs slipped away.

For many young men and women in these "deindustrialized areas," the military offers opportunities that they wouldn't otherwise have. As Patrick told me on the way to the reenactment, "Some guys [in the military] are college educated, but by and large there are a lot of hard-luck cases." Once three years of cumulative duty are completed, vets receive a free education, but after twenty years of service, members can retire with full benefits. Weighing the options in these economically challenged areas, the military looks like a pretty good deal to many eighteen-year-olds, and the U.S. government is happy to have them.

Consider that in 2010, the United States spent $700 billion on defense, more than $2,200 *per U.S. citizen* (not just taxpayers). That's 4.7 percent of our GDP—and amazingly 47 percent of the world's total military spending. But it hasn't always been like this. Between 1776 and the end of World War II, the United States spent only nineteen years at war with other nations, and our spending reflected it, having only been a fraction of what it is now. But since 1950, we've been at war *one-third* of the time, and yet most of those wars haven't been popular with the American public. Many scholars have argued that one of the reasons we have such a big defense budget is to help keep the economy afloat. It's not hard to see how what President Eisenhower called the "military-industrial complex" works: American companies create military products and the U.S. government buys them (while industry lobbyists court politicians on both sides of the aisle). As George Mason University professor Richard E. Rubenstein said on WNYC's *Leonard Lopate Show*, "not only do you have the military-industrial complex supplying demand to the economy, but you have the armed forces soaking up what would otherwise be jobless people." In other words, when manufacturing jobs left town, the military stepped in and provided opportunities where they didn't exist. Some have even called this "Pentagon socialism."

During reenactments I often heard vets talking about how they had a love/hate relationship with the military. As Patrick told me earlier, just boot camp alone was "scary as hell." Yet he found positive sides to his service. "It helped me grow up, it gave me a GI Bill for college, and that's what my family lived off of." Still, despite the attic full of militaria, he's a pacifist and vehemently antiwar. "It's a destructive ugly affair. I've seen death in my job. There's nothing pretty about it."

We've deployed more than 2 million men and women to Iraq and Afghanistan, and most have made it home safely, but that doesn't mean it's easy for them to adjust to life when they return. The army claims 30 percent of all returning soldiers suffer from post-traumatic stress disorder. One Vietnam Medal of Honor recipient has gone so far as to say that the real number is actually 100 percent. Two hundred fifty thousand Iraq and Afghanistan veterans have sought psychological help from the Veterans Administration. Many of these men and women are back home, but not really back at all, to paraphrase the mother of a soldier. Once you've experienced war, it never leaves you. At restaurants, most returning soldiers demand to sit with their back to the wall because they think everyone is out to get them.

Hearing all this, I wondered why, as Rubenstein asked, we haven't "reengineer[ed] the economy for peace." In just over four hours the United States spends more money on defense than the entire *annual* budget of AmeriCorps. Just imagine how different America—and the impoverished areas where most soldiers come from—would be if we spent even the *tiniest* amount—say 5 percent of the defense budget—and "enlisted" young men and women to revitalize the areas in which they live. Instead of giving them American-made guns and training them to kill, exposing them to the horrors of war, we could give them American-made hammers and paintbrushes so they could spruce up old storefronts, turn abandoned warehouses into gathering places—health clinics, recycling centers, playgrounds, you name it—to rebuild their communities, all the while training them so at the end of their service they could receive a free college education. Why isn't that option presented to the cities and neighborhoods that need it the most? It seems so simple and obvious that if you want to revitalize America, you first have to teach kids how to create, not destroy. And from the intensity I saw in "Vietnam" I felt like some of the guys there could benefit from it.

. . . .

I managed to catch a few winks on the air mattress and at dusk, shortly after I'd woken up, a few of us ventured out on a recon mission. "Leave your helmets at base," Ewing ordered. "We won't be seeing any action." I slipped on my floppy hat, heaved the radio on my back and marched back into the woods.

We used our guns as machetes, hacking away at new growth and breaking cobwebs; we ducked under limbs and stepped on briars so the guy behind us didn't get pricked, we crept like cats, we kept our mouths shut. But none of it could help us find whatever it was we were looking for. About fifteen minutes into it Ewing leaned into a mound, spread a map onto the ground and shook his head. "We're sewed up tighter than a tick in here," he whispered in his southern drawl. "Let me see that radio," he said, grabbing the receiver from inside my jacket. "Rumpunch One, this is Hellcat One. Unable to penetrate from Bravo Delta Charlie." He listened for instructions. "Awright, boys," he whispered. "New plan: we're heading to the firebase."

Ten minutes later, we'd finally hacked our way through a few hundred feet of tangled branches and made it to the fortified basketball-court-sized area of red clay. The rest of the GIs were waiting for us. Technically these fortified firebases were built to provide artillery support for infantry, but there weren't any big guns around. In fact, other than a bunch of old bullet casings littering the ground, it was empty. "Just wait until the night battle," Patrick had teased earlier. I realized that the event's climax was just moments away. I leaned into the breastwork and switched my gun off safety.

"I don't like being here," one of the soldiers said.

Another replied, "We're fucked."

Stars twinkled brightly; the Milky Way glowed like a cloud. I thought of something I'd heard earlier that week while driving home from work. It was an old Carl Sagan recording in which he read an excerpt from his book *Pale Blue Dot*. The book's title comes from a 1990 photograph of the earth taken by *Voyager 1.* Later when I looked at the photo, I only saw a few colored streaks, like someone had taken green, brown and red crayons and drawn across black construction paper. They run the length of the photo, and in the brown streak there's a bright speck, like a broken pixel on a screen. But it wasn't a pixel. It was the earth, photographed from 3.7 billion miles away. In one now famous section Sagan considers the humbling photo.

> Look . . . at that dot. That's here, that's home, that's us. On it every-
> one you love, everyone you know, everyone you ever heard of, every
> human being who ever was, lived out their lives. . . . Think of the
> rivers of blood spilled by all those generals and emperors so that,
> in glory and triumph, they could become the momentary mas-
> ters of a fraction of a dot. Think of the endless cruelties visited
> by the inhabitants of one corner of this pixel on the scarcely
> distinguishable inhabitants of some other corner, how frequent
> their misunderstandings, how eager they are to kill one another,
> how fervent their hatreds.

I didn't play much war as a kid, I never had any interest in tactics, uniforms or conquest, I've never wanted something so bad I'd ask *others* to die for it. I didn't understand war before I started reenacting and I understood it even less now.

Phoop!

I heard what sounded like a Roman candle being launched.

"Incoming!" someone yelled. I turned around to see something land just outside the firebase and explode. "Jesus!" I yelled. "Whoa! Holy shit!" others exclaimed. Our enemy had launched a small, but nonetheless real, explosive at us from behind a cluster of very tall trees. It arced high in the air and was followed by a red tail, as if the golf ball Alan Shepard hit on the moon had finally entered the atmosphere and burned up.

Phoop!

"Incoming!"

BAM!

Phoop!

"Incoming!"

BAM!

After only three attempts, the small mortars started landing inside the firebase, scattering the skittish GIs.

Despite the steady bombardment we never received any order to retaliate. There was at least one VC manning their artillery, but where were all the others? I kept my finger on the gun's trigger and hoped it'd all end soon.

Another firework shot up, but this one fell very slowly, like a leaf, then it flared a bright red—so bright that night turned to day. For a couple seconds we all looked at each other, our faces lit up like the taillights of a car. Most of these guys had seen real action and they looked scared.

Then all hell broke loose.

On three sides, from concealed spots in the woods, the VC opened fire. Flames shot out three feet from their big guns. All this time they'd only been thirty feet away, and now their relentless blasts formed a three-walled ring of fire. The concussion was so loud I had to cover one of my ears while blindly firing my gun above the breastwork.

BAM! BAM! BAM! BAM! BAM! BAM!

A couple GIs fired shotguns and .38 specials that were just as loud as the AKs. They made muskets sound like Super Soakers. After a thirty-second barrage, everyone had emptied their first magazine.

Reload.

One of the GIs yelled, "Ho Chi Minh is a fag!"

In his best Kim Jong Il, a VC replied, "Berkcree crass of 1969."

"Buddhists suck dick," a GI responded. Dogs howled in the distance. The smell of gunpowder floated through the air.

Phoop! Another night flare lit us up.

Vietcong blew whistles and from the woods another firestorm raged. Soon my gun jammed. I laid it down, cupped both hands over my ears and curled into a ball, but it was too late: the concussion had given me a pounding headache. I stayed there for the next twenty minutes, waiting for it all to end.

. . . .

Later at base camp, after we'd busted through an estimated three thousand rounds, soldiers cracked cans of PBR and Miller. The radio blared Jefferson Airplane's "White Rabbit." While I waited for Patrick to come pick me up from the VC camp, I deflated my air mattress and stuffed all my supplies into deli bags. One reenactor muttered something about a hookah, grabbed his shotgun and disappeared into the darkness. When Patrick's car pulled up, LeBlanc was entertaining the troops by impersonating Will Ferrell's impression of Harry Caray. Later Patrick would tell me, "In 'Nam the soldiers would celebrate that they'd lived another day." I'm sure many of the GIs—veterans themselves—could identify.

Before we reached the highway, Patrick asked me what I thought of the experience. I wasn't sure how to respond. I'd felt guilty that I'd been undercover, and that I couldn't ask more probing questions. I didn't like being covert. Also, Patrick had been very hospitable. He'd picked me up at the airport an hour from his home, he put me up for two nights at his house, we bonded over '80s new wave music and the surreal British TV show *The Mighty Boosh*; he even took me to Appomattox Court House one afternoon. But I couldn't lie. "To be honest I found it to be really disturbing," I said, staring straight ahead at the curvy, dark country road. His face was lit up by the dashboard, and I could see out of the corner of my eye that he was disappointed.

We didn't talk about it again until early the next morning, while en route to the airport, in his family's old Volvo station wagon. I told Patrick that I found the repeated use of racial epithets upsetting and that I thought LeBlanc needed help. I explained what had happened and that I thought LeBlanc shouldn't be in a situation where accidents can occur, where someone could get seriously hurt by placing a gun against another person's temple. Patrick listened closely and thought about it for a bit, then suggested that LeBlanc should come before a "war crimes trial." I appreciated the sentiment, but wasn't sure how that would help.

As we continued through the early morning sunlight, Patrick told me that many of the participants were sons of Vietnam vets and that they grew up hearing war stories from their fathers, who've never forgotten what happened or what the enemy did to them and their fellow soldiers. The idea of forgiveness entered our conversation. According to Patrick, many World War II veterans have forgiven the Germans— after all, they were just soldiers following orders, like all the other grunts—but not the Japanese. Many Vietnam vets will also never forgive their enemy. "The Americans worship the same God as Germans, they looked like them, they ate similar food," Patrick said. "But a lot of the Vietnam vets and the sons, they carry that hatred around," he said. "It's been passed down their entire lives."

• • • • • • • •

I'll never know what it was like to be an eighteen-year-old kid in boot camp. I've never been taught how to kill someone. I've never been shot at for real. I've never been a kid "with not many opportunities," as Patrick put it to me. I'll never have to come back from war and have trouble readjusting to normal life. Before starting my quest I could count all my military friends on one *finger*.

In the airport, after Patrick dropped me off, I saw a young man, no older than twenty-two, in a wheelchair, his hair shorn short into a military cut, wearing a T-shirt that if I remember correctly just said, "Marines." I felt nervous approaching him. I didn't want him to think that I pitied him for being injured. I feel like the gap between military personnel and civilians has become a chasm in America. The farther it grows apart, the less people understand each other. I'll never know what it's like to be a real man of war, and I'm not sure I ever want to. "You go through scary, difficult circumstances that are physically, emotionally and mentally demanding," Patrick had told me on the way to the reenactment, adding, "Sometimes it's hard to translate that experience to others."

I approached the soldier and held out my hand. "Excuse me," I said. "I just want to say 'thank you' for your service." We shook. It was the first time I'd ever done that.

CHAPTER NINE

History of the Weird, Part I

E arly on while researching this book, I contacted Jack Garrett of the Vikings of Bjornstad, a San Francisco area Viking, Norman and Saxon reenactment group. During our convivial half-hour phone conversation, the sixty-three-year-old and I quickly bonded over our love of all things theatrical. Like many reenactors, Jack's a movie buff. He particularly likes films that depict the era he re-creates. He even devotes space on the Bjornstad website for members to critique Viking movies, and some of the comments made me laugh so hard I spit on my computer screen.

"I can't comment on the quality of the acting, as there didn't seem to be any."
(On the 1978 Lee Majors dud, *The Norsemen*.)

"Worthy of note is that the Native Americans Leif [Ericson] meets either speak Old Norse or he instinctively speaks Algonquian—it's hard to tell which in a silent movie."
(Regarding the 1928 movie *The Viking*.)

"I really didn't need to see the graphic depiction of a guy taking a dump in the woods!"
(On the 2007 Heathen Films production of *Severed Ways: The Norse Discovery of America*.)

Jack, who's an information technology consultant, also moonlights as a playwright. The sixteen-person group sometimes performs his twenty-minute play *The Wedding of Somerled and Ragnhild*, about the marriage of a twelfth-century Viking princess to a Scottish prince, at the Caledonian Club of San Francisco's Scottish Highland Games. In the past the History Channel has even called on Bjornstad—the Scandinavian word translates to "Bear State," a nod to California's state animal—to appear in programs like *Command Decisions: Hastings* and *Conquerors—William the Conqueror*. After chatting with Jack for about half a second I determined that these laid-back and arty Northern Californians would be the perfect group to teach me about the people Merriam-Webster's calls "pirate Norsemen."

During our conversation I briefly mentioned Castra Lafe, the Roman fort in Arkansas, to Jack. He'd never heard of it or the annual reenactment that takes place there, but he was intrigued. "Sounds like the Viking fort that's being built [in the Midwest]," he said. *Viking fort?* I thought. *By Odin, now, that's something I've got to see!*

After we got off the phone I e-mailed the fort's mastermind, a man I'll call "Viking Ted," and asked him if it'd be possible to come visit. He responded promptly and mentioned that I wasn't the first member of the "media" to contact him. Others had requested interviews for film and TV projects, including, according to Ted, the History Channel. However, it turned out that the producers—or whoever they were—didn't think much of him and his hobby. Instead they took the angle of "'look at the nutty reenactors . . . they think they are real Vikings,'" as Ted wrote to me. He told me that if I had the same intention—to basi-

cally tell the world that he was delusional—I should stop corresponding with him immediately. I told him that I didn't.

In between e-mails Ted googled me and listened to some of my
radio stories, including one about the Lingerie Football League and
another about the time I nearly ruined my friends' wedding when I
imitated Borat for the better part of their weekend-long celebration.
Not long after, Ted responded with a brief, mean-spirited critique of my
work.

> [Y]our past work is proof that what you are really
> looking for is to ridicule and demean rather than to
> educate . . . I will recommend again that you not bother
> to contact me.

Wow, I thought. *That's kinda harsh. Demean? Really?* Not once—
okay, once, but I deserved it—had anyone complained about how they
came off in one of my stories.

I read on.

> I will additionally be posting this entire e-mail thread to
> all of the groups that I am in contact with giving them
> fair warning of what I believe your intentions are.

Whoa, I thought. *Now that's just dickish!*

I quickly fired off an e-mail to Jack to tell him what had happened, but to my horror Ted had beaten me to the punch. He'd e-mailed
every Viking in America—all one-thousand-plus of them—via the
hobby's two umbrella groups, Vikings North America and Regia
Anglorum.

That night, anxious and infuriated—and slightly drunk—I sat by
my computer checking my in-box to see how much Viking hate mail

I'd get, but to my relief none ever arrived. Maybe Viking Ted didn't wield as much influence as I'd feared or maybe a thousand Viking reenactors were sharpening their axes and awaiting my communiqué, I don't know. Whatever the case, when I woke the next morning, the only e-mail in my in-box was from a Viking reenactor who'd bravely come to my defense. "Here was an opportunity for us to have spread 'the good word,'" "Bob" wrote to Viking Ted, cc'ing me. "But after this response, I wonder what Mr. Schroeder will write? Nice goin' dude! I hope you did not blow it for all of us." I fired off a quick e-mail to Bob thanking him for trusting me. He fired an e-mail right back. In it he included his theory for why Ted acted so irrationally.

> Unfortunately . . . the world of the medieval re-creationist is somewhat populated with cave trolls . . . who spend they're [sic] waking hours wearing their bathrobe, living in their grandmothers [sic] basement rent free, using a computer to trash the good intentions and ambitions of others when not jerking off while sniffing their mama's underwear.

After I read the e-mail, I noticed that he'd cc'ed Ted on it. *Whoa!* I thought, *these Vikings really mean business.*

While it was nice to know that Bob had my back, I was a little worried that in the twelve short hours since my innocent "Do you mind if I come take a look at your fort?" query, I'd triggered an online Viking melee.

Fortunately all the name-calling soon died down, but not until some damage had been done: Jack, who'd once happily welcomed my participation with Bjornstad, now grew reticent, asking me to present my case in front of the group so they could collectively decide, à la

Althing—the Viking peer judicial system—whether or not they'd let me play. "I . . . recognize there is an unavoidable wackiness in what we do," he wrote. "And even perhaps who we are. (Have you seen the photos on our web site of some of us dressed as hobgoblins?)" But, he said, they didn't want to be made fun of, just like I didn't want my intentions to be judged, so we agreed to reconnect later in the year. "I . . . respect whatever conclusion you all make," I replied in what I now realize wasn't my most grammatically correct sentence, all the while thinking, *Thanks a bunch, Viking Ted. I totally hope some Picts TP your fort.*

· · · · · · · ·

Six months later, in June, during my 420-mile drive to Bjornstad member Ed Berland's house in Santa Rosa, I thought about the Viking Ted incident. I didn't particularly care for the way he'd disparaged me that night, but at the same time, I could understand why he didn't want anybody else writing about him and his hobby. After all, he'd been burned before and didn't want to get burned again. I didn't want to make fun of him; I was genuinely curious about his fort. But maybe deep down inside Ted was aware of what most people think of his hobby: that's it's weird, and that no matter what someone writes about him he'll always come across as "different."

Consider that, over the course of the last year, I heard reenactors described as "weird," "nerdy," "strange," "bizarre," "wacky," "nutjobs," "crazy," "off," "dorks," "fantasists," "insane," "wackos," "geeky" and even "flamin' idiots"—and that was what reenactors called *themselves*. When I told friends and acquaintances that I'd been hanging out with reenactors, some simply pointed at the side of their heads and made circles with their fingers as if to say, "Cuckoo." Over dinner at Old Fort Niagara, John Osinski told me that before someone gets into the hobby, the first thing that he should do is "admit to himself that he's a little crazy" because "most people will look at you like you're crazy anyway." Of course, it's one thing to call yourself crazy and something altogether different when a stranger does it.

While many reenactors—in particular Civil War reenactors—attribute the public's "negative and very, very weird image" of them to Tony Horwitz's book *Confederates in the Attic*, other reenactors acknowledge that the "weird" label is largely the result of their own behavior. Let's face it, dressing like a Nazi and sleeping in subzero temperatures without a sleeping bag or spending one's weekend walking around in a loincloth and getting excited about eating a slice of pork belly with a pig's hairy nipple on its underside—a story I heard while I was on the Big Row—isn't how most people choose to spend their downtime.

But having a "you were there" experience, a time-traveling "period rush," is the point for many reenactors. Over the course of the year I experienced the sensation a bunch of times, as a "Nazi," as a "Rebel," as a "Roman," during the Big Row and in "Vietnam." Sometimes I had to pinch myself to remember where I was. It was as if I'd entered a parallel universe, where all the rules of the normal world suddenly—*jarringly*—no longer applied.

During my meeting with Bjornstad in Ed's suburban mid-'80s split-level, I learned that a couple of its members had experienced the very same sensation. At one point Ed, a sixty-three-year-old graphic designer who looks a bit like a skinnier, bearded Jay Leno, stopped my interview to tell me about an experience that he and another member, Brian Agron, had four years earlier, in Battle, England.

The two men had joined 3,500 other "Saxons" and "Normans" to reenact the Battle of Hastings, the famous clash where, in 1066, William I ("the Conqueror") of Normandy defeated King Harold II of England to become King of England. Before the battle, reenactor priests, with their hair fashioned into "Friar Tuck" tonsures, sprinkled holy water on the troops. It was a ceremonial blessing that put the two

Jewish men in a rather awkward position. Brian and Ed, dressed in chain mail and helmets and wearing quivers on their backs, didn't know what to do. As Ed now said from the comfort of his living room recliner, "I don't know how to genuflect."

But all around them Norman reenactors started to kneel.

"And kneeling is actually forbidden [in our religion]," Brian interjected.

From the opposite side of the battlefield, they heard Anglo-Saxon reenactors pounding their shields and horse hooves thundering on the ground. The two men looked around them at all the kneeling Normans, then back at each other. They had no choice. To give over to the reenactment, to travel back in time, as it were, to experience that period rush, they had to temporarily suspend their disbelief—and, for that matter, their actual belief.

"We took a knee," Ed remembered.

As he knelt down and stared across the very field where, nearly a millennium ago, England and the English language forever changed, he got chills. "You're transported," he told me. "That's the only word I can use to describe it. You're *transported*."

Stories like this might sound strange, but if you're a history buff or simply nostalgic, you've probably asked yourself the question, *Wouldn't it be cool to travel back in time? To walk the streets, at least until somebody emptied the contents of her chamber pot on your head?* Over the year I felt this pull on a number of occasions, typically while reading stories about people I admire: Shakespeare, Bach, Voltaire, Benjamin Franklin, Thomas Paine, Ralph Waldo Emerson. *Wouldn't it be great to hang out with them for an evening? To see how they live, to share a meal with them—even if the water would kill you and they're serving sheep's head for dinner?* When Wendy and I went to art museums I'd find myself staring at paintings and wanting to climb into them, into the homes of wealthy Dutch merchants, or to walk the streets of Renaissance cities or cross the London Bridge when it looked like the Ponte Vecchio and was decorated with the heads of traitors that'd been stuck on pikes. I found it easy to be drawn in by the *romanticism* of the past no matter how well I knew that times were nowhere near as simple as they seemed.

Like me, Ed was drawn to old England, in particular the romance of knights in shining armor. "There's probably more of me that identifies with those historical events than what happened here in the United States," he said. "I find it hard to identify with religious intolerance. That word's not in my lexicon." He paused. " 'Slavery.' Again, racial intolerance, not in my lexicon." At the time I was sitting on his couch next to Brian and facing three other Bjornstad members. In all, in the airy, sunken living room of Ed's house, four members—three men, one woman, all dressed in civvies, all old enough to be my parents—sat in a semicircle around a TV, where a fifth member, Tory Parker, joined us via Skype. (Jack couldn't attend because of a family emergency.)

While tolerance doesn't immediately spring to mind when one thinks of Vikings, it's a mind-set that guides the Bjornstad members. Their group was the only one I met who counted an openly gay couple—Tory and her partner, Kay Tracy—as members. In fact, the two women founded the group in 1999, which, at the time, they called Kyrbyr, a Scandinavian word that translates as "Cow Village," a reference to the area's many cattle ranches. Viking culture holds a special significance for Tory and Kay because, unlike in so many other historical eras, Viking women held strong roles in society. "They owned property, they could divorce, they kept the keys to the treasure boxes," the bespectacled, short-haired Tory told me from the TV screen.

I always thought of Vikings as big hairy dudes who sailed ships, wore horned helmets and enjoyed nothing better than a good pillaging. But, as the Bjornstad members told me, the reality is far more complex than those silly "What's in Your Wallet?" commercials. First off, it was the imaginative nineteenth-century romanticists who painted the Northmen in horned helmets. From there, Wagner borrowed the look for his opera *Tristan und Isolde*. Now it's Minnesota Vikings fans and credit card companies who, perhaps unknowingly, prolong the stereotype. As for their gigantic size, the average Viking stood a towering five foot eight—tall for the time, but well below today's average and only an inch taller than me. (My ancestors were apparently hobbits.) Then there was the raiding, which Ed told me was how the Scandinavians earned the "Viking" moniker. "They went 'a-viking.' That's what it meant, it meant to go out and raid."

"Vikings were one of the most sophisticated cultures of the day," Tory explained. They established trading centers in Dublin and York, England, sailed as far as India and were called "well-groomed" by people in the Mediterranean. So why then do we still picture a bearded barbarous heathen, ax aloft, about to impale a cowering victim? (Aside from the fact that that's the first image that came up when I googled "Vikings.") Why don't we recognize their work as tradesmen, artisans, farmers; the judicial system they created and which the United States adopted; the fact that Leif Ericson stepped foot on the North American continent 491 years before Columbus landed in the Bahamas and exclaimed, "At last, India! Now, does anybody know where I can find a good curry?"

The short answer to those questions can be summed up by Winston Churchill's popular observation, "History is written by the victors." The pagan Vikings, who integrated very well into different cultures, eventually converted to Christianity. In other words, they, and paganism, "lost."

The longer answer lies in words—or rather, in writers. The Vikings didn't write a whole lot down, and when they did, they wrote pretty mundane stuff like, "Rodmar and Herjolf walked by here on Tuesday." They also wrote in runic language, on *stones*, which aren't exactly the easiest medium to distribute. At the time, the most literate Westerners were monks, who didn't exactly appreciate it when a bunch of heathens pillaged their monasteries. In fact the "Viking age" began when a group raided a monastery on Lindisfarne Island, about seventy miles southeast of Edinburgh, Scotland. The monks' tales—written in Latin on parchment and vellum—of godless horror survived and we're still living with the one-dimensional pillaging stereotype.

Still, despite all their relative "sophistication," it's important to remember that Vikings weren't exactly warm and fuzzy. But neither, as Jonathan Clements writes in *The Vikings*, was anyone else in the Dark Ages. "Almost everyone was atrocious. The Angles, Saxons, Irish and Scots were just as bloodthirsty." Between 793 and 1066—the dates that define the Viking era—barbarous behavior was as common as short attention spans are today.

Another handicap to knowing who the real Vikings were is that now antiquated "Dark Ages" label. "It wasn't that dark," Ed told me. But, while it may not have been all that dark, the lights in western Europe had been turned down pretty darn low. When the Roman Empire collapsed, barbarians seized the abandoned lands, and seemingly overnight, an entire millennium of Greek and Roman knowledge pretty much vanished. Books and manuscripts decayed, disappeared or were burned, libraries were destroyed and literacy plummeted so low that only 14 percent of Italy's eight-century social elite could write their name.

Ironically, during the "early Middle Ages," what scholars today prefer to call the Dark Ages, it was the monks that helped preserve many of the texts that were written by their pagan predecessors. And it was the "rediscovery" of those texts that helped to eventually shine the light back on western Europe, during what would later be called the Renaissance, a word that literally means "rebirth." Imagine for a moment what life would be like today if those great thinkers' works hadn't been preserved. Somebody would probably be clubbing you over the head right now and stealing your goats. Your precious, beautiful goats.

In fact, take a moment and think about this: I bet that you know far more about ancient civilizations—Egypt, Greece, Rome, China—than the early Middle Ages. Tutankhamen, Aristotle, Socrates, Sophocles, Plato, Julius Caesar, Antony and Cleopatra and the Bible all probably spring to mind. How about the *I Ching* and *The Art of War*? How about Egyptian pyramids, the Roman Forum, the Colosseum, Roman baths, a manger in Bethlehem, gladiators, chariots and classic Greek drama? Now, what does a Viking house look like? Name a writer or philosopher who lived between AD 500 and 1300. In fact, we don't know if the era's most recognizable figure, King Arthur, even existed or who wrote its best-known piece of literature, *Beowulf*. It's no wonder then that the period spawned—and continues to spawn—so many fantastical tales of dragons and knights and rogue warriors, from *Lord of the Rings* and hobbits to *Merlin*, *Dungeons and Dragons* and much, much more.

. . . .

"You look like a pixie!" Wendy exclaimed. I was standing in my office modeling the Viking outfit that I'd bought from the online reenactment store Historic Enterprises. I looked in our closet door mirror and turned from side to side like a medieval runway model, admiring the muddy hues of my brown linen "Anglo-Saxon trousers" and tunic. I spun around on the slippery-soled leather boots and moonwalked directly into an ironing board, then sized myself up again. "Pixie?" I asked Wendy. "Why did I only buy brown clothing? I look like dragon poo."

Shortly after my meeting with Bjornstad, Jack invited me to become a member of the group, which I happily accepted. I agreed to meet up with them over Labor Day weekend for the 145th Scottish Highland Gathering and Games, an annual event put on by the

Caledonian Club of San Francisco. In the interim, he invited me to help present the "Viking Art of War," the group's fifteen-minute living history presentation on Viking, Norman and Saxon weapons and tactics. I'd talk about the seax (pronounced "sax"), a dagger for which the Saxons—the Germanic people who invaded England after the Romans left—were named. It pops up twice in the epic poem *Beowulf,* including at the end when the heroic Geat uses one against the dragon that eventually kills him.

I rushed to the library, checked out the recent Seamus Heaney translation of the epic poem and started trying to make sense of Old English, a guttural tongue that sounds like Dylan Thomas reading one of his poems backward. While drunk. And with cotton balls stuffed in his mouth.

At night, while lying in bed, I'd read one of its lines out loud, like "Āhlēop ðā se gomela, Gode þancode, mihtigan Drihtne, þæs se man gespræc," then close my eyes and hold the book against my head à la Carnac the Magnificent and attempt to translate it into modern English. "A lob of the gamelan, God Pancake, mitigates Doctor Hytner, so pass the man. Gesture! Wow," I'd say. "That makes no sense whatsoever."

Inevitably Wendy would look up from her book and remark that our next-door neighbors, who can hear everything through our adjoining wall, might think that I was possessed.

"Sorry," I'd say, then I'd whisper Heaney's modern English translation.

"*'With that the old lord sprang to his feet and praised God for Beowulf's pledge,'*" and then cry out, "Shit!"

"Darling! Shh!"

"Sorry, it's just that I refuse to believe that 'Āhlēop ðā se gomela' is the same as 'With that the old lord sprang to his feet.'"

"That's fine, but there's no need for potty mouth."

"This is just remarkable. I mean, if the Normans hadn't conquered England and introduced French into whatever these barbarians were speaking, we'd still be talking like this. Think about it. Instead of saying "I love you" I'd be garbling "Ic lufie þe!"

"You do know that you've officially become the world's biggest history dork."

"Fuck!" I said, failing at another translation.

"Shh! Darling, a fourteen-year-old girl lives right next door and can hear you!"

"You do know that 'fuck' and 'shit' are perfectly fine words. It's the Normans' fault that we think they're crude. They thought the English were vulgar, so they didn't accept their language. That's why it's perfectly fine to take an excrement, but not to take a shit."

" 'Take an excrement'?"

"Or whatever."

Then she turned the light off and that was the end of that.

· · · · · · · ·

Three months after meeting with Bjornstad I drove to the Alameda Fairgrounds about thirty miles southeast of Oakland. After looking for a parking spot in the crowded lot for the better part of fifteen minutes, I settled on a sliver of grass between a customized van with a small Scottish flag stuck to its back window and a white four-door with a bumper sticker that read, "Bagpipers Do It with Guts."

I slipped into my clothing, opened the car door, dinged the van, squeezed out through the six inches of open space, took one step on the grass and nearly fell face-first onto the van's running board. Vikings may have constructed some pretty badass dragon ships, but they couldn't make a pair of boot soles to save their lives.

I practically skated into the sprawling fairgrounds and marveled at all the tanned, trim and beautiful Californians who'd gathered to celebrate Scottish culture. They were about as far from Mike Myers's Fat Bastard character as you can get. Many wore kilts and T-shirts printed with their clan names—"Clan Donnachaidh," "Clan MacKinnon," "Clan MacDonald," and there were, of course, even a few that identified themselves as "Clan Inebriated." To my surprise no one seemed to notice—or care—that I resembled a medieval UPS driver, because most were too busy dancing to a group of sweaty, tatted-out Scottish folk rockers. Past the fleet of classic Morris Minor automobiles and a man named Digeridrew who sold, rather incongruously, *Australian* didgeridoos, I spotted a wide yellow "Living History" banner strung between two poles. In a broad circle formed around a tree, a couple dozen reenactment groups had set up their encampments. After sifting through a few Renaissance and Roman soldiers—any group that even *touched* Scotland was invited to the event—I located the Bjornstad encampment erected between another Viking reenactment group, called Dark Boar, and a bearded "medieval prince" who was knighting a middle-aged Asian man from the comfort of his throne.

I introduced myself to Jack, a gray-bearded man with teardrop eyes. A pendant of the Norse god Odin hung around his neck. In all, about twelve members were there, dressed in natural, drab and loose-fitting medieval clothing. They lounged under the canopy of a canvas fly, snacked on fruit, bread and cold cuts and chatted amiably with one another, as if they were all hanging out on the beach. The only pillaging I witnessed took place when one member grabbed a handful of grapes *and* apricots.

For a couple of hours I hung out and watched the members interact with the public. Viking booty, Dark Ages armor and an old Anglo-Saxon map of the world that Jack had painstakingly reproduced on goatskin lay on a display table. For Jack, who got into the hobby because he wanted to know what it was like to wear chain mail, dressing strangers in Viking battle gear was an opportunity not only to educate and entertain, but maybe even to alter the public's perception of reenacting. "We have such a terrible culture that says enthusiasm for learning is reserved for children," he told me. I couldn't agree more and, by the looks of things, the public liked the interactive 3-D history lesson. "If only history would have been taught like this in school!" adults exclaimed.

Soon it was my turn to get into kit and help the group put on a show. I slipped on a heavy steel helmet, fastened a seax on my thick leather belt and, along with ten other members, helped form a "shield wall"—essentially a group of guys holding shields in front of them and looking surly. In front of us, on a wide lawn, Bjornstad member Rick Mantegani, a retired food industry worker, paced back and forth and delivered a rousing monologue about honor that was meant to attract an audience for our "Viking Art of War" presentation. I was the only person without a shield so I hid in the second row, struggling to see through the helmet's ocular protection and above the men in front of me. I silently rehearsed my speech, making sure that I didn't forget any of the key points: *A seax handle was made from either bone, wood or antler. They were worn horizontally on one's person. They were a single-edged all-purpose knife. Beowulf stabbed the dragon with one. Saxons were named for them.*

I'd thought that immersing myself in history would inspire me to connect to my heritage like all those people in front of us wearing tartan, that I'd want to trace my family tree and discover all my long-lost relatives, that I'd dress in lederhosen and amble through Germany knocking on every Schröder's and Graf's door exclaiming, *"Ich bin ein lost relative!"* I thought that I'd feel so German that I couldn't go one more day, nay one more *second*, without wearing a watch. But none of that ever happened. Outside of a brief conversation with an uncle about a distant relative, my connection to Germany or to my German heritage seemed far, far away. The more I read about old Germanic tribes and Holy Roman Empires and bisexual Prussian kings, the less identifiable it all felt. I mean, which facets do I co-opt? Which do I politely decline?

For many people identifying with their heritage helps them make sense of the world, of their past, of their identity. But for me it couldn't have felt more forced or fake, like I was standing at a salad bar and could pick and choose what I liked the most—beer, pretzels, Kraftwerk—and leave all the other stuff—Nazis, weird porn, Kraftwerk—out. I could place stickers on my car, or hang a flag in my apartment, but no matter what I'd dig up, I'd always feel about as German as a Wienerschnitzel drive-through.

Whap! Thump! Whap! Thump!

The sound of sword-on-shield action—technically a "holmgang"—interrupted my musings. Ed and Henrik Olsgaard, who were both forty years older than the average Viking, had broken off from the shield wall and were now beating the living excrement out of each other. A crowd gathered to see what all the fuss was about. After a dozen or so fierce blows, Jack broke away from the wall and cried, "Halt!"

With a decent-sized and attentive crowd now assembled, the members speedily transitioned into the Viking Art of War. One by one, they stepped forward to talk about their weapons, how they were made, how they were used: the spear, the bow and arrow, the ax. It'd been almost eight years since I'd been in front of an audience. Over the years the part of my brain that stores lines had atrophied, and now only snippets of Shakespeare remained: a Romeo monologue, a sonnet, maybe two. I feared that in a moment of panic, I'd launch into the balcony speech and mistakenly start to woo some dude in a kilt.

> *But soft, what light through yonder window breaks?*
> *It is the east and Aidan McMahon is the sun!*

While thinking of all the terrible things that could happen to me I looked up and saw Rick, a shortish man with a gray mustache, looking at me as if to say, "You're on." Which made sense because I was.

I gingerly placed one foot in front of the other, like a tap dancer walking across a sheet of ice, took a couple deep breaths, adjusted the helmet so my eyes wouldn't cross and held the seax aloft for all to see. I paced in front of the crowd, presenting its uses, its meanings and cultural references. When I finally finished, dropping the "Saxons were named for it" bombshell, a few folks in the crowd nodded the way people do when they think quietly to themselves, *Huh, never knew that.* In less than a year I'd gone from ignoramus to educator, from student to teacher. I'm not going to lie, it felt kind of nice.

I spun around and walked back to the shield wall, where I resettled in the second row. As I skidded in, Ed, Jack and Brian nodded at me as if to say, *"Wilcume."* Later, as the sun disappeared behind a nearby mountain range, a few of us gathered under the tent to drink mead from a cow horn. It'd been a refreshingly pleasant reenactment experience (except for the mead, which tasted like dirty socks), and as mellow as one can imagine. There weren't any carcinogens or exploding tennis balls; nobody fired blanks or poked a pilum in someone's eye. I didn't see any night flares, swastikas or tanks; it wasn't freezing cold; nobody triple-charged her musket and broke my eardrum or farted in my face; and the losing side didn't win. There was no period rush. But that was okay with me. It'd been a nice change from the intensity of 'Nam and besides, things were about to get a little crazy.

CHAPTER TEN
Friar, Walk with Me

In late September, I flew to Pennsylvania and went to the same Renaissance faire where I'd worked seventeen years earlier. I thought that by returning to the place where I first became acquainted with reenactors, I'd be coming full circle and would be able to assess how far I've come in the past year—you know, how "living" through two thousand years of Western civilization had changed me. I even thought that by dressing up in the colonial garb I'd worn with Schuyler's Company, I'd have completely morphed into the type of person who voluntarily dresses in historical clothes and attends faires—the person I'd made fun of so many years ago.

As I shuffled up and down the shire streets, I marveled at all the changes that'd taken place since I was last there. Now it seemed like there were twice as many merchants, the streets that were once dirt were now paved and an inviting brew pub had opened in a newly built corner near a massive, red "pyrate" ship store. Flipping through the program outside a new medieval dungeon, I noticed that even *Romeo and Juliet*, once an embarrassingly short thirty minutes, had doubled in length to a somewhat more respectable sixty. Like everything else in America over the last couple decades, the faire had boomed.

And yet, walking around, it was clear to me that something was rotten in the state of Pennsylvania. At the Globe Theater I plopped down on a long wooden bench to watch two swashbuckling comedians—"sixteenth-century" Abbott and Costellos—perform their routine. Dressed in conquistador helmets and speaking in fast-paced Speedy Gonzales accents, the duo flung jokes back and forth at one another.

"How can you tell if there's a Mexican pirate in your neighborhood?" the mustachioed Spaniard asked. "He's doing your yaaarrd."

"What do you call four Spaniards in quicksand?" the bearded one replied. *"Quatro cinco."*

"What did the fish say when he hit the wall?" they both asked. "Dam!"

When I worked at the faire it was admittedly pretty schlocky, but at least we tried our hardest to make it historically accurate. In fact, we weren't allowed to reference anything past the year 1587, which isn't easy. But it was clear that those days were over. What little dignity the faire had back then had clearly disappeared.

Even worse, it seemed as though today's costumed visitors now think of the faire as an extension of Comic-Con. Once upon a time they were the ones who were so into history that they showed up as knights in shining armor or Renaissance "gentlemen." But now guys dressed as pointy-eared elves and girls looked like "Harajuku" misfits, in bright red wigs and tartan miniskirts. Some wielded cartoonishly oversized broadswords, while others carried big plastic chain saws. I even saw an imitation Paul Stanley from the glam rock band KISS— large black star painted over his right eye, unbuttoned leather vest, tight black pants and all. *Just who are these knot-pated clotpoles? I wondered, And wherefore were they in Elizabethan England?*

After only two hours in the shire, barely enough time to work up an appetite for a turkey legge, I made haste for the arched sandstone front gate. As I galloped apace toward my rental car I looked over my shoulder to see a banner printed with the faire's motto: "Fantasy Rules!"

It doth not, I thought. *History doth.*

• • • • • • • •

Throughout the year reenactors often asked me if, when I finished my journey, I would join a group and become one of them. The question always made me feel a bit uncomfortable because I never thought that I would actually become a reenactor. I figured that this adventure would just be one of many. I assumed that once I'd finished, I'd immerse myself in something else fun like spelunking or bread making. But on the flight home from Pennsylvania, smooshed between what I assume were two former professional wrestlers, I had a thought: *What if I did become a reenactor? What would I do? Who would I be?*

I'd fought in a lot of fake battles, but I wasn't particularly fond of military tactics or "killing" people. And though the Renaissance faire was better, after my two experiences with "Justin Bieber" and "Paul Stanley," I never wanted to step foot in the "sixteenth century" again. I'd witnessed reenactors' obsessive attention to detail, making sure their clothing looked as authentic as possible. This appealed to me even less. I can't sew and I certainly can't make shoes or tools. I'd reenacted the eighteenth century three times and it emerged as my favorite time period, but I didn't feel compelled to re-create one particular event from it. I was at a loss. I didn't know what to do.

Then a lightbulb went on. Literally. The guy to my right had turned on his reading light and its glow was spilling onto my tray table. And there, on my boarding pass, was my answer—or at least my partial answer. "Destination: Los Angeles." *I'll reenact something that happened in Los Angeles.*

I opened my notebook and started to brainstorm. But nothing came out. I'd lived in L.A. for eight years but didn't know a thing about its history. I'd spent the last year crisscrossing the country, traveling back in time to broaden my knowledge, but had neglected to learn about the very place I live.

When I got home I determined to change all that.

· · · · · · · ·

The suburb where Wendy and I live isn't very old. In fact, it's really new. It only celebrated its centennial in 2011. Suffice it to say, it hasn't been around long enough to accumulate much of a history. Consider that our local historical society is only open for six hours each *week*. On our one visit to it, shortly after I had the idea to create my own reenactment, we walked through its roomy hangarlike space and took in the items that businesses and residents had donated: old film editing equipment and phonographs, early televisions and typewriters, cameras and household appliances. In one display case I even saw the battery-powered memory game Simon, with its four big colored buttons that I used to play with as a kid.

After our brief visit I felt dejected. Despondent, really. *Mopey.*

"I don't know. Do you think that people will want to watch me splice old film?" I asked Wendy as we left.

"No," she said. "Unless it all caught on fire. That'd be exciting."

For the rest of the day I tried to think of what to do: I could rent an old T-Bird and swing by the Friday night carhop at the country's oldest Bob's Big Boy; I could dress as the Tramp and reenact the horse ride Charlie Chaplin and Douglas Fairbanks used to make from their homes in Beverly Hills to Hollywood; I could squeeze into a pair of old swim trunks and re-create an aerial stunt at the original Muscle Beach. But as quickly as the ideas came to me I shot them down. They all seemed so new, so *recent*. Not to mention that I'd likely perish attempting two of them.

One morning later that week, however, while riding the elevator to work, I spotted something that I'd never noticed: the L.A. city seal, stamped in the center of the inspection certificate. Curling around its bottom half were the words "Founded 1781." *Seventeen eighty-one?* I thought. *Don't they mean 1881?* I looked again: "1781." *Who in God's name was here in 1781?*

At the time I didn't realize it, but I'd just answered my question.

• • • • • • • •

When Wendy first moved to L.A. I took her to Chinatown to show her that she could still find lots of things that she had in Hong Kong. I pointed out the smattering of dim sum restaurants and stores that sold ginseng, tea and dried foods. After five minutes we'd pretty much seen the whole gritty neighborhood. I turned to her and asked, *"Jung, mm jungyi?"* ("Do you like it?") But all the color had drained from her face. She stared straight ahead at a shuttered gas station, its red-tiled roof built to look like a traditional Chinese one. "Sorry, darling," she said. "It's just that it looks like an abandoned amusement park here."

Fortunately we soon discovered the bedroom communities of the San Gabriel Valley, about ten miles east of downtown. On its surface the area is indistinguishable from the rest of L.A. It has one-story '50s-era homes and strip malls where orange groves used to be, traffic clogs the streets and palm trees stretch up toward azure skies. But when you look closer—not even really *that* close—you'll see Chinese characters adorning virtually every storefront. The first time we drove through the broad swath I realized that the San Gabriel Valley and its cities of Monterey Park, Alhambra, San Gabriel, Rosemead, Arcadia and Rowland Heights hadn't so much spawned a newer, larger Chinatown, but rather a decent-sized "China City." Today, more than 150,000 Chinese call it home.

For the last seven years, we've visited the "SGV" to dine on a smorgasbord of regional Chinese cuisines and foods: steamed pork buns, dim sum, Peking duck, hot pot, noodles, seafood, even Muslim-Chinese lamb. We buy our groceries there. Around Chinese New Year we go to its nurseries for festive flora, like kumquat trees and narcissus. But despite having gone there hundreds of times, I never noticed the small beige sign that greets drivers as they enter the city of San Gabriel. The one with the city's motto, "City with a Mission," a reference to the 1775 Spanish mission for which the city and valley are named.

On an overcast Saturday in mid-November, however, I did notice it and soon Wendy and I were driving down Mission Drive. For a while it carved a path like any other L.A. street, straight and at a ninety-degree angle to the ones that intersect it, but after a few blocks it started to snake and the area's architecture morphed from single-story dwellings to long "mission-style" rancheros. On our left a spacious plaza led up to a grand Spanish-style playhouse; farther down, an old brick wall peeked out of a restaurant's arched doorway. Finally, as the street bent so severely that I had to slow the car to a crawl, we came upon the Moorish-style mission itself. Towering palm trees framed a thirty-foot-high belfry with a small cross planted on its top, like a candle on a cake. On a well-manicured lawn two young Chinese newlyweds posed for photos, and nearby a Latino wedding party waited to have theirs taken against the area's most photogenic backdrop.

After I parked the car, Wendy and I meandered back through the mission's courtyard located between its gift shop and the long beige church. For a while we took in the abundance of native plants and read placards that told stories of how the Spanish friars and native Tongva people made clay aqueducts to funnel water into the mission grounds. Then Wendy spotted what turned out to be a 236-year-old grapevine.

While she traced its gnarled tentacles, I noticed a sign located at the far end of the church, near its museum entrance. "Come in and experience a time capsule of California history," it said in a kind, "teacherly" hand. "Welcome 4th graders."

The faint sounds of a recorded mass filtered into the dimly lit room. Framed essays written on yellow notebook paper hung low on walls, targeting the ten-year-olds who study California's mission history. I scooted by some display cases, one filled with memorabilia from celebrity visits, another that displayed a Franciscan friar's habit, sandals, rope belt and staff. Original native depictions of the stations of the cross hung high on walls, and in a long, low case a small placard read, MASS HAS BEEN CELEBRATED IN THE MISSION EVERY DAY SINCE IT WAS FIRST FOUNDED IN 1771. For the first time since I moved to L.A., I felt like I'd stepped back in time. Well, at least further back than *Happy Days*.

· · · · · · · ·

In 1769 the once mighty Spanish empire found itself in a difficult spot. It was burdened with high debts from the Seven Years' War and had recently learned that the Russians were starting to explore what's now the Pacific Northwest, an area the Spanish had claimed back in 1513. To kill two birds with one stone, as it were—to settle the land and help pay off their debts—the Spanish needed to do what they'd been doing "south of the border": convert and "civilize" the natives into tax-paying, Christian subjects.

Leading this "spiritual conquest" was Father Junípero Serra, a Franciscan missionary who possessed an indefatigable zeal not only for spreading the word of God, but for walking. After founding Spain's first "Alta California" mission in San Diego in 1769, he walked 450 miles north to oversee the construction of ones in Carmel (1770) and Monterey (1771). Later that year he walked back south and founded Mission San Gabriel Arcángel, as the Spanish called it, at a location five miles south of its current one. After a flood destroyed it, it moved to its present location in 1775.

In all, between the years 1769 and 1823, Spain—and later Mexico after winning its independence—would build twenty-one California missions from San Diego to Sonoma, each spaced roughly a day's journey apart. Today the "Mission Ladder" ranks as one of the state's most popular tourist attractions.

While the missions might be "must-see" destinations, opinions about the missionaries' work have changed since we've recalibrated our moral compasses. Consider that the missionaries lured the aboriginals with baubles and trinkets and then essentially enslaved the "childlike" people to construct the missions and farm their land. And while it may have been their objective to save the "aboriginal heathens" from damnation and hellfire, the holy men ended up unintentionally killing a great number by infecting them with European diseases that the natives had no immunity to. When you factor in that many Indians converted to Christianity, the result was a rapid eradication of native life. Before they made contact with the Spanish, California's native population stood at 300,000, but by 1900—131 years later—it'd dwindled to just 16,000. So it comes as no surprise that Padre Serra's beatification in 1988 by Pope John Paul II didn't sit well with many modern-day Californians.

Despite now being a controversial figure, Serra will forever be known as the "founder of California." He's one of two Californians—the other is Ronald Reagan—whose likeness is cast in bronze and represents the state in the U.S. Capitol's Statuary Hall, a curious inclusion given that Serra was Spanish, first stepped foot in California before anybody had even *thought* of the United States and died sixty-six years before California was admitted to the union.

But regardless of how one feels about him now, the "indefatigable little friar" remains one of history's most compelling characters. The thirty-six-year-old Majorcan arrived in the New World from Spain in 1749 after a ninety-nine-day-long voyage at sea. Despite being weary and in all likelihood unable to walk in a straight line, he turned down a ride to Mexico City on a horse because the Franciscan Rule dictated that friars "must not ride on horseback unless compelled by manifest necessity or infirmity." He ended up walking 250 miles from Veracruz through all sorts of challenging terrain, only to be bitten by a mosquito on his left foot. His leg swelled to twice its normal size and the condition plagued him for the rest of his life. Despite qualifying for "infirmity" he never stopped hoofing it. Never. His devotion to God and saving pagans from eternal hellfire was so powerful that during a seven-year stretch in Mexico he hobbled a blisterific 5,500 miles on his bum leg, earning him the nickname "Friale Andariego," the Walking Friar.

Perhaps the only thing he did with more zeal was mortify his flesh. Consider some of the stories that I read in Katherine and Edward M. Ailsworth's biography of Serra, *In the Shade of the Juniper Tree*: he "lacerated his body with rough pieces of sackcloth made either of bristles or woven with broken pieces of wire," occasionally "beat his breast" with a stone and "publicly scourged himself with chains . . . and applied flames to his naked flesh to epitomize the horrors of hell fire to his hearers." Add to everything else that his prayer sessions lasted until four in the morning and you have the portrait of a man who was literally trying to beat, burn, tear and will impurity from his being.

Walking through the mission I wondered what Serra would think of L.A. today, home to the Church of Scientology Celebrity Centre, the adult film business and tranny prostitutes cruising Melrose Boulevard. Or, for that matter, what he'd think of the California he founded, a place that used to be considered the end of the earth and is now home to 37 million people and the world's eighth largest economy. A place that was once barren, except for missions and native huts, and is now crisscrossed with ribbons of freeways and urban sprawl, a place that

Serra traversed on foot, walking on dirt paths with only Spanish soldiers and a burro to protect and keep him company.

As I thought of this utterly contrarian lifestyle, I realized that I'd
found my reenactment. It'd be simple, really. All I'd do is dress like a
friar and walk between the two L.A. area missions—San Gabriel and
San Fernando. Okay, so it wasn't all that simple. It was downright
crazy, and I'd probably get shot, but at least it'd make people turn their
heads and wonder who I was. Like the Big Row crew, I'd ambush them
with history. Because if it's one of your goals as a reenactor to educate—
and it certainly isn't for all—sometimes you have to launch a sneak
attack, to stick out and call attention to yourself so people inch up to
you and say, "Who are you?" and then, when they least expect it, pass
out a history lesson that will completely change the way they look at the
world. (Then again, maybe nobody would blink an eye when they saw
me. When I told Jack Garrett of the Vikings of Bjornstad my idea, he
mentioned that he'd attended the San Francisco premiere of the movie
Beowulf and Grendel in full Viking kit. Afterward he rode public trans-
portation home, but nobody even looked at him. Then again, he lives
in San Francisco.)

· · · · · · · ·

The first order of business was to map my route. Spanish friars wore
down a trail between the missions and called it "el Camino Real," or the
King's Highway. I would have loved to follow in their footsteps, but
unfortunately today in many parts, it's the ten-lane 101 Freeway. Seeing
as how walking on the 101 would result in certain death, I did what any
educated man of the day would do. I let MapQuest route my journey.
One day, I opened my laptop, entered the two addresses and traced the
26.7-mile path as it zigzagged northwest from San Gabriel through
familiar terrain: the neighborhoods and communities of Alhambra, San
Marino, South Pasadena, Eagle Rock, Glendale, Burbank, Sun Valley

and Pacoima. I zoomed in to look closer at what lay in its route: residential and commercial districts, arroyos, freeway overpasses, airports, schools and rec centers, busy six-lane boulevards and the sinewy tree-lined streets of affluent suburbs. To my surprise I saw that it even passed within three hundred feet of our apartment. For nearly seven years I'd lived right in the middle of history and didn't know it.

Once I determined my course I set about planning all the logistics, which were virtually impossible to replicate in the twenty-first century. Whenever the friars walked between missions—out in native territory—soldiers accompanied them and burros carried all their food and supplies. I decided to combine the two companions into a "Sherpa-soldier," and to enlist friends who wouldn't mind carrying a backpack filled with water, food and informational flyers that I'd pass out along the way. I divided each Sherpa-soldier's shift into a five-mile stretch, roughly one-fifth of the total journey. Wendy volunteered to be my first one and I was excited for her to join me. It was the first reenactment she'd seen me do and after a year of leaving town, time and space I was happy to share some of the experience with her.

During those two months I read a number of books on the missions, but was surprised to find one of my favorite factoids while reading a children's book. Apparently at one point rats had infiltrated the San Fernando Mission's granary. To get rid of them, the friars borrowed cats from San Gabriel. When I read it I decided to incorporate the episode into my walk, as a sort of objective for my "character." You know, just in case somebody asked me what I was up to. The day after I read this, Wendy and I headed to Toys "R" Us, where I bought a small stuffed black and white cat.

After nailing down the logistics I started assembling my kit. For reenactors this is the most important step. If you don't look good in "authentic" gear, then really what's the point? While a hard-core reenactor would have found a sheep, sheared it, spun the wool and sewed his own habit, I opted for a more efficient approach. I ordered my brown habit from an online costume store. "Vow to have a good time in this!" its description read. "Even the most imperfect soul can achieve the look of spiritual perfection with this costume!"

The habit came with a rope belt, an oversized cross and a silly "Friar Tuck" wig. But I figured if I was going to cut corners on my garb, I had to go hard-core on the hair. So I decided to shave it into my very own tonsure, a "Friar Chuck," if you will. All I can say is that it sounded like a good idea at the time.

The night before the walk, on a cool Friday in early January, I went back to the salon where I'd gotten my Nazi haircut. In the intervening fifteen months the price had risen from seven dollars to eight and Loreta, who'd styled my Hitler do, no longer worked there. To give my hairdresser a visual idea of what I wanted I'd printed out a few pages of monk haircuts from the Internet. After waiting nervously for five minutes, I was approached by a woman with shoulder-length auburn hair, named Anita.

"Are you ready?" she asked in an Armenian accent.

I stood up and looked her in the eye. "Yes, I think. But are *you*?"

I handed her the images, fearing that'd she'd think I was a plant in a hidden-camera show, but to my surprise she didn't flinch. In fact, she studied them closely, like a cook consulting a recipe.

"I'm, uh, I'm walking between the missions," I said nervously. But she didn't respond. She just continued to consider the monks' strange hair. "You see, uh, I don't really want to do this. I'm writing a book and it's going to be the last chapter and what's funny is that I like my hair far too much to just shave it off." She lifted her eyes toward me, but kept her head down. She studied my head like a great painter looking at a blank canvas. Finally she spoke, whispered really.

"Is okay," she said. "I used to work in salon in Hollywood. Many people want strange hair. But I think when done, you must wear hat."

I pulled one out of my back pocket. "Already thought of that."

It's hard to believe but the medieval practice of tonsuring was only abolished in 1973 by Pope Paul VI. Shaving one's scalp until only a fringe of hair remained was meant to resemble the crown of thorns on Jesus's head and designated that a monk had been received into the clerical order. It wasn't, as so many people surmise, a massively hideous bald spot made famous by a tubby friar from Sherwood Forest.

While the Nazi haircut took a mercifully short time to style, my tonsure took the better part of an hour. By the time she'd finished it I looked like a cross between St. Francis of Assisi and Jim Carrey in *Dumb and Dumber*. Clumps of brown hair slid down the front of the barber's cape and a cool breeze chilled my newly exposed pate. After some time I finally summoned up enough courage to look in the mirror.

"Wow" I muttered, too shocked to scream or cry. "Eleven years of Propecia down the drain." I'm sure none of Anita's instructors at cosmetology school ever asked her to fashion a tonsure and yet despite this being her first effort it was flawless. Scarily flawless. She was my St. Paul Mitchell.

I handed her the mirror back and she looked at me very sincerely and said, "Now would be good time for hat."

I ended up paying her double for her hard work and slipped outside into the darkened alleyway that leads to our apartment. When I reached our door I slid the key in slowly so Wendy wouldn't hear me. Once inside I left my baseball cap on, kicked off my shoes and snuck toward the bathroom so I could wash off all the itchy hairs. But halfway there she spotted me.

"Let's see!" she said.

"Um, just a minute. I gotta take a quick shower first," I said, dashing to the bathroom and shutting the door.

I hurriedly took off my clothes and lathered up my temples with shaving cream, to tidy up the remaining stubble.

"Darling, I want to see," Wendy cried from the other side of the door. "Not now, I'm naked."

"Uh, we're *married*," she said and flung open the door.

"Oh no," she said, seeing my bumpy white scalp. "Oh no."

I could have closed the door, but I figured she needed to see me in all my nastiness so she could start acclimating. "I just need to tidy up my temples a bit," I said, dragging a razor down the side of my head. "They're a bit stubbly."

"Oh, darling, oh, darling," she said, tearing up. "Oh no, oh no."

"It's okay," I said. "It should grow back."

"No, no," she said. "No, no. No, no. No, no."

The only time I'd seen her like this was the time when I—moronically—told her that, one day, our cats would die. "I'm just saying it's inevitable that one day Duster and Jassy won't be here," I'd said. That momentary hiccup of emotional unintelligence launched an unstoppable shower of tears from her and nothing I said could stop them. Now it was happening again.

"I feel cold," she said, grabbing her stomach. "I'm shivering in my tummy. I feel like I'm standing on the edge of a cliff."

"Hey, hey," I said, approaching her with outstretched arms. "It'll only be for a day."

But by the time I'd uttered those words she'd bolted out of the bathroom. A couple months earlier she approved of my mission walk idea. She'd known for a while that I was going to get my hair cut like Serra's. So I couldn't understand why she was so upset. I turned around to resume shaving, but when I looked in the mirror I didn't recognize the person staring back at me. He was buck naked and a ring of hair encircled his bald head. Shaving cream was smeared all around his ears. I raised my hand and he raised his. I slid the razor down my face and so did he. But that guy in the mirror . . . that guy looked like a crazy person. I flashed back to the time at Old Fort Niagara when John

Osinski said that to be a reenactor the first thing you have to do is admit to yourself you're a little crazy. I'd officially arrived.

. . . .

A few weeks earlier I'd e-mailed 850 of my closest friends and asked them to join me on the walk. "You can walk for 26 feet or 26 miles," I wrote, blithely spamming their in-boxes. Most ignored my missive, but nearly thirty RSVP'd; two even promised to dress up like nuns. But even though I sent it to every single person in my address book, I didn't expect anyone to come from far away. Then I received an e-mail from the Big Row's David Manthey. "Reb and I are going to join you for your walk," he wrote. When I read it I nearly tumbled off my chair. In a year in which I was on the receiving end of many reenactors' benevolent gestures, this one—flying in from Albany, New York, and Waterville, Maine, to walk an uncomfortably long distance with me—topped the list.

They arrived late on the night before the walk and stayed at our apartment. In the morning we all rose early and slipped into our garb, I in my habit, they in their eighteenth-century slops. The four of us arrived at the San Gabriel Mission at 7:00 a.m. on a cool, overcast Saturday morning. There we met Chuck Lyons, the mission's director of publicity, near a bronze statue of Serra. The padre held a walking stick and looked beatifically into the distance. After posing for a few Abbey Road–esque photos in front of the bell wall, we started to walk. As we made our way down a snaking walkway, Lyons scurried inside to ring the church bells. Hearing them echo through the mission district sent a shiver swirling around my chilly bald head.

For the first hour all was quiet. David, Reb and I chatted about all that had transpired since we last saw each other on the St. Lawrence River. During lulls in the conversation Reb took note of the region's different vegetation, while David remarked on how different the roadway engineering was from streets back east. I struggled to adjust my gait to accommodate what was essentially a very long dress. My Sherpa-soldier, Wendy, along with her friend Arthur, trailed us. I feared she was trying to stay as far away from me as possible.

Together as we strode through the sleepy streets of a residential neighborhood, we noted the sights of an early January morning: chirping birds, inflatable snowmen that lay collapsed on front lawns, Mexican gardeners trimming bushes, a peloton of cyclists whizzing by too fast for me to distribute the informational flyer I'd made.

About an hour after we started, we entered the village of San Marino. I'd yet to hand out a flyer, but brimmed with confidence upon seeing a smattering of muffin-munching pedestrians. I figured if anyone would want to learn about the area's history, it'd be the people who live in this highly affluent city, a place that's home to the Huntington Library and one of the country's finest collections of rare manuscripts.

So when I saw a yuppieish man of about forty-five with dark curly hair approaching me, I expected that he'd welcome me to his neighborhood as a sort of cultural emissary. "Hi," I said, clearing my throat and proffering a flyer. But to my surprise he held up his hand and turned away. *That was awkward*, I thought. I continued on down the quaint tree-lined strip and approached a speed-walker, her arms by her sides like wings.

"Greetings, would you like a fl—?" I asked.

"No! No!" she said, flapping away.

Around that time a car drove by.

"Did you see that?" David asked, turning to follow it down the street. "That woman crossed herself when she saw you."

"Huh," I said, a bit distractedly because while that was happening, a short, blond woman walked by and muttered, "God bless you," too fast for me to turn and hand her a flyer.

Mission Walk Reenactment
(Or, "Why in the world am I dressed like this?")

WHAT IN THE WORLD AM I DOING? I'm reenacting a typical walk between two Los Angeles area missions, Mission San Gabriel Arcángel and Mission San Fernando Rey de España. It's 26.7 miles. Please join me. My feet are killing me.

WHY AM I TAKING THIS ROUTE? Typically Spanish friars would have followed the "El Camino Real" (now the 101 Freeway). But that adds another 4 miles to my trip and would result in certain death if I attempted it.

WHAT'S UP WITH MY FUNNY HAIRCUT? It's called a "tonsure." Spanish friars fashioned their hair this way when they were received into the clerical order. No, it's not a bald spot.

WHAT YEAR IS IT? It's 1798. The San Fernando Mission just opened last September. Everybody's talking about it.

WHY DO I HAVE A CAT WITH ME? The San Fernando Mission has a rat problem in their granary. I'm bringing them a cat to "address the issue." Meow.

WHO'S THE PERSON CARRYING MY BACKPACK? My "Sherpa-soldier." Soldiers accompanied friars during their travels; Sherpas carry people's gear that climb Mt. Everest. I don't know, it just seemed like a good name at the time.

WHAT'S THAT SKETCH AT THE TOP OF THE PAGE? That's Mission San Fernando Rey de España and the San Fernando Valley, in 1853.

WHERE AM I? "Alta California" in New Spain.

SPAIN? YOU'RE CRAZY. THIS IS THE UNITED STATES OF AMERICA. No, the United States is that new country way over that way (he says, pointing to the east). Last I heard the farthest Western state was called Tennessee or something. As if that country will ever amount to anything. No state sponsored religion? Good luck with that one, Yankees!

WHY ARE THE SPANISH IN ALTA CALIFORNIA? Our government heard that the Russians were starting to explore the land up north from here. But we consider it ours. Here's the deal: we need to grow our empire. We're still smarting from that expensive Seven Years' War. (Who said war was good for business?) To do that we've set up missions from San Diego to Sonoma to convert the natives to Christianity. Unfortunately, we brought diseases with us that the natives have no immunity to. We've tried to "civilize" them, but in the process have killed many of them off.

"Thanks!" I said, not knowing how else to respond.

It never occurred to me that people might actually think *I* was on a mission and that it was *my* goal to save *twenty-first-century* heathens. But as I caught my reflection in a Lilly Pulitzer store window, I saw it too: the sandals, the robe, the rope belt, the stupid cat tucked under my armpit, the ream of flyers. What I'd thought of as an ambush lesson in local history looked more like a proselytizing Hare Krishna. *I may have seriously miscalculated,* I thought. *This could be a very long day.*

. . . .

History books are filled with tales of people making long one-day journeys on foot. Roman legionnaires typically traveled twenty miles in back-breaking armor; toward the end of the Civil War, Union forces trudged up to an unbelievable thirty-five miles a day; and perhaps the most famous message ever delivered arrived via the fiery-footed Greek messenger Pheidippides, who ran twenty-five miles from Marathon to Athens to announce that Greece had defeated Persia in the Battle of Marathon—only to keel over from exhaustion. Or so the legend says.

I'm obviously none of those people. They all lived a long time ago, when human beings still put one foot in front of another to get somewhere. I'm a soft, twenty-first-century American with a body unsuited for even the most casual stroll. I'm short, my butt grows a little bigger every day and one of my legs is three-quarters of an inch longer than the other, an affliction that causes my right foot to shoot out at a thirty-degree angle when I walk. Follow me down the street, and you might mistake me for a duck. I don't so much walk as waddle.

So it came as no surprise that after nearly seven miles of trudging on the world's most unforgiving surface, a sharp pain shot down my legs and hot spots flamed up on my feet. I could handle the leg pain for the time being, but no matter how much cream I massaged into my feet, I couldn't stave off the encroaching blisters. After another mile I feared I'd lose my feet to gangrene, so I stopped by the side of the road and changed into a pair of hiking shoes.

Modern Life: 1

Historical Accuracy: 0

During the break Wendy retired as my Sherpa-soldier and my friend Hiro took over her duties. "Darling, I love you," Wendy said, "but my legs are killing me. Arthur and I are going to have breakfast."

"Of course, I understand. Can I come with you?"

She kissed me. "You've got nineteen more miles to go."

"I guess that's a no."

I watched her go and envied the two of them for being able to sit down on cushioned seats.

After scaring off most of San Marino I decided to change the way I approached my "converts," which was a good idea because we were entering the gritty hipsterville of Eagle Rock. By now we'd transitioned out of a eucalyptus-tree-lined hillside neighborhood into the congested, noisy commercial swath of the six-lane Colorado Boulevard. Cars whizzed by and trucks exhaled noxious fumes that choked our lungs. Homeless people pushed shopping carts; a few haggard-looking men huddled around a rehabilitation center. When I spotted some wide-eyed slackers chilling outside a coffee shop I approached them, doing a silly little dance so they wouldn't run away from me.

"Hey, we're doing this whacky reenactment thing," I said, handing a flyer to some dude in Deee-Lite glasses.

"Cooool," he said. I was surprised that he dug it. Although to be honest I'm pretty sure he was coming down off ecstasy because all he really wanted to do was rub my scalp.

"You shaved your head," he said. "That is effing hard-core, boss."

Soon I was inside the shop passing out flyers to a posse of Mac nerds and getting my photo taken. "Have another flyer or twelve," I said, handing them a bunch and shouting "Whoo-hoo!" every time I did so. I'm not sure why, but dropping a "Whoo-hoo!" always puts strangers at ease.

I'd found my stride.

. . . .

Over the next ten miles the size of our posse swelled and shrank. Friends joined us, friends dropped out. Many who only knew fragments of my quest couldn't believe their eyes when they saw me. My friend Jay said in his usual droll tone, "Wow. Charles, that's a whole new level of weird." Another friend, Ian, muttered, "Talk about commitment." For a few miles our ranks swelled to eight and our ambush history lesson turned into a "happening." My friend J. Ana even kept her promise to dress as a nun. The circus had come to town and together we all walked down the six-lane Glenoaks Boulevard, occasionally handing out flyers to that rarest of sights, an ambulatory Angeleno.

While our posse slowly marched on into the overcast afternoon, the unforgiving pavement proved too much for Reb. After nearly twelve miles, Wendy picked her up and drove her back to our apartment. Soon thereafter, our mob broke up. Hiro passed on the Sherpa-soldier duties to my friend Drew, who a few miles later handed off the backpack to my friend Loren. My grand idea may not have been a historical facsimile and I'm not sure if I changed many lives, but it had an unintended effect: a group of friends came together and did something that few people in L.A. ever do—walk. At times I couldn't tell if people were looking askance at the costumed characters or just at the people putting one foot in front of the other.

At mile sixteen most of my friends hopped back in their cars. They thanked me for getting them outside and walking, for the exercise and camaraderie. David, Loren and I soldiered on into a pedestrianless industrial area behind the Burbank Airport. Adrenaline fled our bodies and the conversation faded away. Exhaustion hit us hard. I hadn't been eating enough food or drinking enough water and started to feel delirious. It was a little after four in the afternoon and we'd been walking for nine hours straight. We still had another ten miles before we reached San Fernando. The streets were empty. There was no one to hand flyers to. Soon it'd be dark. The air cooled; so did my head. My legs felt like cracked rubber.

"Serra must have been the Bionic Man," I said, astonished that the afflicted friar could hike so far.

"Are you positive the missionaries did this in one day?" Loren asked.

"That's what I remember reading," I said.

"I'm finding that less and less likely," David said. "Think about how challenging the terrain must have been."

"Yeah," I said, but I didn't want to admit that I was starting to doubt my research, that I may have misread something along the way. In my excitement to create a reenactment I realized that I'd overlooked the most important detail, the truth. (I'd find out later that it took them *three* days.) At that moment I did know one thing for sure: Junípero Serra owned exactly one worldly possession, a collapsible bed that he took with him on his journeys. And I wished I had one now.

During a lull I thought about one of the questions I always asked reenactors: "Why is it important to learn about history?" The most common response I heard was a famous quote from the philosopher George Santayana, "Those who cannot remember the past are condemned to fulfill it." I heard so many different versions of it so often, in fact, that it started to lose all its meaning. It seemed too cliché, too pat, too easy. After hearing it for the umpteenth time I started asking people if, as a result of learning about the past, they stopped making mistakes, but they all said no, they still did.

I found studying history to be the perfect antidote to our times. In an age when "stories" are told in 140 characters or less and so many people's imaginations are, as the historian Simon Schama says, "held hostage in the cage of eternal Now: the flickering instant that's gone as soon as it has arrived," I *needed* to immerse myself in complex historical tales. They grounded me, they told me where I came from, they told me where I was. They helped me look at the world in a completely new light. And despite all these wonderful epiphanies, what I really liked most were history's stories. As Angie Potter once told me,

> History is about storytelling. It gives us a perspective on things. About where we come from and the stories we tell each other. And in this world, where we're caught adrift—we don't live in the same towns our whole lives and we certainly don't live with our families—it's a way to create stories and understand who we are and where we are.

"Ah, just missed the walk signal," David said, pulling me out of my reverie. We were at mile nineteen and had been approaching a busy intersection when the Don't Walk sign started to flash. I leaned on my walking stick, eyes cast down, struggling to remain lucid, when I heard the low rumble of a car hissing and wheezing. "There's Jay Leno," Loren said, matter-of-factly. I looked up. Was my mind playing tricks on me? I rubbed my eyes and refocused. Indeed, there was Jay Leno in his trademark denim work shirt puttering by in an open-air hundred-year-old steam-powered car. He looked at us in disbelief. I looked at him in the exact same way. I waved. He waved back.

Not long ago I feared that I'd be walking down the street and Leno and his crew would ask me elementary questions about history. Of course I wouldn't be able to answer him and of course he'd end up show-ing it later that night on an edition of "Jay Walk All-Stars," embarrassing me in front of the entire country. But standing there, bent over at a ninety-degree angle and watching the King of Late Night cruise by, I'd have done anything for him to stop and ask me questions. *Bring it on, Leno,* I thought, *I want to show America who knows his history.*

EXT. INDUSTRIAL WASTELAND—DAY

JAY LENO, 60, big-chinned talk-show host, hops out of his antique car and approaches CHARLIE SCHROEDER, 38, intrepid historical reenactor, dressed as a Spanish friar. Leno holds an old-time microphone. Schroeder, a stuffed cat.

Jay

Okay, Mr. Weirdy Pants, pop quiz. What percentage of Civil War battles were fought in Virginia?

Charlie

Oh, come on, Jay, that's an easy one. Sixty percent.

Jay

What did a medieval person's teeth look like?

Charlie

Ah, tricky. You're thinking of *Monty Python and the Holy Grail*, right? Blackened teeth and all that? Actually a typical medievalist had pretty decent teeth because the sugar trade between Europe and the Caribbean hadn't commenced.

Only wealthy folks could afford sugar back then, so they were the ones who suffered, not the lowly peasants.

Jay

Okay, what's the world's first global currency?

Charlie

The Spanish pieces of eight. Spaniards came to the New World looking for gold and found silver instead. What's amazing is that the pieces of eight were legal tender in the United States until 1857. Oh, and did you know that the Spanish brought horses with them too? Before that there weren't any in America.

"Charlie," Loren said, snapping me back to reality.
"What?"
"We've got the walk signal." He and David started to march across the intersection.
"Wait, wait," I cried. "Don't go. We've walked nineteen miles in nine hours, we've seen maybe two hundred people and I don't know how many more we're going to see. It's getting dark and I'm pretty sure I've lost my mind. I'm taking the Jay Leno sighting as a sign from the comedy gods."
"Exactly what kind of sign?" David asked.
"That it's okay to hitch a ride."
I dug into the backpack, pulled out my phone and dialed Wendy.
"My love, can you pick us up, please? And drive us to San Fernando?"
I still had one more part of my mission to complete.

. . . .

Now, I know this must sound a little strange, but I never told anyone at the San Fernando Mission that we were coming. I wasn't sure what time we'd arrive, whether it'd be 5:00 p.m. or 8:00 p.m. or no time at all, and I didn't want anyone to expect us, or for there to be a big "welcome mat" placed out in the parking lot. And yet as Wendy pulled in, I felt elated to have made it. Forget history, this had been a monumental achievement. We'd managed to walk nineteen miles—and neither David nor I had trained. And now it was over. Finally.

So imagine my disappointment when Wendy, Reb, David, Loren and I, with a stuffed cat still tucked under my arm, walked into the icon-laden gift shop and were met with a look from the cashier that might best be described as disbelief.

Wide-eyed and delirious, I hobbled toward her and proudly announced that David and I had just walked from the San Gabriel Mission.

"Okayyy," she said suspiciously. I couldn't tell if she was shocked or pissed.

"And," I continued, "I really need to use your bathroom."

She pointed toward a door that led to the courtyard. "Around the corner."

"Thank you," I said, shuffling by a display case of Franciscan friar statuettes.

I entered the low yellow building's grassy courtyard and felt blissfully serene, as if Scotty had just beamed me into eighteenth-century New Spain. I soaked it all up, then hiked up my habit and headed for the john.

When I reentered the gift shop a few minutes later, everyone looked really uncomfortable. "Let's go," Wendy said, grabbing my hand.

"But I need to drop off the cat," I muttered.

"No, darling, let's go."

As we walked into the parking lot I learned why Wendy was so insistent. While I was in the restroom, David had walked into the courtyard to take a photo. But the cashier stopped him. "Get out!" she snapped. "You can't take pictures in there!" Her wary look could now be explained: she clearly thought we were kooks.

I was angry that she'd yelled at David. He'd flown across the country and the next day walked nineteen miles to help educate Angelenos about their history, only to get booted out. I couldn't believe that after reenacting for a year and three months it'd ended with an eviction. After a while, I calmed down. *What do you think she thinks?* I thought. *It's fifteen minutes to closing and in walks some dude dressed in a robe, sporting a chrome dome and carrying a stuffed cat. You're lucky she didn't call the cops.*

In the parking lot I embraced Wendy. Practically suffocated her, really. "Thank you for everything," I muttered, burying my nose in her shoulder. She couldn't have been more supportive over the past fifteen months. While I disappeared back in time, vanished into history books and fashioned my hair into all sorts of ridiculousness, she was right there encouraging me, accommodating me, loving me. I'd traveled close to forty thousand miles, reenacted ten different time periods, read upward of sixty books, dressed like a Roman, a Viking and a friggin' Nazi, been attacked by the British, French and Russians, nearly froze to death, nearly capsized a bateau, got heckled by "Justin Bieber" and even made some new friends. And yet not once did she doubt my sanity. She doubted it about a dozen times.

"I love you," I said.

"I love you too, darling, but I don't think we should be hugging in the parking lot like this. You know, me and a 'friar.' It looks pretty creepy."

"Good point," I said.

"Here, let me put the cat over by the gate," she said.

"No, you know what, I kind of like him. Let's keep him. Duster and Jassy will have a new friend."

As I limped toward the car she asked me if there was anything special I wanted to eat that night.

"No," I said, turning to look at her. "All I want is for you to help me shave off the rest of my hair. I can't stand to look like this for another second. I just want to be myself again."

Epilogue

It's been nearly five months since I dressed as a friar and limped my way from the San Gabriel Mission to Jay Leno. My hair's grown back, my feet have healed and I don't feel like I'm nearly as bonkers. The brown habit now shares space with the rest of my reenacting gear—tunics and colonial garb, slippery Viking shoes and burlap sacks—in a plastic storage container underneath our bed.

Since the walk I've been firmly planted in the twenty-first century, spending my weekends away from the battlefield, with Wendy, doing the things we used to do before I started traveling back in time. We go to the movies, read books, visit museums and take walks around the neighborhood. Ours is a quiet, simple life free of conflict, danger and Russian snipers and that's just how I prefer it.

Recently we went to see Woody Allen's movie *Midnight in Paris*. In it, Owen Wilson plays a Hollywood screenwriter who's writing a novel about a man who works in a nostalgia shop. While on vacation in Paris, Wilson magically travels back in time to the 1920s. There, in apartments and dance halls, he meets his Jazz Age heroes F. Scott

Fitzgerald, Ernest Hemingway and Gertrude Stein, just to name a few. He parties with them, seeks their writing advice and even falls for a flapper girl named Adriana. It's a great movie, and I couldn't help but draw some parallels between Allen's premise and what I'd experienced over the last year: what would happen if we could travel back in time to the periods we identify with the most?

Wilson spends the movie crossing back and forth between the past and present, much to the consternation of his fiancée, who wonders why he's so aloof. While he's in the present, a pretentious acquaintance named Paul tells Wilson that he's suffering from "Golden Age thinking," an affliction in which someone believes that the past is better than the present. "Nostalgia is denial," Paul says. "Denial of the painful present . . . the erroneous notion that a different time period is better than the one one's living in—it's a flaw in the romantic imagination of those people who find it difficult to cope with the present." Later, when the flapper Adriana tells Wilson that she'd rather live in the Belle Epoque of late nineteenth-century Paris, the pair is transported there and meets Degas, Toulouse-Lautrec and Gauguin. During a conversation at the Moulin Rouge, the three artists all agree that the time they live in is no good and that things were better during the Renaissance. This bit of perspective, that *everyone* romanticizes the past, causes Wilson to realize that we all do it because "[present] life is always a little disappointing."

I understand what Wilson—or rather, Allen—means. After spending a good portion of the year in the past, I better understand why people reenact. Because the world most reenactors create allows them not only to temporarily escape the drudgery of modern life but to fulfill our most primal desires: to fight, to be the hero, to feel remarkable, to be brave men, to feel a sense of human accomplishment, to escape our responsibilities.

• • • • • • • •

I may no longer dress up in historical clothing and take to the battle-field, but I'm still hooked on history. Since I limped into Wendy's car at the San Fernando Mission, I haven't stopped gobbling up great historical stories. At a time when most contemporary stories fail to excite me I'm glad to have these narratives. They remind me of how we all live in a long shadow of past events.

Most of what I learned came from history books and the historians who've spent countless hours in libraries and museums piecing together the past so we can better understand it. That's not to say that I didn't get a lot out of play-acting. I did. Reenacting shrinks the broad subject of history to a personal scale, away from dates and ideas to something we can all relate to, the human experience. As Tony Horwitz has written, "No matter how much you read about the misery of long marches . . . or the tedium of camp life, you'll appreciate it a little better after trudging for ten miles in heavy wool and ill-fitting boots." By stripping away the present, you can start to get a sense of what it must have been like "back then." How one cooked, traveled, cleaned, ate, battled, believed . . . how one survived. It's a way to lift history off the page, to temporarily inhabit it and to consider not only who we were but what we've become, to marvel at our ancestors and ourselves. Although many reenactors may be nostalgic for a "simpler time" or, in the most troubling cases, lost causes, I defy anyone to spend a weekend in the past and feel as though things were better back then.

• • • • • • • •

The reenactment world is much larger than the one I've documented in these pages. Out there, likely not far from where you live, are reenactors linking together tiny bits of steel into chain mail, sewing clothing and preparing for a "battle" or parade, Renaissance faire, heritage day or living history event. Your neighbors might be soldiers from ancient Greece, the War of 1812 or Wild West gunslingers; they might be fur traders, Anglo-Zulu War soldiers or doughboys; they might work at interpretive museums like Historic Williamsburg and Plimoth Plantation, spending their days tending fields with period farm equipment or demonstrating how old printing presses work. I suggest attending a public reenactment and interacting with them. Ask them questions about who they are and what time period they're re-creating. Most will be happy to talk to you and share their knowledge. I promise they won't bite. Well, maybe one will.

While I'll definitely continue to visit historical sites and the occasional reenactment, today all my clothing is stowed away. But I still stay in touch with some reenactors. Legion VI was recently hired to portray Roman soldiers in a National Geographic Channel documentary about history's greatest parties. Rik Fox and his wife, Tarrah, are "sacking out" their horses to desensitize them to the hussar's wing racks and the Fort Lafe staff has already issued an e-mail advising attendees to "un-round" their "overlarge" bodies for next year's strenuous Boudiccan Revolt. The Vikings of Bjornstad are prepping for an upcoming workshop in the "impalement arts" (an ax- and knife-throwing session) and David Manthey told me that this year's Big Row crew will row eighty-seven miles from Rome, New York, to the Mabee Farm Historic Site in Rotterdam Junction. This five-day adventure is part of his "grand plan to cover all of the waterways that [this] type of bateau originally traveled." Just thinking about it makes my butt hurt. That said, I wonder if they have room for one more crew member.

7/12